THE ETIOLOGY OF ALCOHOLISM

THE ETIOLOGY OF ALCOHOLISM

Constitutional, Psychological and Sociological Approaches

By

JULIAN B. ROEBUCK, Ph.D.

Professor of Sociology
Mississippi State University
State College, Mississippi

and

RAYMOND G. KESSLER, M.A.

Research Associate
Family Court Division
Common Pleas Court of Philadelphia

CHARLES C THOMAS • PUBLISHER
Springfield • Illinois • U.S.A.

Published and Distributed Throughout the World by
CHARLES C THOMAS • PUBLISHER
BANNERSTONE HOUSE
301-327 East Lawrence Avenue, Springfield, Illinois, U.S.A.

©1972, *by* CHARLES C THOMAS • PUBLISHER
ISBN 0-398-02392-1
Library of Congress Catalog Card Number: 71-87672

With **THOMAS BOOKS** *careful attention is given to all details of
manufacturing and design. It is the Publisher's desire to present books
that are satisfactory as to their physical qualities and artistic possibilities
and appropriate for their particular use.* **THOMAS BOOKS** *will be true
to those laws of quality that assure a good name and good will.*

Printed in the United States of America
A-2

To

Elizabeth Gonzalez Roebuck
and
Lori Cobalis,

the most important women
in our lives.

PREFACE

T HE IDEAS AND SOME OF THE DATA for this monograph evolved
from a university interdisciplinary seminar in deviant behavior
entitled *Alcoholism and Drinking Practices in the United States.*
The authors have, among others, maintained for some time that
no one or two disciplines may claim exclusive expertise in this very
broad and complicated area. Moreover, unlike some of his col-
leagues, he contends here and elsewhere that sociologists must be
concerned with causation as well as with social process. A cursory
examination of the literature quickly revealed that the works on
alcoholism comprise a mixed bag of theory and research (design
and data) at various levels of analysis. The authorship determined
that the various "relevant" theories of alcoholism postulated by
different behavioral scientists would have to be articulated (not
mixed) sooner or later. The first step in this required articulation
seems to call for a *current delineation* of the primary approaches to
the etiology of alcoholism, along with accompanying theoretical
frames of reference and research data. This first step of critical
classification marks the major focus of this book. A review of the
literature suggested a rough model of analysis for this endeavor
in three parts: *the constitutional approach, the psychological approach, and the sociological approach.*

The problem of definition is considered in Chapter I; however,
one aspect of our schematic position is initially required. The
classification and analysis model adopted includes problem drinkers
as well as alcoholics. Many scholars with some justification will
disagree with this apparent, forced reductionism; however, we
assumed that the embracement was necessary for typological
reasons. The terms "alcoholic" and "alcoholism" are ambiguous;
many scholars disagree about their meanings. The terms "problem
drinkers" and "problem drinking" are also ambiguous in that they
contain a membership of alcoholics and non-alcoholics. This sometimes pervasive overlap is glaringly obvious in the literature and

vii

therefore precludes any clear-cut heuristic differentiation for our classificatory purpose. Throughout this work we note the demarcation when (and how) it is made.

The authors thank the many graduate students for the stimulation they gave to this work. We are indebted to Mark Keller of the Center of Alcohol Studies for his critical statements on the manuscript in its early stage, and to Douglas Spanier, a colleague psychologist, for his critical review of the chapter on the psychological approach. Lori Cobalis of Temple University's Institute for Survey Research and Robert Quan proved of great assistance in typing, proofreading, and checking references. Other appropriate acknowledgements are made in footnotes for material quoted at various places in the monograph.

JULIAN B. ROEBUCK
RAYMOND G. KESSLER

INTRODUCTION

PURPOSE

T HE PRIMARY PURPOSE OF THIS BOOK is to examine recent (1940-1971) theories and research data concerned with the etiology of alcoholism. More specifically, the authors were interested in (1) the formulation of a categorical framework reflecting the theoretical approaches and related research bearing on the etiology of alcoholism as found in the literature and (2) the presentation, analysis, and evaluation of representative theories and research findings within this classification.

Methodology

The representative material reviewed was that published between the 1940's and early 1971 in scholarly journals in the fields of sociology, psychology, psychiatry, and the biological sciences (as well as books and monographs within these disciplines bearing directly or indirectly on alcoholism). No attempt was made to review all the literature in the area. The review and analysis focus on two major tasks: the delineation of patterns or trends in, and an evaluation of (1) research results and reports on alcoholism and (2) causation theories. A limited amount of descriptive background information, not directly related to the etiology of alcoholism, is included for clarification purposes.

CATEGORIES

Many postulates in the literature about alcoholism do not qualify as well developed systematic theory, and a plethora of material exists in terms of implicit hypotheses or loose hypothetical statements. Nonetheless, many of these postulates were included in our analysis. The major focus, however, was on the more specific and explicit theoretical and research collections which were found to exist (roughly) within three categorical approaches: (1) the constitutional—focusing on genetic, physiological, and biochemical factors; (2) the psychological—focusing on the relationship of alcoholism to psychological mechanisms and personality; and (3) the sociological—relating alcoholism to sociocultural and demographic factors.

We disclosed a number of subapproaches within this schema, many of which were not mutually exclusive. Therefore, at points our classification is by necessity arbitrary. Furthermore, it is not wholly novel since similar frameworks in a loose and scattered sense exist elsewhere. Although the review includes an examination of a wide range of substances on alcoholism, the works presented herein meet one or more of the following criteria: (1) those representative of a given approach in terms of theory, analytic assumptions, methodology, or results; (2) those contradicting (systematically) representative works or theories; (3) those constituting other reviewers' evaluations or summations of theory and research in the area of alcoholism; and (4) those providing supportive knowledge and classification substance to causation theories.

CONTENTS

THE ETIOLOGY OF
ALCOHOLISM

Chapter I

ALCOHOLISM: DEFINITIONS AND INCIDENCE

In examining the literature on the causes of alcoholism, one comes across many different terms denoting alcoholism. Some authors simply use the term "alcoholic" while some use the term "chronic alcoholic" in an attempt to emphasize the frequent and long-term aspects of alcohol. Others use the term "alcohol addict" or "addictive drinker." In general, the differences in terminology reflect each author's theoretical orientation.[1]

One term which seems to have gone out of style in the recent literature is "dipsomania." Tahka[2] states the following:

> Although the concept of dipsomania originally included all forms of pathological drinking today it refers exclusively to periodic forms of inebriety. Dipsomania is characterized by remittent alcoholic bouts, often preceded by alterations in mood, and lasting from a few days to several weeks. In the intervals, which may amount to several months, the affected person usually remains abstinent.

There is no universally accepted definition of alcoholism, and many scholars contend that the term encompasses a wide range of pathological behavior syndromes associated with alcohol use. In short, it might be more appropriate to speak of "alcoholisms" rather than alcoholism, since there are a number of distinct disorders whose major common characteristic is the pathological seeking for, and reaction to, the effects of alcohol. Specifications in the literature are mixed and vary from the disease concept to pure sociological frames of reference. Some suggest formulations in terms of community standards and social reaction, e.g. the utilization of frequency of arrests for drunkenness and contacts with social agencies, clinics, mental hospitals, Alcoholics Anonymous, and so on.[3]

Many designations of alcoholics and alcoholism deal almost exclusively with the idea of the damage caused to the individual himself and to society, e.g. Williams[4] describes an alcoholic as anyone whose drinking behavior interferes with his or her activities as a useful and productive citizen; Jellinek[5] views alcoholism as any use of alcohol that causes damage to the individual or society or both; Coleman[6] sees alcoholics as individuals whose alcohol consumption seriously impairs their life adjustment.

Other authors, in their definitions, have added the concept of loss of control to the basic idea of damage. Diethelm[7] considers a person to be an alcoholic if his alcohol use interferes with a successful life in the physical, personality, or social spheres, and if he is unable to recognize the deleterious effects of alcohol or is unable to control his alcohol consumption even though he recognizes its negative effects. Chafetz and Demone[8] consider alcoholism to be a chronic behavioral disorder signified by undue preoccupation with alcohol to the detriment of physical and mental health, by a loss of control when drinking has begun, and by a self-destructive attitude in life situations. Jellinek[9] earlier (1952) pointed out that the disease conception of alcohol addiction does not apply to the excessive drinking of many drinkers but solely to the "loss of control" which occurs in only one group of alcoholics, namely "alcohol addicts."

Keller[10] adds the idea of "implicative" or "suspicion-arousing drinking," emphasizing the part that labeling of an alcoholic by others play in defining alcoholism. He sees alcoholics as those whose frequent and repeated drinking is in excess of the customary dietary and social drinking practices of the community. Drinking habits interfere with the drinkers' health, interpersonal relations, and social or economic functioning. Alcoholics suffer from stress or tension resulting from physiological, psychological, and/or social pressures. Alcohol provides temporary relief. Initially, the alcoholic is unable to refrain from drinking, and after he starts he is unable to quit.

Clinard,[11] utilizing a sociological approach, envisions alcoholism in terms of the culture in which the individual resides. He designates alcoholics as excessive drinkers who deviate markedly from drinking norms, as evidenced by the frequency and quantity of their consumption of alcohol and by the unconventional times and places they select for drinking.[12]

The World Health Organization's formula contains many features of the preceding definitions. Its position is that definitions should be free of theoretical bias, pending the development of more precise etiological knowledge.[13]

> Alcoholics are those excessive drinkers whose dependence upon alcohol has attained such a degree that it shows a noticeable mental disturbance or an interference with their bodily and mental health, their interpersonal relations, and their smooth social and economic functioning; or who show the prodromal signs of such development.

The Alcoholism Subcommittee of the World Health Organization delineates two basic types of alcoholics: "alcohol addicts" and "habitual symptomatic excessive drinkers." Excessive drinking in both groups is considered to be symptomatic of underlying psychological or social pathology. After several years of excessive drinking, "loss of control" over the alcoholic intake occurs in the case of the "alcohol addict," but is absent among "habitual symptomatic excessive drinkers." The disease concept applied to the "alcohol addict" is related to his loss of control and not to his excessive drinking. The nonaddictive alcoholic may be a sick person, but his ailment is not excessive drinking. He suffers from psychological or social difficulties from which alcohol gives temporary relief. Loss of drinking control by "alcoholic addicts" is a disease condition resulting from an abnormal personality of which excessive drinking is a symptom. Some nonaddictive alcoholics ("habitual symptomatic excessive drinkers") drink as much as, or more than, some "alcohol addicts."

THE DISEASE CONCEPT OF ALCOHOLISM CONTROVERSY

The major controversy in the alcoholic literature centers on the disease concept of alcoholism. The World Health Organization's nomenclature is criticized by many because of its vagueness, lack of operational significance, and disease concept. The disease prototype is deprecated by many scholars throughout the literature from several standpoints:[14]

1. It is confusing to the public and for research purposes.
2. It is difficult to operationalize for research purposes.
3. It is ambiguous.
4. It is difficult to separate symptoms from disease concept.
5. It is difficult to separate the "so-called" symptomatic drinker from the "so-called" addictive drinker.

6. There is the idea that alcoholism is an irreversible disease.

7. There is the possibility that alcoholism may be a symptom of a number of quite separate conditions.

8. The "so-called" alcoholic may be reacting to social, rather than personal cues.

9. The emphasis on alcoholism as a disease steers attention to the individual and away from the social labeling process, and the social consequences resulting from his drinking behavior.

10. Alcoholism does not fit a medical model and has not been defined in terms of treatment.

11. The concept of alcoholism as a disease may drive a wedge between the alcoholic and society and provide the problem drinker with an alibi for failure to change his behavior.

Wittingly or unwittingly some chief exponents of the disease concept (e.g., E. Morton Jellinek and Mark Keller) have met many of the foregoing criticisms by definitions which include, though transcend, alcoholism as merely a physical disease entity; and by distinguishing between specific types of alcoholism. Jellinek makes a distinction between "alcoholic addicts" and "habitual symptomatic excessive drinkers" in keeping with the two basic types proposed by the Alcohol Subcommittee of the World Health Organization. Keller[15] deviates from the classical disease concept in that he views alcoholism as a psychological disablement rather than a result of physical dependence, tolerance, or altered cell metabolism. He recognizes that there are various stages in alcoholism, a variety of development courses, various degrees of severity, different orders and combinations of manifestations, and varying symptoms, but he still maintains that alcoholism is a disease.

Jellinek[16] outlines the phases of alcoholic addiction indicating the progression of malign symptoms: prealcoholic phase, the pro-dromal phase, the crucial phase, and finally the chronic phase. Though he does not claim that every drinker inevitably progresses through these phases of action, such an implication is hard to overlook. He perceives alcoholism as a disease in which various body systems are progressively involved. Etiology varies and depends upon the alcohol-use syndrome presented by the alcoholic. Jellinek's logical typology follows: "Alpha alcoholism" is character-ized by "a purely psychological continual dependence to relieve bodily or emotional pain." There is no loss of control or progressive process with this type of drinker. "Beta alcoholism" occurs with organic disturbances, such as cirrhosis and polyneuritis. Dependence may be based on physical, psychological, or social conditions. Withdrawal symptoms are absent. "Gamma alcoholism" involves tolerance to alcohol, adaptive cell metabolism, withdrawal symptoms, and loss of drinking control. "Gamma alcoholism" is progressive and moves from psychological to physical dependency. Of all types, it results in the greatest harm to health and social relations. "Delta alcoholism" is similar to gamma, but is characterized by greater loss of drinking control. Withdrawal symptoms are more frequent and intense. Finally, "epsilon alcoholism" refers to periodic or episodic drinkers. Jellinek's typology is eclectic. He includes cultural and socioeconomic factors as well as physiological and psychological factors among the variables involved in drinking and alcoholism. Moreover, he recognizes that alcohol usage, in part, leads to the observed characteristics of alcoholics.

PROBLEM DRINKING AND PROBLEM DRINKERS

The concept of alcoholism as a disease survives, despite its limitations, especially in medical circles. It appears that further qualification is likely. Recently, a group of social scientists proposed that to label a person alcoholic and alcoholism a disease, implies that he (the alcoholic) suffers from a specific biological derangement and obscures the social and psychological aspects of his problem. The Cooperative Commission on the Studies of Alcoholism in its 1967 report (a report by T. F. Plaut) proffers the term "problem drinking" rather than "alcoholism." "Problem drinking is a repetitive use of beverage alcohol causing physical, psychological, or social harm to the drinker or to others."[17] Don Cahalan,[18] a social psychologist at the University of California at Berkeley, who recently published the results of the first nationwide survey ever conducted on the prevalence of alcohol-connected problems (*Problem Drinkers*, 1970), explains that this definition is compatible with Knupfer's more general definition that, "a problem connected fairly closely with drinking—any problem—constitutes a drinking problem."[19] In the first chapter of his book,

Cahalan makes a strong brief for use of the term "problem drinking," rather than alcoholism. He also discusses several sample surveys in the United States which have measured some aspects of problems associated with alcohol.

Cahalan's *Problem Drinkers* presents an analysis of the various types of problems relating to alcohol which developed in the lives of Americans, and describes which subgroups are most susceptible to problems associated with drinking. The data from this study of the correlates of drinking evolved from two probability samplings of the U. S. household population of adults (21 or older) in which a sample of persons who were initially interviewed in 1964-1965 (1,359 persons) were reinterviewed in 1967. The first stage of interviewing conducted in 1964-1965 resulted in a descriptive survey of drinking practices (Cahalan, Cisin, and Crossley, *American Drinking Practices,*[20] 1969); the second stage conducted in 1967 focused upon problems associated with drinking. Data from both sets of interviews were combined at certain junctures, thus providing fuller background information on respondents than could have been accomplished in a single interview. The sampling procedures for both stages skipped most institutionalized and "derelict" alcoholics, unless they were living in a household (census definition) at some time during the period of the initial field work in 1964-1965. This sampling method was based on the belief that many of the phenomena measured in studies of alcoholics actually reflect the process of institutionalization and de-socialization more than they measure the correlates of problem drinking per se. The plan was to follow up an adult population over a period of years in order to chart the course of the development or decline of drinking-related problems as they occur. This study represents the second phase in a longitudinal program of research which will be completed (Stage III) in 1975. Though dealing with problem drinkers rather than alcoholics per se, Cahalan expects his findings to be helpful in understanding the process of becoming an alcoholic.[21]

Cahalan's rationale, accepted by many social scientists, for the use of the term "problem drinking" instead of "alcoholism," may be summarized by the following points:

1. The disease notion of alcoholism as a physical entity is

unsupportable.

2. From an etiological standpoint, more can be gained by analyzing the prevalence of a range of specific, operationally defined problems associated with alcohol than by a nose count of alcoholics. Problem drinking in this context must be defined in terms of a specific kind of problem related to alcohol.

3. Problem drinking places emphasis upon behavior rather than on the person and thus avoids the more permanent label, "alcoholism," which tends to be attached to the person.

4. The idea of problem drinking encourages inquiry into a typology of drinking problems and problem drinkers.

5. The problem drinking concept indicates that clear-cut distinctions may be made between the problem drinker and the nonproblem drinker, whereas alcoholism may imply that causation inheres excusively in the alcohol rather than also involving individual and environmental factors.[22]

CAHALAN'S DEFINITION OF PROBLEM DRINKERS

Cahalan's "problem drinkers" concept is very important for two reasons: his definition encompasses the elements of many other researchers' definitions, and he has recently completed the only nationwide survey on problem drinkers. He constructed his definitions of drinking-related problems from three sources: the hypotheses of Jellinek and Keller; T. F. Plaut's definition of problem drinking; and the types of drinking problems measured in past U. S. surveys.[23] He selected eleven specific types of problems for analysis in the data from the national survey:

1. Frequent intoxication, or exceeding what was defined as a moderate level in a combined frequency and amount-per-occasion measure, or getting intoxicated fairly often.

2. Binge drinking (being intoxicated for more than one day at a time).

3. Symptomatic drinking behavior (symptomatic dependence upon alcohol) as inferred from finding it difficult to stop drinking, sneaking drinks, etc.

4. Psychological dependence on alcohol.

5. Problems with current spouse or with relatives because of one's drinking.

6. Problems with friends or neighbors caused by one's drinking.

7. Problems concerning one's work or employment occurring in relation to one's drinking.

8. Problems with the police, or accidents in which someone is hurt or property damage occurs, owing to one's drinking.

9. Health (for example, physician advises patient to cut down on drinking).

10. Financial problems connected with one's drinking.

11. Belligerence or fighting associated with one's drinking.

These categories were concerned with drinking behavior itself and reasons for drinking, problems connected with interpersonal relations, and miscellaneous problems or potential problems not classifiable into either drinking behavior or interpersonal relations. Two principles underlying the definitions of drinking-related problems in this survey are (1) the selection of socially defined problem behaviors that are regarded by the individual himself or by his significant others as problems and (2) the selection of problems indicating addictive drinking from the public health or medical point of view. The data for scoring each interviewee on each of eleven types of problems were secured from approximately seventy-five items applied at the time of the second interviewing stage in 1967. The prevalence of the eleven types of drinking-related problems was measured in terms of occurrence within three years (1964-1967).

DEFINITIONS UTILIZED IN THE ANALYSIS OF THE LITERATURE

The foregoing discussion reveals that the authors faced a problem of selection and classification in their attempts to analyze theories and data on alcoholism, since scholars employ a melange of definitions which make cross-studies research comparisons difficult. Social scientists and other nonmedical scholars interested in alcoholism have negated the disease concept in connection with the study of alcohol-related problems. A growing number of researchers direct their attention to problem drinkers rather than to alcoholics. Though vehemently denied by representatives of several approaches, the alcoholic-problem drinker controversy, in part, is a semantic one. The researcher, of whatever persuasion, may operationalize his perception of alcoholism or problem drinking to meet (his own) specific research needs.

Keller and Jellinek are justified in retaining the disease concept of alcoholism. Both realize and appreciate the fact that alcoholism is more than just a medical problem and that psychological and sociological factors are involved it its etiology. All diseases do not have to have a biological base and, as Keller notes, many diseases including alcoholism manifest inconstant characteristics. (This of course does not gainsay constitutional factors in alcoholism.) Keller claims that alcoholism is a disease because the alcoholic is unable to consistently choose whether or not he should engage in a self-injurious behavior. The chief issue here is again semantic. How de we define disease? Obviously, even by the criteria used by those advocating the appellation, "problem drinking," a number of problem drinkers are alcoholics and need medical as well as other kinds of attention. Additionally, a number of those labeled "problem drinkers" will eventually become alcoholics.

Perhaps those who prefer to deal with drinking-related problems are in a better position to study drinking practices over time than those who deal with alcoholics. Cahalan has shown that large numbers of people, at one time or another, have drinking problems and that many of these same people "mature out" of these difficulties. On the other hand, some people might "mature out" of alcoholism or into alcoholism from problem drinking. Cahalan's claim that a study of problem drinking places more emphasis on the individual's behavior than does the study of alcoholics is not necessarily the case. Various kinds of behaviors or behavior models may be used as a dimension of study in the analysis of alcoholics. Researchers who study alcoholics are not compelled to concentrate on "the alcoholic effects" of alcohol on a subject to the exclusion of the subject's personality and environment. In fact, few do. In sum, various students of alcoholism have devised drinking typologies which appear to meet many of Cahalan's criticisms, including different kinds of problem drinkers.

The point is not made that alcoholics and problem drinkers constitute the same class of individuals. Obviously, all alcoholics would appear to be problem drinkers. Some problem drinkers are alcoholics, however, and some are not. Some problem drinkers will become alcoholics and some will not. Some problem drinkers and some alcoholics "mature out" of their difficulties. Whether one researches the etiology of alcoholism or of problem drinking, longitudinal surveys are necessary. The correlation of excessive drinking to problems at one point in time does not answer the question, "Which came first, the problem or the drinking?"[25] Finally and importantly, some definitions of alcoholism and certainly all definitions of problem drinking involve a behavior dimension excluding drinking and alcoholic effects per se.

Since the works in the literature concerned with research data and the etiology of alcoholism involve definitions pertaining to alcoholics and to problem drinkers, and since in many instances these materials reflect an overlap, we decided to analyze research data and theories within both categories. We utilize the definitions given by the various authors, and we make the demarcations between problem drinkers and alcoholics when they are made.

In summary, most of the theoretical formulations on alcoholics and alcoholism deal with the following aspects of alcohol usage:

1. Self-destruction.

2. Interference with the individual's physical, mental, or social functioning or adjustment.

3. Exceeding the norms (or dietary or social customs) of society in terms of quantity, frequency, and time and place of alcohol consumption.

4. Loss of control.

5. Noticeable or suspicious behavior in a drinker.

6. Problem drinking.

The operational definitions (in the literature) used to define the alcoholic for research purposes generally fall into three general categories related to the type of sample utilized:

1. *The captive sample.* These are persons who have been designated alcoholics because of arrest for offenses involving alcohol consumption, or those who are inpatients or outpatients with a diagnosis of alcoholism or a closely related condition. In general, incarceration or institutionalization caused by alcohol consumption or diagnosis defines the alcoholic.

2. *The located sample.* These persons defined as alcoholics or

problem drinkers are found through various surveys. They are usually located in a larger nonalcoholic sample chosen by various probability sampling procedures. In most cases, the individual is classified as an alcoholic or problem drinker because of his attitudes toward alcohol, his consumption of alcohol, or by reports from friends or family members. Problem drinkers may be determined by interviewing techniques (specific questions on drinking-related problems) with large probability samples.

3. *The longitudinal sample.* The persons involved in a longitudinal study may be defined as alcoholics or problem drinkers when followed up for some time by diagnosis; institutionalization or incarceration, as in the case of the captive sample; or by their behavior and attitudes, or reports thereon, as in the case of the located sample.

DRINKING PATTERNS IN THE UNITED STATES

Historically speaking, Americans have been ambivalent in their attitudes toward alcohol, and alcohol usage in the contemporary United States still represents a conflict of values.[26] Excessive drinking and alcoholism now, as in the past, signify deviant behavior. The Calvinistic tradition, though not as viable as in yesteryear, still survives among some religious and regional groups. At one time or another, moralists, religionists, and even some students of human behavior (as separate entities or in combination) have attacked alcohol usage as a major contributor to many problems, including physical and mental ill health, divorce and family problems, sexual immorality, poverty, delinquency, crime, and auto and other accidents.[27]

Despite the Calvinistic influence, an increasing number of people view social drinking as useful and even necessary. Alcoholic beverages are used to celebrate holidays and other special events, to negotiate social and business encounters, and simply to entertain. In many homes and in many social situations one is expected to proffer drinks. To many people of varied age groups, having a "good time" is synonymous with "getting high." Drinking behavior today is either more appropriate or more acceptable in a larger number of social situations than it has been in the past.

The measurement of alcohol use varies with the descriptive

criteria utilized, e.g. the frequency of drinks, the frequency of drinking occasions, the number of persons admitting to drinking, the amount consumed per drinking occasion, the kinds of alcohol used, and the time span of drinking behavior. The type of drinker or drinking poses another dimension of measurement—social or controlled drinking, heavy drinking, alcoholic drinking, chronic alcoholic drinking, problem drinking.

Most national and local surveys record that approximately two-thirds of the population over 21 drink alcoholic beverages to some extent. Add to this 10 million youth (16-20) drinkers and we have approximately 90 million Americans over 15 who drink. Some investigators estimate that we have as many as 128 million drinkers. Mulford,[28] in a 1963 study, reported that approximately 71 percent of the adult population, or 80 million persons, drink some type of alcoholic beverage during the year. Several studies of teen-age alcohol use in various parts of the United States between 1953 and 1963 find that most high school students have consumed alcoholic beverages. Straus and Bacon[29] reported in 1953 on the drinking practices of 16,300 students in 27 American colleges throughout the country. They estimate that 74 percent of their sample used alcoholic beverages. Various studies of drinking in high-school and college-age groups[30] disclose that from 8 to 10 million young people (aged 16-20) drink as a group. High-school student drinkers are not heavy drinkers.

Mulford,[31] in his survey of 1963, utilized both an index of drinking frequency and the amount of alcohol consumed. He found that 30 percent of the population are abstainers (22% of the men and 38% of the women); 28 percent drink infrequently (24% of the men, 32% of the women). He classified 32 percent of his sample as light drinkers, 30 percent as moderate drinkers, and 8 percent as heavy drinkers. He reported that among heavy drinkers, males outnumbered females by four to one.

Cahalan and Cisin,[32] in a study of drinking behavior utilizing a sample of 2,746 adults (1964-1965), discovered that 32 percent of the population are "abstainers" (drink less than once per year, if at all). Most of these abstainers are lifetime abstainers. Cahalan, Cisin, and Crossley[33] in *American Drinking Practices* report that 32 percent of Americans are abstainers, 28 percent are light drinkers, 15 percent are infrequent drinkers, 13 percent are moderate drinkers, and 12 percent are heavy drinkers. Twenty-one percent of male drinkers are heavy drinkers; five percent of women drinkers are heavy drinkers.

"Abstainers"—drink less than once a year or not at all; "Infrequent drinkers"—drink at least once a year, but less than once a month; "Light drinkers"—drink at least once a month, but typically only one or two drinks on a single occasion; "Moderate drinkers"—drink at least once a month, typically several times, but usually with no more than three or four drinks per occasion; "Heavy drinkers"—drink nearly every day with five or more per occasion at least once in a while, or about once weekly with usually five or more per occasion.[34]

Mulford's[35] comparisons of the prevalence of drinkers in 1963 with those of earlier studies show the present rate of drinking (1963) to be slightly higher in the total population (as well as by sex, age, and education). Clinard[36] reasons from this and other studies that the rate of drinkers is increasing, that each generation tends to have a larger proportion of persons who drink, and that most persons who drink remain drinkers throughout life. Clinard also describes the various types of public drinking houses found in the United States and the patterns of drinking behavior that occur within them. He points to the large number of bars and taverns (over 200,000) and their continual proliferation to meet the needs of various kinds of drinkers and drinking groups as additional evidence of the extent of drinking. Clinard estimates that one-third of all liquor sales are made in taverns. Cavan,[37] in an ethnographic study of bar behavior in San Francisco, found that in 1964 the California Department of Alcoholic Beverage Control listed about 2,000 establishments in that city as licensed to sell alcoholic beverages for consumption on the premises (792 of these were strictly bars and did not serve food).

The amount of money spent on alcoholic beverages and excise taxes, and the rate of alcoholic consumption are additional indicators of alcoholic drinking. In 1959, $9.6 billion was spent on alcoholic beverages. In 1960, the Treasury Department collected $3,193,714,000 in excise taxes on liquor, more than was collected on gasoline, tobacco, or automobiles. In 1960, the per capita consumption of distilled spirits was 1.90 gallons; of wine, 1.32 gallons; and of beer, 21.95 gallons—for a total per capita consumption of 2.07 gallons of absolute alcohol. This figure has barely changed since 1850. The consumption of spirits has decreased in this time span, while the use of wine and beer has grown.[38] Drinkers consumed an estimated 370 million gallons of distilled spirits in 1970—up from 362 million gallons in 1969, reports the Licensed Beverage Industries, Inc., in the *Wall Street Journal*.

EXTENT OF ALCOHOLISM

The number of alcoholics in the United States is difficult to determine because there is no universally accepted definition of alcoholism, and because the condition is frequently denied or hidden. Various methods have been used to estimate the incidence of alcoholism: clinical case studies; local surveys; national surveys; epidemiological studies of specific age, sex, class, religious and regional groups; morbidity and mortality rates for certain diseases; deviant behavior associated with drinking, and arrests for drunkenness. The best known method of estimating rates of alcoholism is Jellinek's formula:[39]

$$A = \left(\frac{PD}{K}\right) R$$

A = Total number of alcoholics alive in a given year.

D = The number of reported deaths from cirrhosis of the liver in that year.

P = The estimated percentage of such deaths attributable to alcoholism.

K = The estimated percentage of all alcoholics with complications who die of cirrhosis of the liver.

R = The estimated ratio of all alcoholics to alcoholics with complications.

This formula is based on the annual number of deaths due to cirrhosis of the liver, which is a common ailment among alcoholics. A proportion of these deaths are assumed to be due to alcoholism. This proportion times the total number of deaths yields the total number of alcoholics who die of cirrhosis of the liver. From this, an estimate is made of the number of living alcoholics with cirrhosis of the liver. To obtain an estimate of the total number of alcoholics (in the United States), this last figure is multiplied by 4. The figure 4 is derived from the estimate that alcoholics with cirrhosis of the liver constitute only 25 percent of the total number of alcoholics. According to this formula, there were an estimated 3,760,000 men and 710,000 women (totalling 4,470,000) alcoholics in 1960.[40] This total figure is equivalent to a rate of 4,000 alcoholics per 100,000 adults age 20 and over, which is equivalent to at least 1 in 15 adult persons who use alcohol. Keller[41] contends that if corrections were made in the population for groups who do not have high rates of alcoholism, the rates would be higher. Assuming the total number of alcoholics to be around 6.5 million, a rate based on white, urban, non-Jewish, non-Italian, non-abstaining males age 25 years and over would involve one in five or six as alcoholics.

Many critics of the Jellinek formula maintain that it under-reports alcoholics.[42] In fact, some regional surveys report twice as many alcoholics as would the Jellinek formula. Local survey reports or estimates of rates of alcoholism throughout the United States[43] vary from 14 to 50 per 1,000. Cisin and Cahalan[44] in a national survey estimated that 9 percent of the U.S. adult population were heavy "escape" drinkers. Cahalan[45] reports in his national survey, *Problem Drinkers,* that 9 percent of his sample (15% of the men and 4% of the women) had a relatively high percentage of drinking problems. When asked about their past experiences, Cahalan found an additional 9 percent of the total sample (16% of the men and 3% of the women) said that they had had drinking problems in the past. Coleman[46] estimated that 6 percent of the adult population, or 5 million people, were alcoholics. Keller and Efron,[47] on the basis of cross-country comparisons, report that in terms of total population, the United States has the highest rate of alcoholism (4,390 per 100,000—alcoholics with and without complications), followed by France and Sweden. Rates for chronic alcoholism (with compli-aations) are highest in Switzerland. The United States, in this area, ranks fourth. Most students of alcoholism would agree that approximately one out of every sixteen drinkers in the United States becomes an alcoholic. The term *alcoholic* in this estimation includes nonaddictive as well as addictive alcoholics.

NOTES AND REFERENCES

1. Straus, Robert: Alcohol. In Merton, Robert K., and Nisbet, Robert A. (Eds.): *Contemporary Social Problems,* 2nd ed. New York, Harcourt, Brace & World, 1966, pp. 259-262.
2. Tahka, Viekko: *The Alcoholic Personality.* Helsinki, The Finnish Foundation for Alcohol Studies, 1966, p. 18.

3. McCord, William, McCord, Joan and Gudeman, John: *Origins of Alcoholism.* Stanford, Stanford University Press, 1960, pp. 10-11.
4. Williams, Roger J.: *Alcoholism; The Nutritional Approach.* Austin, University of Texas Press, 1959, p. 3.
5. Jellinek, E. Morton: *The Disease Concept of Alcoholism.* New Haven, College and University Press, 1960, p. 7.
6. Coleman, James C.: *Abnormal Psychology and Modern Life.* Chicago, Scott, Foresman, 1964, p. 421.
7. Diethelm, Oskar: Research in chronic alcoholism. In Diethelm, O. (Ed.): *Etiology of Chronic Alcoholism.* Springfield, Thomas, 1955, p. 5.
8. Chafetz, Morris E., and Demone, Harold W.: *Alcoholism and Society.* New York, Oxford University Press, 1962, pp. 38-39.
9. Jellinek, E. Morton: Phases of alcohol addiction. *Quarterly Journal of Studies on Alcohol, 13:*674, December, 1952.
10. Keller, Mark: Definitions of alcoholism. *Quarterly Journal Studies on Alcohol, 21:*125-134, March, 1960. See also Keller, Mark: The definition of alcoholism and the estimation of its prevalence. In Pittman, David J., and Snyder, Charles R. (Eds.): *Society, Culture, and Drinking Patterns.* New York, Wiley & Sons, 1962, pp. 310-329.
11. Clinard, Marshall B.: *Sociology of Deviant Behavior,* 3rd ed. New York, Holt, Rinehart & Winston, 1963, p. 32.
12. Clinard, Marshall B.: *Ibid.,* pp. 414-415.
13. Expert committee on Mental Health, Alcoholism Subcommittee: *Second Report, World Health Organization Technical Report Series,* No. 48, 1952. An additional definition is found in Cooperative Commission on the Study of Alcoholism: *Alcohol Problems.* New York, Oxford University Press, 1967, p. 39. For further discussions of definitions of alcoholism, see Jellinek, E. Morton: *The Disease Concept of Alcoholism, op. cit.,* pp. 37-45; Chafetz, Morris E., and Demone, Harold W.: *Alcoholism and Society, op. cit.,* pp. 33-39; and Tahka, Veikko: *The Alcoholic Personality, op. cit.,* pp. 16-19.
14. Cahalan, Don: *Problem Drinkers, A National Survey.* San Francisco, Jossey-Bass, 1970, pp. 3-10.
15. Cahalan, Don: *Ibid.,* p. 5.
16. Jellinek, E. Morton: *The Disease Concept of Alcoholism, op. cit.,* pp. 36-41.
17. Plaut, T. F.: *Alcohol Problems: A Report to the Nation by the Cooperative Commission on the Study of Alcoholism.* New York, Oxford University Press, 1967, pp. 37-38.
18. Calahan, Don: *op. cit.,* p. 13.
19. Knupfer, Genevieve: The epidemiology of problem drinking. *American Journal of Public Health, 57:*973-986, August, 1967.
20. Cahalan, Don, Cisin, Ira H., and Crossley, Helen M.: *American Drinking*

Practices. New Brunswick, Rutgers Center of Alcohol Studies, 1969, pp. 1-17 (Ch. I presents methodology).

21. Cahalan, Don: *op. cit.,* pp. 167-176.
22. Cahalan, Don: *Ibid.,* p. 12.
23. Cahalan, Don: *Ibid.,* p. 26.
24. Cahalan, Don: *Ibid.,* pp. 26-27, pp. 35-37.
25. Cahalan, Don: *Ibid.,* p. 13.
26. Myerson, Abraham: Alcohol: A study of social ambivalence. *Quarterly Journal of Studies on Alcohol, 1*:13-20, June, 1940.
27. Clinard, Marshall B.: *op. cit.,* pp. 389-391.
28. Mulford, Harold A.: Drinking and deviant drinking U.S.A., 1963. *Quarterly Journal of Studies on Alcohol, 25*:634-648, December, 1964.
29. Straus, Robert, and Bacon, Selden D.: *Drinking in College.* New Haven, Yale University Press, 1953.
30. See Bacon, Margaret, and Jones, Mary Brush: *Teenage Drinking.* New York, Crowell, 1968; and McCarthy, Raymond G.: High school drnking studies. In McCarthy, Raymond G. (Ed.): *Drinking and Intoxication.* New Haven, College & University Press, 1959, pp. 205-211. Teenage drinking rates below 50% were found in a study in Kansas; see McCluggage, Marston M. et al.: Summary of essential findings in the Kansas study. In McCarthy, Raymond G. (Ed.): *Ibid.,* pp. 211-218. See also Maddox, George L.: Teenage drinking in the United States. In Pittman, David J., and Snyder, Charles R. (Eds.): *op. cit.,* pp. 230-245.
31. Mulford, Harold A.: *op. cit.,* pp. 634-648.
32. Cahalan, Don, and Cisin, Ira H.: American drinking practices: Summary of findings from a national probability sample, I. Extent of drinking by population subgroups. *Quarterly Journal of Studies on Alcohol, 29*:130-151, March, 1968; and American drinking practices: Summary of findings from a national probability sample, II. Measurement of massed versus spaced drinking. *Quarterly Journal of Studies on Alcohol, 29*:642-656, September, 1968.
33. Cahalan, Don, Cisin, Ira H., and Crossley, Helen M.: *op. cit.,* p. 19.
34. Cahalan, Don, Cisin, Ira H., and Crossley, Helen M.: *ibid.,* p. 19.
35. Mulford, Harold A.: *op. cit.,*
36. Clinard, Marshall B.: *op. cit.,* pp. 401-406.
37. Cavan, Sherri. *Liquor License, An Ethnography of Bar Behavior.* Chicago, Aldine, 1966, p. 23.
38. Gold, Harry, and Scarpitti, Frank R. (Eds.): *Combating Social Problems.* New York, Holt, Rinehart & Winston, 1967, p. 465. See also *Wall Street Journal,* June 3, 1971.
39. Popham, Robert E.: The Jellinek alcoholism estimation formula and its application to Canadian data. *Quarterly Journal of Studies on Alcohol, 17*:559-593, December, 1956. See also Keller, Mark: Alco-

holism: Nature and extent of the problem. *The Annals of the American Academy of Political and Social Science, 315*:1-11, January, 1958.

40. Keller, Mark: *op. cit.,* pp. 310-329.
41. Keller, Mark: *ibid.,* pp. 319-320.
42. See Seeley, John R.: Estimating the prevalence of alcoholism: A critical analysis of the Jellinek formula. *Quarterly Journal of Studies on Alcohol, 20*:240-254, June, 1959. Also Brenner, Berthold: Estimating the prevalence of alcoholism: Toward a modification of the Jellinek formula. *Quarterly Journal of Studies on Alcohol, 20*:225-265, June, 1959; and Keller, Mark: *op. cit.* In light of these criticisms Jellinek suggested modifications of the constants in his formula. He had even suggested that the formula no longer be used. See Jellinek, E. Morton: Estimating the prevalence of alcoholism: Modified values in the Jellinek formula and an alternative approach. *Quarterly Journal of Studies on Alcohol, 20*:261-269, June, 1959.
43. Blum, Richard H., assisted by Braunstein, Lauraine: Mild altering drugs and dangerous behavior: Alcohol. In *Task Force Report: Drunkenness,* publication of Commission on Law Enforcement and Administration of Justice. Washington, U. S. Government Printing Office, 1967, pp. 29-49. See also Bailey, Margaret B., Haberman, Paul W., and Alksne, Harold: The epidemiology of alcoholism in an urban residential area. *Quarterly Journal of Studies on Alcohol, 26*:19-40, March, 1965; and Mulford, Harold A., and Miller, Donald S.: Drinking in Iowa, V. Drinking and alcoholic drinking. *Quarterly Journal of Studies on Alcohol, 21*:483-499, September, 1960. Also see Seeley, John R.: The ecology of alcoholism: A beginning. In Pittman, David J., and Snyder, Charles R. (Eds.): *op. cit.,* pp. 331-334.
44. Cahalan, Don, and Cisin, Ira H.: American drinking practices: Summary of findings from a national probability sample, I. Extent of drinking by population subgroups; and American drinking practices: Summary of findings from a national probability sample, II. Measurement of massed versus spaced drinking.
45. Cahalan, Don: *op. cit.,* pp. 37 and 142.
46. Coleman, James C.: *op. cit.,* p. 421.
47. Keller, Mark, and Efron, Vera: The prevalence of alcoholism. *Quarterly Journal of Studies on Alcohol, 16*:634, December, 1955.

Chapter II

THE CONSTITUTIONAL APPROACH

RESEARCHERS EMPLOYING THE CONSTITUTIONAL APPROACH view alcoholism as a form of addiction defined in terms of the pharmacological criteria of tolerance and dependence. They deem it imperative to differentiate between the pharmacological and sociocultural criteria of alcoholism in order to avoid the confusion generated by the ritual polemics over definitions. To them, the objective pharmacological criteria of addiction is a more important province than the social consequence of alcohol. Therefore, they prefer a disease model, and the social consequences of drinking are viewed in terms of alcohol effects.

Many constitutionalists are not primarily concerned with etiological factors, but rather analyze those variables that combine to perpetuate and maintain drinking behavior once the syndrome of alcoholism has been established. Constitutionalists explicitly or implicitly maintain that the cause of alcoholism is basically physiological. Many of their theories stipulate the existence of a biochemical predisposition involving some physiological or structural defect which causes the individual to become physically addicted to alcohol. Once a person with such a proclivity begins or continues drinking, he becomes addicted because of peculiarities of his biochemical makeup. Among physiological causes that have been proposed are genetic propensity, metabolic defects (such as abnormal enzyme levels), disturbed glandular functions, abnormal levels of various body chemicals, and allergic reactions.

INHERITED PREDISPOSITION
Studies on Human Heredity and Alcoholism

A number of investigators have studied twins and other relatives of alcoholics in an attempt to determine a hereditary base for alcoholism.

Bleuler[1] investigated the family backgrounds of 34 male and 16 female Americans undergoing treatment for alcoholism. Fourteen of the fathers and 10 of the siblings (of the sample) were alcoholics. He discovered that the incidence of alcoholism among the parents and siblings of the alcoholics in his study was higher than that in the general population.[2] In a similar study of 38 male and 12 female alcoholics undergoing treatment for alcoholism in Zurich, Bleuler[3] again found alcoholism more frequently in the parents and siblings of the alcoholics than in the general population.

E. M. Jellinek[4] has reviewed several studies postulating a hereditary basis of alcoholism. From a total sample of 4,372 chronic alcoholics, he noted that 52 percent had been reared by one or more alcoholic parents. He notes that in 15 studies of alcoholics an average of 35 percent of the respondents (alcoholics) had been submitted to a "hereditary liability." Exclusive of alcoholic parentage, 35 percent of this sample had deviant (criminal, psychotic, other aberrations) parentage. Jellinek concludes from his analysis of these studies that it is not a disposition toward alcoholism that is inherited, but rather a weak constitution which is unable to resist the social risks of inebriety. Jellinek finds that the "hereditary factor" does not become operative without other "social factors," but he does profess a constiutional basis. Kinsey[5] and Moore and Ramseur[6] report alcoholic parents in the backgrounds of 15 of 46 hospitalized female alcoholics and 45 of 100 hospitalized male alcoholics.

Kaij[7] drew a sample of twins by comparing data on a listing of twins kept at the University of Lund with data on registers kept by two County Temperance Boards in Skane, the southernmost part of Sweden. Swedish Temperance Boards are responsible for the social care of alcoholics and keep records of reports from police, courts, friends, family doctors, and other sources relevant to temporary or continuous cases of alcohol abuse. The sampling was performed in 1953 and the Temperance Board register yielded the names of 23,221 men who had been born in the area since 1890. Opposite-sex and female-twin pairs were excluded and the comparison yielded 310 male-twin pairs, in which at least one partner was registered. Errors in the registers and exclusion of persons whose twin had died before the age of 15 further reduced the sample.

The final sample consisted of 146 dizygotic pairs and 59 monozygotic pairs in which, at best, one partner was registered with the Temperance Board. Concordance for registration with the Temperance Board was 54.2 percent for the MZ twins and 31.5 percent for the DZ twins. (p<.01).

Kaij personally interviewed 292 of the twins. On the basis of the interviews and analysis of Temperance Board records, individual twin pair members were placed into 1 of 4 classes of drinking behavior: (0) abstainers and below-average consumers; (1) average consumers who have a drink now and then; (2) weekend drinkers and above-average consumers; (3) heavy abusers;

TABLE I
RATES OF CONCORDANCE
AMONG MZ AND DZ
TWIN PAIRS AT FOUR LEVELS
OF DRINKING BEHAVIOR

Twin Pair Types	All Classes	Drinking Behavior		
		Class 2,3,4	Class 3,4	Class 4
MZ pairs	53.5	55.6	63.0	71.4
DZ pairs	28.3	20.0	26.7	32.3
Difference MZ - DZ	25.2	35.6	36.3	39.1

Adapted from L. Kaij, *Alcoholism in Twins: Studies on the Sequels of Alcohol.* Stockholm, Almquist and Wiksell, 1960, Table 14, p. 3.

and (4) chronic alcoholics (see Table I). "Chronic alcoholics" were defined as such by one or more of the following criteria: those experiencing frequent blackouts, extended drinking binges, trouble with families, police, jobs; those subjected to the intervention of Temperance authorities; those continually intoxicated; and those suffering from cirrhosis of the liver or alcoholic psychoses. There were 31 DZ pairs in which at least one twin was a chronic alcoholic. In 10 of these pairs, both were chronic alcoholics, making a concordance of 32.3 percent. There were 14 MZ pairs in which at least one twin was a chronic alcoholic. In 10 of these pairs both were chronic alcoholics, making for a concordance of 71.4 percent.

Kaij calculated rates of concordance for MZ and DZ pairs by classes of drinking behavior. The data in Table I indicate that concordance for MZ pairs increases with alcohol abuse, while the concordance for DZ pairs remains at roughly the same level.[9] Kaij claims on the basis of his data "that common genetical factors are the main cause of the higher concordance rate of drinking habits and of chronic alcoholism in MZ twins."[9] The data clearly support the heritability of alcoholism from Kaij's major premise.

Partanen et al.[10] conducted a multi-stage twin study which began with a target population of all-male twin pairs born in Finland between 1920-1929 (both of whom were alive and residing in Finland in 1958). Analysis of data and records from parish and population registers showed that 2,393 male pairs had been born in that time period. Of these, there were only 1,044 pairs in which both were surviving and living in Finland. Addresses were obtained through the National Pension Institute and from local census authorities. In 142 pairs either or both refused to cooperate or could not be located. The final sample consisted of 902 pairs: 198 MZ, 641 DZ, and 63 of unknown zygosity, all of whom were interviewed by male employees of the State Alcohol Monopoly.

An individual was classified as an abstainer if he stated that he had never consumed alcohol or if he estimated that the average interval between two consecutive drinking occasions exceeded three years. Concordance rates for abstaining from alcohol were .944 for the MZ pairs and .894 for the DZ pairs (significantly different at the 5% level by chi-square analysis). These figures showed that abstaining from alcohol was influenced by hereditary variation.

Factor analysis of responses to a number of questions on drinking revealed three primary drinking behavior variables: *density, amount,* and *lack of control. Density* (frequency of drinking and duration of drinking occasions) and *amount* (amount of alcohol consumed per average drinking occasion) showed significant heritability while *lack of control* (ability to control amount and ability to stop drinking) showed no significant heritability.

A "social complications" score was derived from nine items on the interview schedule concerned with the consequences of drinking. The respondents reported on financial difficulties resulting from drinking, job difficulties as a consequence of drinking, arrest history involving drinking, and subjection to official measures aimed against abuses of alcohol. No significant hereditary variations were found for social complications.

An individual was classified as a heavy user if he admitted consuming more than the equivalent of 7.5 cl absolute alcohol on both of his last two drinking occasions. The percentage of heavy users constituted 31.2 percent of the total sample. Concordance rates for heavy use of alcohol were .753 for MZ pairs and .633 for DZ pairs (significantly different at the .001 level by chi-square analysis). Definite evidence of the heritability of heavy alcohol usage was found (see Table II).

Complete records on arrests for drunkenness had been kept by the Finnish Alcohol Monopoly since 1945 and these records were utilized to calculate rates of concordance for arrests for drunkenness. About one-sixth of all respondents in the sample had at least one arrest for drunkenness. There were 135 MZ pairs in which at least one twin had been arrested for drunkenness and 409 DZ pairs in which at least one twin had been arrested for drunkenness. The rates of concordance were .800 for the MZ pairs and .778 for the DZ pairs. These two rates were not significantly different and did not indicate hereditary influence (see Table II).

TABLE II
RATES OF CONCORDANCE
FOR HEAVY USE OF ALCOHOL,
ARRESTS FOR DRUNKENNESS, AND PRESENCE
OF ADDICTIVE SYMPTOMS

	Heavy Use of Alcohol		Arrest for Drunkenness		Presence of Addictive Symptoms	
	MZ	DZ	MZ	DZ	MZ	DZ
No. of pairs	198	641	135	409	198	641
Concordance	.753	.633	.800	.778	.737	.686
Chi-square	9.59		.30		1.86	
	(p < .001)		(p > .05)		(p > .05)	

From J. Partanen et al., *The Inheritance of Drinking Behavior. Helsinki, The Finnish Foundation for Alcohol Studies*, 1966, adapted from Tables 30 and 31, p. 104.

By use of a "hierarchial grouping procedure,"[11] all subjects were placed into six distinct, but internally homogeneous groups, on the basis of drinking behavior. Four of these groups, comprising nearly one-third of the sample, differed from normal users in almost every dimension of alcohol usage and its consequences.[12] Items related to social consequences of drinking seemed to discriminate best between normal users and other drinkers. Other discriminating items referred to blackouts, age at first hangover drink, frequency of drinking, lack of control, etc. The individuals comprising the four deviant drinking behavior groups were considered to have "addictive symptoms." The rate of concordance for addictive symptoms was .737 for the MZ pairs and .686 for the DZ pairs (not statistically significant; see Table II).

Partanen's results on several dimensions support the operation of hereditary factors in alcoholism; on other dimensions the relevance of hereditary factors is found to be questionable or irrelevant. Partanen maintains that the discovery of hereditary differences between individuals relating to alcoholism is a complex problem. Various methodologies utilize different definitions and employ different operational indicators. Partanen found hereditary differences when he used indicators of alcoholism based on "drinking behavior and dependence on alcohol." On the other hand, when he used "social consequences of drinking" as a criterion of alcoholism, he did not find significant statistical evidence for hereditary differences.

Eysenck,[18] in a recent review of European twin studies, reports a concordance of 65 percent for alcoholism among 26 MZ twins and a concordance of 30 percent for 56 DZ twins. As part of a larger study, Amark[14] investigated alcoholism, alcohol abuse, and other illnesses in the families of alcoholics. The sample consisted of 103 male alcoholics treated at a psychiatric clinic in Stockholm during the years 1945-1947, and 103 male patients treated at ten Swedish institutions for alcoholics in 1947. Basic information on the parents and siblings was obtained from local parish records. These records also contained information on causes of death as well as names of all insane and mentally defective persons. With the help of this basic information, extracts were procured from the Law Court Records of the Royal Board of Prisons and from the records of the Liquor Control Board. Data was also obtained from the Swedish alcohol-control System Companies.[15] The country is divided into 41 selling areas and in each of these there is a so-called System Company which has a monopoly on sales in that area. Anyone desiring to buy spirits or wine must have a passbook which entitles him to purchase a certain quantity of liquor per month. Anyone under 21 years of age or anyone who has been convicted of drunkenness or offenses connected with the abuse of alcohol may not possess a passbook. These System Companies maintain careful personal data records. Every passbook owner in the area is registered with the company. This record contains data on the individual's purchases of liquor, economic situation, and conviction for drunkenness and other offenses. Persons who do not own a passbook are registered if they have been convicted of drunkenness or other criminal offenses. When anyone applies for a passbook, a detailed inquiry is made into his background. The data was incomplete for some parents because data collection was inadequate during their early years. The data for mothers and sisters was incomplete because married women rarely receive passbooks. The data for the brothers, on the other hand, was almost complete. Additional information on parents and siblings was gained through interviews. Information was available on 349 brothers, 365 sisters, 186 fathers, and 200 mothers. There were 53 cases of alcoholism among the brothers, none among the sisters, 48 among the fathers, and 4 cases among the mothers.

Morbidity rates for alcoholism were computed for the general population and compared with the rates for the parents and siblings. For brothers and fathers, the rates were significantly higher than those of the general population of males. The rates for sisters and mothers were not significantly different from the rate for females in the general population. Brothers of alcoholics showed higher frequencies of abuse of alcohol, suspension of passbook due to intemperance, and conviction for drunkenness than males in the general population. Sisters, on the other hand, did not differ appreciably from the general female population in regard to these indicators.

Amark[16] utilized Weinberg's Proband method in his data analysis and concludes, from the statistically significant differences found, that among alcoholics there are certain groups in which heredity factors play an essential role in the origin of alcoholism.

Winokur and Clayton[17] studied the family backgrounds of 69 male and 45 female alcoholics admitted to a psychiatric ward of a general hospital in St. Louis. The greater frequency of alcoholism and other psychiatric disorders in the parents of the female alcoholics led them to suggest that one possible explanation was an X-linked recessive gene.[18]

Roe[19] compared the adult adjustment of 36 children of alcoholic fathers with the adjustment of 25 children of non-alcoholic parentage. All subjects were white, non-Jewish and had been placed in foster homes (with nonrelatives) before the age of ten. The alcoholic parentage group consisted of 21 males and 15 females; the nonalcoholic parentage group included 11 males and 14 females. At the time of the study the former group averaged 32 years of age while the latter averaged 28 years of age. In most cases, the subjects as well as the foster parents were interviewed. Information about the use of alcohol was obtained from 27 subjects of alcoholic parentage and from 22 in the other group. There were no excessive drinkers or alcoholics in either group and differences with respect to the use of alcohol were insignificant. Although the possibility of some of the subjects becoming alcoholic in later life could not be ruled out, Roe thought that this was equally unlikely for either group due to the generally satisfactory life adjustment and low rates of alcohol usage in both groups. Roe[20] did not report a high incidence of inebriety among children of alcoholics. She points to environment rather than heredity as determining alcoholism.

Roe's findings appear unique since other studies in this area suggest a blood relationship in alcoholism. Few studies in the United States since the turn of the century deal specifically with the familial incidence of alcoholism, and these few suffer from severe methodological weaknesses. In many of these studies, a family is considered "tainted" if one person other than the index case (or proband) is an alcoholic. Taint estimates range from 33 to 82 percent. Jellinek questions the assumption of "nonspecific heredity" common to these studies (e.g. the studies of Amark, Kaij, Partanen, Brun and Markkanen, Eysenck).

A recent study by Lucero, Jensen, and Ramsey[21] lends indirect evidence to a relationship between genetics and alcoholism. Forty probands, 40 abstaining alcoholics, and employees of the Hazelden Rehabilitation Center, Center City, Minnesota, were asked to classify their blood relatives as teetotalers, light drinkers, moderate drinkers, heavy drinkers, and alcoholics. A total of 119 grandparents, 356 parents, aunts and uncles (sisters and brothers of the parents), and 165 siblings of probands were identified. They found a strong relationship between teetotalism and alcoholism—as teetotalism decreases in the families under study, alcoholism increases. Eight alcoholic grandparents (when one grandparent was an alcoholic, the family was studied) produced 34 offspring of whom 19 (56%) were alcoholics; 10 alcoholic parents had 45 children of whom 22 (49%) were alcoholics. Applying the label "family taint," if one member of a family was an alcoholic, Lucero found that 82 percent of the time there was at least one other alcoholic in the family. The authors concede that the separatism of hereditary predisposition and social learning and combinations of these are complex. They recommend several types of family studies. The study did disclose that 50 percent of the descendants of alcoholics were also alcoholics, *a highly significant proportion.*

E. Jonsson and T. Nilsson[22] (1967) sent questionnaires regarding drinking habits to 1500 pairs of twins of the same sex born before 1925, taken from the registry of twins at the Karolinska Institute in Stockholm. Concordance within a pair of monozygotic twins was considered due to inheritance; that within dizygotic twins, to environment. The number of concordances was larger than expected in both groups in men as well as women. Preliminary analysis of results shows that drinking patterns depend primarily on social conditions but *genetic factors* are relevant in regards to the *consumption or nonconsumption of large* quantities. This is a large study and its final results may prove significant.

The existence of genetically determined racial differences in reaction to alcohol has been suggested by Wolff.[23] In this investigation he compared the alcohol-induced facial flushing responses of both adults and infants from Caucasoid and various Mongoloid groups.

In the adult portion of the study the subjects were healthy Mongoloid and Caucasoid men and women between 25 and 35 years of age. All subjects were randomly selected, the Caucasoids from the United States and the Mongoloids from Japan, Taiwan and Korea. Flushing was determined by optical densitometry of the earlobe and inspection of the face. Because the densitometric response was linear in the range of values tested, it was assumed that differences in baseline optical density due to variations in skin pigmentation did not affect the results. The densitometer also provided an indicator of pulse pressure. Room temperature was maintained at a comfortable level. All subjects drank beer (5% alcohol by volume) and were tested at least two hours after a meal. The Caucasoids received consistently more alcohol per unit of body weight (0.36 to 0.45 ml/kg) than Mongoloids (0.14 to 0.30 ml/kg). During the test they were asked to report any subjective symptoms that might be related to alcohol. Finally, the subjects filled out a short questionnaire including questions about the incidence of facial flushing in their families.

The results for the Caucasoid and the three Mongoloid groups are found in Table III. The differences between each Mongoloid group and the Caucasoid group were statistically significant ($p < .001$). Eighty-three percent of the adults in the total Mongoloid sample responded with a marked visible flush and an increase of optical density greater than 5 mm. The mean increase for the Mongoloids was 34.3 mm and the range was 14 to 78 mm. Only 2 of the 34 Caucasoid adults (6%) showed an increase in optical density greater than 5 mm and only one flushed visibly. An

TABLE III
FACIAL FLUSHING RESPONSES, INCREASES
OF OPTICAL DENSITY AND PULSE PRESSURE
AFTER INGESTION OF ALCOHOL FOR ADULT
AND INFANT CAUCASOIDS, JAPANESE, TAIWANESE
AND KOREANS

Group	Sample size (No.)	Visible flushing (No.)	Optical density Increase ‡5 mm (No.)	Optical density Mean increase for total (mm)	Pulse pressure Measurable increase (No.)	Pulse pressure Mean increase for total (%)
Caucasoid						
Adults	34	1	2	1.1	1(?)	5(?)
Infants	20	1	1	1.7	0	
Japanese						
Adults	38	32*	34*	36.8†	33*	257†
Infants	25	17*	17*	16.8†	9	
Taiwanese						
Adults	24	19*	20*	37.7†	19*	246†
Infants	10	9*	9*	14.6†	4	
Korean						
Adults	20	14*	10*‡	17.41†‡	9*‡	161†

In each case the Caucasoid group is compared to a corresponding Mongoloid group.
*Group differences significant at $p < .001$ chi-square. †$p < .001$ t-test.
‡The records of six Korean subjects could not be analyzed because of line voltage disturbances.
Adapted from Peter H. Wolff: Ethnic differences in alcohol sensitivity. *Science, 175*: 449 January 28, 1972. With the permission of the American Association for the Advancement of Science.

inspection of the data on elapsed time between drinking and the onset of flushing and optical density suggests the observed differences in these responses were not due to group differences in rates of absorption or metabolism of alcohol. The greater incidence of facial flushing among Mongoloids was also found in the adults' reports on their parents. Ninety-four percent of the Mongoloid adults reported that at least one of their parents flushed consistently after drinking. In contrast, only one percent of the Caucasoids reported that either of his parents flushed consistently after drinking. The Mongoloid adults also reported a greater number of symptoms of intoxication than Caucasoids (see Table IV).

In the second portion of the study, Wolff attempted to control for cultural differences in alcohol consumption, diet and other postnatal influences by comparing the facial flushing responses of full-term Caucasoid infants with those of Japanese and Taiwanese infants. The infants received small amounts of port wine in 5% glucose solution. The Caucasoid infants received consistently more alcohol per body weight (0.34 to 0.45 ml/kg) than Mongoloid infants (0.16 to 0.23 ml/kg).

The results for the infant groups are found in Table III. The differences in facial flushing and optical density between each group of Mongoloid infants and the Caucasoid infants is statistically significant (p < .001). Of the 35 Mongoloid infants tested, 74 percent responded with a visible flush and an increase in optical density greater than 5 mm. Changes in pulse pressure could not be measured reliably in the infants but were noted in one third of those who flushed visibly. It was suggested that since newborn infants showed the same group variations in alcohol responses as adults, postnatal dietary factors and cultural variations in drinking habits did not account for the differences.

On the basis of the adults' reports of subjective symptoms (see Table IV), Wolff contended that the differences in alcohol sensitivity were not limited to vasodilation of the facial vessels but extended to other physiological systems and particularly those under autonomic nervous system control. It was hypothesized that the vascular response and subjective symptoms experienced by Mongoloids prevent many of them from consuming even moderate quantities of alcohol. Wolff concluded that population differences in facial flushing caused by alcohol may reflect a genetic difference in autonomic nervous system responsivity that can also be inferred from reports of racial differences in autonomic response to other pharmacologic agents.

TABLE IV
SUBJECTIVE SYMPTOMS AFTER ALCOHOL
CONSUMPTION REPORTED BY CAUCASOID
AND MONGOLOID ADULTS

Symptom	Group			
	Caucasoid N = 34		Mongoloid N = 78	
	%	No.	%	No.
Hot in stomach	5.8	2	52.5*	41
Palpitations	0		25.7*	20
Tachycardia	2.9	1	43.5*	34
Muscle weakness	2.9	1	25.7†	20
Dizzy	8.6	3	37.2†	24
Sleepy	5.8	2	33.4†	26
Falls asleep	0		18.0†	4

*p<.001 and †p<.01.

Adapted from Peter H. Wolff: Ethnic differences in alcohol sensitivity. *Science, 175*: 450 January 28, 1972. With the permission of the American Association for the Advancement of Science.

Studies of Heredity and Alcoholism
Utilizing Nonhuman Species

Animal species are quite similar in mechanisms of inheritance; many researchers looking for indirect evidence of the heredity of alcoholism in humans have studied the effects of heredity on alcohol ingestion and metabolism in other species. Almost all of these experiments have utilized rats and mice. Generalizations of their results to *homo sapiens* are often left unexplored. Nonetheless, their results may eventually prove important in understanding the relationship of genetic factors in humans to alcoholism.

McClearn and Rogers[24] experimented with 4 male and 4 female rats from each of 5 strains that had long histories of inbreeding. Water and 10% ethyl alcohol solution were available to the rats ad lib. Liquid consumption was monitored for 14 consecutive days. One strain was found to prefer the 10% ethyl alcohol solution over water, three strains were found to prefer water, and one strain showed a mixed reaction. The authors concluded that these strain differences in liquid preference might be determined by genetic differences. These same authors conducted a similar study with 3 male and 3 female rats from each of 4 strains.[25] The rats were given a choice of tap water or any of 6 concentrations of alcohol solutions: 2.5%, 5%, 7.5%, 10%, 12.5%, or 15% (alcohol by volume). Liquid consumption was measured over a three-week period. Two strains showed progressive increases in proportional amount of alcohol consumed and a preference for the 10% solution. The two other strains tended to avoid all concentrations of alcohol. This preference for water tended to increase over the three-week period. Variance analysis indicated that the highly significant differences were almost entirely attributable to strain. The results manifest to Rogers and McClearn "that alcohol preference of mice is influenced by multiple allele or a multiple-gene system or both."[26]

Karla Thomas[27] attempted to test the extent to which the mice strain difference in spontaneous consumption of a 10% alcohol solution could be generalized to other concentrations. Free-choice tests were conducted to determine selective thresholds and degrees of selection of alcohol solutions varying in concentrations. She assumed that differences in alcohol selection are genetically determined in certain strains of laboratory mice. DBA/2 and CSB1 mice and derived generations were examined for agreement with a simple genetic model. Two inbred strains of mice were used for most observations: C57B1/Crgl and DBA/2Crgl. Generations derived from these strains (F_1, F_2, and backcrosses to C57B1 and DBA/2) were bred and weaned at the Cancer Research Genetics Laboratory, University of California. Animals of both sexes were brought to the psychology laboratory at 50 to 90 days of age and testing began within 2 weeks after they arrived. Thomas used the same apparatus as McClearn and Rogers. In all experiments each animal had free access to two drinking tubes, one containing an alcohol solution and the other containing twice-distilled water. Alcohol concentrations varied for different experiments, but generally covered the range between 0.00001 percent and 30 percent by volume. An alcohol selection score, representing degree of selection of alcohol, was defined as the percentage of alcohol solution in the total daily fluid consumption. Alcohol selection thresholds were measured by a method of limits.

Thomas conducted two experiments. The purposes of Experiment 1 were to define the general limits within which alcohol selection thresholds might fall; to verify the predicted drop in selection of high alcohol concentration by the C56B1; and to discover whether serial order of presentation would be a major determinant of the alcohol selection-avoidance function. The RIII strain was included for comparison purposes; Rogers and McClearn identified this strain as moderate in spontaneous consumption of 10% alcohol. Thomas used thirteen test solutions ranging from 30% to $10^{-10}\%$ ethanol by volume. The interval of separation between concentrations was one log unit, except for the addition of 30% alcohol solution 1.5% above the 10% solution. Daily alcohol selection scores were averaged at each test solution for each animal.

The results of Experiment 1 identified the range of alcohol solutions appropriate for later experiments. The expected decrease in C57B1 alcohol selection was noted at the 30% alcohol solution, and the large effect of presentation of this solution on subsequent consumption of 10% alcohol suggested a second experiment. Experiment 2 investigated the effect of prior presentation of 30% alcohol on the C57B1 response to 10% alcohol solution. As was expected, the intake of 10% alcohol was depressed below normal level in those animals having immediate prior experience with 30% alcohol solution.

Experiment 3 was designed to verify the apparent avoidance of alcohol shown by DBA/2 mice over all concentrations above threshold, and to estimate selection thresholds for DBA/2 and C5B1 mice and generations derived from them. Important summary results of these three experiments disclosed that DBA/2 Crgl mice avoided alcohol at all concentrations above the selection threshold; C57B1/Crgl mice chose alcohol solutions over water at some concentrations, but avoided a stronger solution (30% alcohol); and experience with 30% alcohol produced a temporary decrease in C57B1 consumption of 10% alcohol. Significant differences in alcohol selection thresholds occurred between the two strains of mice. The DBA/2 threshold was lower than that of the C57B1. The average scores secured for generations of mice obtained by crossing the two strains fell in the order hypothesized by simple genetic model. Alcohol selection scores and alcohol selection thresholds were positively related to the proportion of C57B1 genes in a group. Thomas' findings support the conclusion of McClearn and Rogers that differences in alcohol selection and laboratory mice are genetically determined.

Eriksson[28] selected at random 20 pairs of rats from the F_{10} generation of a special bred "drinker" strain of rats. Of these, 38 parents and 177 offspring were maintained for 10 days with 10% (V/V) alcohol as their only drinking fluid, and then were put on a free choice between 10% alcohol and tap water for three weeks. Alcohol consumption during the third week was utilized to calculate alcohol preference (alcohol solution consumed as percent of total fluid consumption), absolute alcohol consumed (m1/100 g of body weight), and caloric intake from alcohol (alcohol cal/100 g/day). The correlation coefficient of alcohol preference was .40 in parents and offspring, .16 in males and offspring, .43 in females and offspring, .19 in males and male offspring, .36 in females and female offspring, .01 in males and female offspring, and .13 in females and male offspring. The high correlation between parents and offspring suggests that the degree of voluntary alcohol consumption is highly heritable in this strain. The highly significant correlations between female parents and all offspring, and female parents and female offspring, indicate that voluntary alcohol consumption is inherited through the females. The low exploration level of the regression models shows that the random variance in self-selection functions is great.

Sheppard[29] and his associates demonstrated a systematic relationship between the behavioral trait of *ethanol selection* and the activity of aldehyde dehydrogenose and the activity of alcohol dehydrogenose (both inherited). Alcohol dehydrogenose and aldehyde dehydrogenose, the two principal *enzymes* of alcohol metabolism, were assayed in the livers of the inbred mouse strains C57B1 and DBA. Previous tests showed that animals of various C57B1 substrains prefer a 10% ethanol solution to water in a two-bottle choice test and that animals of various DBA substrains avoid alcohol. Sheppard discovered in his study that C57B1 mice had 300 percent more aldehyde dehydrogenose activity than DBA mice and 30 percent more alcohol dehydrogenose activity. His hybrid F_1 generation was *intermediate* to the parents in preference for the 10% alcoholic solution and had *intermediate* levels of alcohol and aldehyde dehydrogenose activity.

Theories and Studies on the Hereditary
Mechanisms in Alcoholism

A number of theorists have attempted to identify some inherited mechanisms involved in the causation of alcoholism.[30] Roger J. Williams formulated a "genotrophic" theory of alcoholism. He hypothesized that a biochemical defect, a genetotrophic dearth of nutritive elements, can be traced to an inherited metabolic defect which impairs enzyme production. These enzymes function in the metabolism of certain nutrients, but their paucity results in nutritional deficiencies which cause a derangement of the hypothalamus. This derangement leads to a craving for alcohol in much the same manner as a thirsty man craves water.[31] The initial drink gives rise to the urge for additional drinks because of deranged cellular metabolism. Williams recommended nutritional, dietary supplements and extreme dietary care as part of an alcoholic prevention and treatment program. He based his theory on numerous studies in which rats on nutritionally deficient diets consumed more alcohol than rats on standard diets, and on at least one human experiment involving 22 hospitalized alcoholics and 20 controls (other nonalcoholic patients). He found significant metabolic differences (e.g. the alcoholics were higher in total leucocytes, urinary sodium, and unidentified diazonium coupling compound).[32]

Brady and Westerfield[33] examined the relationship between nutrition and alcohol intake in an experiment involving 36 rats. Rats on purified diets, with all known members of the vitamin B complex plus a liver additive, did not consume alcohol under autoselection conditions. Rats on the same diet, except without the liver additive, gradually increased their alcohol consumption. Those rats on diets deficient in members of the vitamin B complex consumed relatively large amounts of alcohol. Once the alcohol intake increased on a deficient diet it could not be permanently reduced. For these rats, inclusion of the missing nutritional elements brought about only a temporary decrease in alcohol intake. Brady and Westerfield concluded that their results confirmed observations that deficiencies of the B-complex vitamins increase the voluntary consumption of alcohol by rats.[34]

Mardones[35] found that rats on diets which deprived them of thermolabile elements of the vitamin B complexes increased their intake under conditions of self-selection. Additional testing showed that alcohol consumption could be reduced by dietary additives. These diet-alcohol intake interactions were found to vary with the strain of rat. Mardones explained this variation on the basis of different combinations of genes belonging to several alleles. He compared his results with those of Brady and Westerfield, Williams, and others, and concurred with Williams on the operation of genetic factors in alcohol consumption. Mardones differed, however, with Williams on the interpretation of the "trophic" factors involved.

In a more recent study, Brown[36] utilized 50 male and 50 female mice from a strain bred and selected for low alcohol preference. All mice were given a standard diet for three weeks. Ten mice of each sex were placed on a three-week diet deficient in (only) one of the following vitamins: pantothenic acid, pyridoxine, thiamine, or niacin. The remaining 10 male and 10 female mice constituted a control group and were continued on a standard diet. The rats had a choice of plain water or a 10% ethyl alcohol solution. The results indicated that rats of both sexes on diets deficient in pantothenic acid, as well as male mice on diets deficient in pyridoxine and thiamine, did not consume more alcohol than controls. Both male and female rats deprived of niacin increased their alcohol intake, although the latter consumed twice as much alcohol as the males. Only females on diets deficient in thiamine and pyridoxine showed increased alcohol intake. Brown concluded that his results indicated that the internal environment, (sex-specific factors such as hormonal level) causes different responses to some vitamin deficiencies.[37]

Dr. J. J. Smith[38] hypothesized that alcoholism is a symptom of an underlying metabolic disturbance. This hypothesis developed from observations of the similarity between Addisonian crisis and delirium tremens. Smith reported encouraging results in the treatment of patients having delirium tremens and acute alcohol intoxication with desoxycorticosterone and whole adrenal cortex extract. He conducted at least four studies in which there were from 30 to 150 alcoholics and found a number of physiological abnormalities among them (e.g. lymphocytosis, expanded or contracted blood volume, low blood chloride level) which he traced to an adrenal cortex insufficiency. He also presented his clinical impressions of 1,800 male alcoholics and concluded that the alcoholic is a specific constitutional type and that the tendency to alcoholism is transmitted genetically. He based this claim on the observation that Celtic and Scandinavian peoples are most susceptible to alcoholism while Semitic and Chinese people are rarely alcoholic. The general inbreeding patterns of these groups supposedly perpetuated these patterns. Smith suggested that these group differences were not due to cultural but to genetic factors.

THE ENDOCRINE GLANDS, BRAIN DAMAGE, AND BIOCHEMISTRY

A number of other investigators infer that the predisposition to alcoholism is either unknown or acquired in some other manner than genetic.[39] In some cases a predisposition is assumed, while in others it is alcohol itself which creates (supposedly) the conditions predisposing to alcoholism. The classification of studies within this category proves even more difficult since some are mixed, i.e. based on both acquired and hereditary origins.

Alcoholism and Endrocrinological Functioning

Some hypotheses hold that alcohol proneness is related to endocrinological functioning. Many of these are similar to Selye's[40] general-adaption-syndrome formulations, a few of which follow.

Tintera,[41] and Tintera and Lovell[42] conceive of alcoholism as a symptom of a glandular disorder, in a theoretical position similar to that of J. J. Smith. Adrenal cortex insufficiency, a symptom of hypoadrenocorticism, is the basic cause of alcoholism. This condition may be the result of constitutional or other factors, or it may be brought on by drinking itself. In the latter case, alcoholic intoxication represents a stressful condition which brings on a sudden increase of adrenocortical hormones followed by a decrease to subnormal levels. Repeated depletions in cortical reserve result in adrenal insufficiency and other glandular dysfunctions. Alcohol temporarily relieves the insufficiency, but it also increases the stress and further aggravates the condition so that a vicious circle of uncontrolled drinking results. Tintera recommends extensive use of injections of adrenal cortical extract and other substances to restore endocrine and chemical balances in the body of the alcoholic.

Goldfarb and Berman,[43] from their own observations and a review of the literature (on the interaction of alcohol and glandular dysfunction), developed a hypothesis similar to that of Smith and Tintera and Lovell. A person predisposed to alcoholism is one who needs the initial effects of alcohol as a "stressful agent" to stimulate a secretory response of the adrenal cortex. This initial need may be brought on by neurosis or other constitutional or acquired factors. Although alcohol initially stimulates the necessary secretory responses, its continued use causes glandular dysfunction and creates further need for glandular stimulation. This alcohol-caused need for stimulation invites ingestion of further alcohol to stimulate new secretory responses, and a vicious circle develops. Alcoholism is thus seen as a self-perpetuating progressive disease.

Kissin[44] compared a group of active alcoholics, a group of ex-alcoholics who had been abstinent for two or more years, and a group of controls matched on age (with the alcoholics). The number of subjects involved varied, with different types of examinations, from 3 to 78. Kissin closely examined endocrine activity, the autonomic nervous system, and muscle tension in all groups. He assumed that emotions are characterized by specific physiological changes in all three areas. Both alcoholic groups showed physiological patterns in all three areas different from that of the controls. The active alcoholics were given alcohol and their physiological patterns were changed in the direction of normal. Chlorpromazine had effects similar to that of alcohol. These results suggest to Kissin that the alcoholic is an emotionally disturbed individual and that these emotions lead to physiological tensions. Alcohol reduces these tensions and thus the reduction of physiological tension is the motivation for drinking.

The findings of Kissin are supported in a study by Fleetwood[45] who isolated substances in the blood correlated with the emotional states "tension" and "resentment." The "resentment" substance was found to be more characteristic of alcoholics than of normals or nonalcoholic psychiatric patients. Ten alcoholics undergoing treatment were given alcohol which reduced or eliminated the "resentment" substance in their blood. The "tension" substance was reduced in six of ten cases. Five of the nonalcoholic psychiatric patients also received alcohol and the comparative results showed that alcohol reduced both substances more significantly in the alcoholic group.

Alcoholism and Brain Pathology

Several investigators have concentrated on brain pathology as a factor in alcoholism. Lemere[46] claims that the common denominator for all types of alcoholism is loss of control over drinking. The histories of most alcoholics show a number of years of normal controlled drinking followed by a gradual slip into uncontrolled pathological drinking. One of the factors that Lemere thinks could lead to such a loss of control is brain damage caused by years of heavy drinking. The first brain cells to be affected would be those that are first anesthetized by alcohol—those subserving the higher cerebral levels of willpower and judgment. These brain cells are gradually destroyed until a stage is reached where any alcohol in the system will immediately paralyze the drinker's judgment and willpower. The portion of the brain which usually tells the drinker when to stop is unable to function. This irreparable brain damage is the reason why chronic alcoholics, once cured, can never resume drinking without relapsing completely to alcoholism. Social or moderate drinking is an impossibility once brain damage has occurred. Lemere also hypothesizes that prolonged drinking may alter the drinker's metabolic patterns, so that the presence of alcohol is a temporary necessity for optimum brain functioning. Brain cells may become so dependent upon alcohol that its sudden withdrawal throws them into disequilibrium which is translated into symptoms of hangover and tension. The alcoholic then continues drinking in an attempt to ward off these symptoms.

Davis[47] compared the electroencephalograms of 15 hospitalized nonpsychotic alcoholics with those of a group of psychotics and normals. Only 2 of the alcoholics had the alpha type of pattern which is one of the most common for normal persons. The other 13 alcoholics had mixed frequency patterns which seemed to be intermediate between known normal and abnormal patterns. On the basis of these and other comparisons, Davis concluded that the alcoholics appeared to lie between the normals and psychotics with respect to normality and stability of EEG patterns.

Little and McAvoy[48] gathered electroencephalographic data on

34 confirmed alcoholics and 55 apparently unmatched controls. Routine readings of the records revealed little in the way of significant differences between the two groups. Significant differences were found, however, in alpha activity. Seventy-two percent of the normals, as compared to 46 percent of the alcoholics, showed alpha activity. These results were similar to those of Davis et al. Good amplitude modulation of alpha activity was found in 86 percent of the controls and in only 50 percent of the alcoholics. This amplitude modulation was poor in 38 percent of the alcoholics and only 4 percent of the controls. Little and McAvoy submit that these differences might be caused by a cerebral condition which is not the result of alcoholism but is in fact a predisposing condition.

Tumarkin, Wilson and Snyder[49] studied 7 high-ranking Army enlisted men who had been using alcoholic beverages for 7 to 17 years. All had been admitted to a hospital because of inability to perform their duties. All 7 presented abnormal EEG patterns, although in only one case were alpha waves among the most prominent abnormalities. Pneumoencephalographic findings revealed that parietal atrophy was marked in all cases, although the patterns of atrophy were not identical for all patients. These authors concluded that periodic acute alcoholic intoxication led to a gradual loss of cells in the frontal and parietal regions. The cumulative loss of cells led to increasing intolerance to alcohol in which subjective feelings of intoxication were elicited by increasingly smaller amounts of alcohol.

Skillicorn[50] studied 6 male alcoholics with cerebellar dysfunction admitted to a U. S. Navy hospital. In contrast to the results of Davis, Little and McAvoy, and Tumarkin, Wilson and Snyder, none of the 6 alcoholics examined showed abnormal electroencephalographic patterns. Pneumoencephalographic examniations suggested cerebral atrophy in all cases. Skillicorn proposes that alcohol consumption over a prolonged period might result in permanent cellular damage within the cerebrellum in susceptible individuals.

Other Formulations

Two rather dissimilar approaches follow, which illustrate the wide variety of constitutional perspectives. Rogers and Gawienowski [51] extracted blood samples from 30 male hospitalized alcoholics and 20 healthy (apparently unmatched) male controls. Comparisons of these samples revealed that the alcoholics had significantly higher serum copper levels. These authors reasoned that because 90 percent of the copper in human serum is known to exist in the form of ceruloplasm (suspected to be involved in schizophrenia), a similar relationship might exist between high serum copper concentrations and alcoholism. Rogers and Gawienowski addressed themselves to the question of whether these higher concentrations were contributing factors in the etiology of alcoholism or were the result of long years of excessive drinking. The possibility that drug therapy was responsible for the increased serum copper levels was ruled out when similar results were obtained from an additional group of alcoholics that had not been receiving drug therapy. There was no evidence available to suggest that alcohol ingestion or any type of diet might lead to increased serum copper levels. Finally, within their own group of subjects, there was no correlation between duration of excessive drinking and concentration of serum copper. These authors maintain that the high copper levels found in the alcoholic group were not solely the result of years of excessive drinking, but were involved in a predisposition to alcoholism.

Randolph[59] hypothesizes that alcoholism is a manifestation of a "food addiction." Food addicts are persons who are highly sensitized to certain foods, to which they become addicted; however, the origin of the initial sensitivity has not been precisely delineated. Such addiction is a process similar to other addictions in that the addict is "picked up" temporarily after a meal and is "let down" by subsequent withdrawal or hangover-like effects. The alcoholic is seen not to be addicted to alcohol, but to the malt, corn, or other food elements in the beverage. Frequent consumption of the food, or an alcoholic beverage derived from it, gives temporary relief from the "let down" (or "hangover"). When the food element is taken in the form of an alcoholic beverage, absorption is more rapid; the "pick up" is gained more quickly, and the "let down" can be rapidly alleviated. However, increasingly large doses become necessary to prevent the "let down," and alcoholism may result. Randolph claims some support for his theory from a study of 40 alcoholics. He discovered they were highly sensitive to the highest concentration of food elements found in their favorite drink.

COMMENTS ON THE CONSTITUTIONAL APPROACH

Studies on human heredity and alcoholism utilizing a number of twin studies and studies of alcoholics' relatives (who are also alcoholic) strongly indicate (indirect evidence) that there is a hereditary predisposition to alcoholism. The problem remains, "How does one specify the hereditary predisposition?" and "How does one study this phenomenon in its association with social learning and environment?" Perhaps as we learn more about the mechanism of heredity, our indirect evidence of alcoholic predisposition will become more direct.[53] The probability also exists that there is not an inherited predisposition to alcoholism per se, but that there is an inherited physiological-pattern type of personality which predisposes an individual to many types of pathological behavior patterns. One of these pathological behavior patterns, under certain environmental conditions, might be alcoholism.[54]

Though studies of heredity and alcoholism employing nonhuman species (primarily rats) demonstrate that alcohol preference and degree of ingestion (at times under stressful conditions) are strongly influenced by genetic factors, vigorous critics have questioned their results. Lester[55] reviewed many of these studies and criticized them on methodological grounds. He stipulated that some of the variables should have been subjected to stricter control, e.g. bottle position and rat paw and position preferences. He reasoned that smell and taste preferences for water, different water and alcohol mixtures, and foods may have confounded some of the experiments. According to him, investigators should have taken blood samples from the animals during and after testing period instead of assuming (on the basis of the rate of alcohol ingestion) that the alcohol had an effect. He holds that in the absence of knowledge about alcohol concentration in the blood, no conclusion can be drawn as to whether the drinking resulted from taste preference or a search for a pharmacological effect. He mentions several other factors that must be controlled in rat studies, including sex, strain of animal, and animal quarter conditions. After examining large numbers of rat studies reporting "contradictory results," he concludes that "biochemical measures correlated with varying degrees of alcohol selection have not been found."[56] Lester is also concerned with the small number of rats used in many experiments (in small samples, individual rat preferences may distort the data). He finally notes the danger in generalizing from the behavior of rats to the behavior of humans. These criticisms, though appropriate in part (e.g. on increase in the number of subjects in study samples), appear too severe. Roger J. Williams, among other researchers, has met many of them and he, among others, has obtained biological and chemical results.

Theories and studies concerned with the mechanisms involved in alcoholic causation (be they inherited, unknown in origin, or acquired) have come under heavy fire. Many studies in this area deal with nutritional, metabolic, endocrinological, and neurological differences in their relationships to alcohol. Some include lower animals, some include humans. Lester,[57] among others, has pointed out that many human studies have no control groups. Therefore, the biochemical and biological characteristics reported among alcoholics may also exist in the general population. In many instances where controls are used, the alcoholics and controls are not matched on important variables such as age and physical condition. Many times, controls are selected from people readily available. Frequently, in metabolic studies, the controls and experimentals are not on the same diet before being tested. Thus, the metabolic differences found between alcoholics and nonalcoholics might have resulted from factors that were not controlled. Lester stresses that as long as positive findings are more frequently published than negative ones, we will continue to receive reports on biological differences between alcoholics and nonalcoholics. Contrariwise, it could be that positive findings may be more frequently published than negative ones, because there are more positive findings than negative findings.

Wexberg[58] (March 1950) critically analyzed the findings and hypotheses of Smith, Williams, Goldfarb and Berman, and Tintera and Lovell. He submits, after a review of the literature, that there is no support for the contentions of Smith and Williams that the alcoholic possesses a metabolic individuality which predisposes him to alcoholism. Wexberg recommends a longitudinal study to solve this problem. He negates Williams' parallel between craving for alcohol and other physiologically determined appetites on several bases; first, such cravings refer to substances lacking in the body. Since alcohol does not constitute an essential normal substance in the human body, there can be no craving for it. The so-called cravings for alcohol are experienced in the olfactory and gustatory apparatus. Many alcoholics dislike the taste and smell of whiskey. In fact alcoholics often drink shaving lotion and other solutions that taste and smell repulsive. Additionally, some alcoholics utilize other drugs, such as barbiturates, interchangeably with alcohol. Wexburg states: "It is obvious that what the alcoholic is craving is not the stimulation of gustatory or olfactory end organs, as in physiological appetites, but the toxic effect of alcohol on his nervous system, i.e., relaxation, sedation, removal of inhibitions, euphoria."[59]

As Lester, Wexberg, and other critics have observed, investigators who find nutritional, metabolic, or endocrinological conditions prevalent in alcoholics may not be sure that these conditions are not caused by the alcoholism instead of vice versa, e.g. there is much evidence that alcoholism leads to glandular dysfunction, but less evidence that glandular dysfunction leads to alcoholism. Again, longitudinal studies are advocated by many researchers as an answer to this problem of cause and effect.

McCord's Longitudinal Study

We have at least one in-depth longitudinal study on alcoholism utilizing human beings. McCord et al.[60] received data from the Cambridge-Somerville Project on a number of subjects which they reexamined in an attempt to arrive at the origins of alcoholism. They conducted the first published longitudinal study on the etiology of alcoholism.[61] The Cambridge-Somerville Project began in 1953 with two matched groups of 325 boys each from Cambridge and Somerville, Massachusetts. At an average age of 9, all 650 boys were given medical and psychological examinations. Social workers interviewed parents and teachers, evaluated home atmosphere and neighborhoods, and devised delinquency proneness profiles. One group of 325 boys, the treatment group, received regular guidance from a friendly adult counselor as well as medical and educational assistance. Treatment began at an average age of eleven and continued until most of the boys were in their middle teens. The other group, the control group, was left to the usual services of the community. The original purpose was to determine if such guidance would prevent later delinquency or antisocial behavior. Sixty-five boys in the treatment group were dropped from the program; two had died and three moved away from Massachusetts. This left 255 boys from the original treatment group and 255 matched partners in the control group. Follow-ups were conducted in 1948 and in 1956.

In 1957, McCord decided to use these records in a longitudinal study of alcoholism; at this point in time the subjects were in their early thirties. Alcoholics were defined as those who met at least one of the following criteria: (1) had been a member of Alcoholics Anonymous, (2) had been referred to a hospital in Massachusetts for alcoholism, (3) had been known as an alcoholic by the Boston Committee on Alcoholism or other social agencies, or (4) had been convicted by the courts for public drunkenness at least twice. Fifty-one alcoholics were found in the study, exactly 10 percent of the sample of 510 for which complete data was gathered. Twenty-nine of these subjects came from the treatment group and 22 from the control group.

After coding the backgrounds of the original 255 treatment and 255 controlled subjects (initially matched pairs equated in terms of physical health, intelligence, emotional adjustment, home atmosphere, neighborhood, and delinquency prognosis), McCord recorded case data information on each together with a coded report of adult behavior on I.B.M. cards. The data recorded came from case-file "items" on socioeconomic and cultural factors, family structure and family interaction, parental attitudes and behavior, child-rearing practices, and miscellaneous information. Additionally, factors pertaining to the boys' health, attitudes, and behavior were recorded under the headings entitled health, attitudes and behaviors, and miscellaneous information.

All of these cases were broken down into four groups: alcoholic noncriminals, alcoholic criminals, nonalcoholic criminals, and nonalcoholic noncriminals. To distinguish the alcoholics from a nondeviant population, McCord omitted the criminals from all analyses, except those dealing specifically with differentiation among deviants. Therefore, for the majority of comparisons,

McCord considered the differential factors that distinguished the 29 alcoholic subjects from the 158 nondeviant (nonalcoholic noncriminal) subjects in the treatment group. He utilized the chi-square test, two-tailed, to ascertain the likelihood that differences were due to chance.

McCord selected from the literature a varied number of hypotheses concerning the genesis of alcohol and then analyzed his data in such a way that these hypotheses were tested. He claims that his own hypothetical schema based on a stress, dependency conflict, role confusion, and collapse of self-image "model" evolved from the data analysis.[2]

At this juncture, we are only interested in McCord's etiological findings related to nutritional, glandular, and hereditary factors. He formulated three hypotheses to test for these three variables:

1. Roger J. Williams and members of his school would predict that a significantly greater proportion of people who, as children, exhibit signs of nutritional deficiency and metabolic dysfunction would, as adults, become alcoholic more frequently than those not having these disorders.

2. Tintera, Lovell, Smith, and Bleuler, advocates of a glandular interpretation, would predict that children suffering from glandular disorder would, as adults, have a significantly greater tendency to become alcoholic than those not suffering from such disorders.

3. Scholars advocating the genetic approach would predict that close blood relatives of alcoholics would be more frequently alcoholics than those without alcoholic blood relatives.

McCord concludes from his analyses of the subjects' medical records (based on physical examinations by physicians between 1935 and 1945) that nutritional deficiencies and glandular disorders were not significant in the etiology of alcoholism. For these analyses, the 29 alcoholics from the treatment group were compared with 158 men (also from the treatment group) who appeared to be neither alcoholics nor criminals (see Table V).

McCord also claims that his data demonstrate the unimportance of heredity factors in the causation of alcoholism. Fifty-one fathers of the 510 subjects under study were themselves alcoholics. The data in Table III indicate a tendency for the son to follow the father's pattern, but the pattern is not statistically significant.

TABLE V
NUTRITIONAL DEFICIENCIES,
GLANDULAR DISORDERS,
AND LATER ALCOHOLISM

	Percent Who Be-came Alcoholics
Nutritional deficiencies present (N: 28)	11
No nutritional deficiencies (N: 159)	16
Glandular disorder present (N: 21)	0
No glandular disorder (N: 166)	17
	Percent of Sons Who Became Alcoholics
Alcoholic fathers (N: 51)	22
Nonalcoholic fathers (N: 126)	12

Adapted from William McCord, Joan McCord, and John Gudeman, *Origins of Alcoholism.* Stanford, Stanford University Press, 1960, pp. 25, 27.

McCord found that alcoholism was more strongly related to parental criminality than to parental alcoholism (31% of the sons of criminals became alcoholics). He states that this finding supports an environmental rather than a hereditary explanation.[63] He did find that neural disorder (51 boys had indications of neural disorders—15 boys had definite neural disorders as evidenced by abnormal EEGs; 36 had either abnormal EEGs or had experienced convulsions, had noticeable tics or tremors) remained constantly associated with alcoholism even when other petrinent factors were controlled. McCord assumed that neurally disordered persons are under greater stress, both physiologically and environmentally, than normals and are therefore more likely to use alcohol to reduce stress. He thought that had his subjects been subjected to current neural exams more of them would have demonstrated neural damage.[64] McCord therefore recognizes the importance of constitutional factors.

McCord's methodology and, therefore, findings are questionable from several standpoints. We are primarily interested, at this point, in his biochemical findings. One wonders if the "gross physical examinations" to which the Cambridge-Somerville boys were submitted were sophisticated enough in type to reveal the possible nutritional and glandular differences existing between the experimental and controlled groups.

Current extensive and intensive biochemical and physiological examinations involve the analysis of blood, saliva, urine, and biopsy materials. To expedite investigations in this area, we need automated equipment and computer techniques to aid in the interpretation of the complex data. McCord's subjects were certainly not subjected to this type of medical examination. Hypothetically accepting McCord's "gross medical findings," the subjects may have developed glandular and nutritional malfunctions and disorders following the Cambridge-Somerville study experience (they were in their middle teens when last seen), but antedating their alcoholism.

In reference to McCord's negation of hereditary predisposition to alcoholism, one could argue that his findings suggest hereditary predispositions to deviant behavior, including criminality as well as alcoholism. McCord finds striking similarities among the backgrounds of his alcoholic and criminal subjects. He discovered many similar personal and social characteristics among alcoholic noncriminals, alcoholic criminals, and criminal nonalcoholics. These three deviant groups were markedly different from nonalcoholic noncriminals. Perhaps the most important crticism of McCord's methodology has to do with a condition which he could do little about, that is, his subjects were in their early thirties at the time of his analysis. Since many alcoholics are not diagnosed as such until after 35, McCord's data may be contaminated; some of his controls may have been prealcoholics. This criticism is made more important by the fact that McCord's experimental group (29), for many comparisons, was small. In fairness to McCord, he was aware of and acknowledged most of the preceding criticisms. He made clear that his statistical findings were tenuous and tentative because of his small sample.

Needs for Improvement

The entire constitutional approach is characterized by a large number of competing, and at times, conflicting theories. Jellinek[65] lists over 30 different published theories in this area in his 1960 review of the field. There appears to be a nonspecific predisposition to alcoholism, whatever its origin might be. Moreover, several EEG studies indicate that some people develop abnormal brain waves after long periods of excessive drinking. These EEG studies suggest that following neurological damage caused by alcoholism, many individuals are unable to control their drinking behavior.

Assuming a predisposition to alcohol of whatever type, an essential question remains unanswered: Why did a predisposed individual take the alcohol (or not take it) in the first place? Social and psychological factors are required to explain the initial usage. Goldfarb and Berman, Lemere, and some of the other investigators in this field have not completely ignored this crucial question. It still awaits an empirically based answer.

The authors think that the implementation of the following methodological procedures might strengthen research efforts in the constitutional study of alcoholism: (1) the exertion of greater control over more variables in animal and human experiments, (2) the utilization of a large sample of animals and/or humans in experimental studies, (3) the more frequent use of matched or randomly selected control groups in human and animal studies, and (4) the use of longitudinal studies.

Jack H. Mendelson and Nancy K. Mello[oo] recently offer a disease model of alcoholism involving the interaction between host, agent, and environment that seems to comply with most of the above suggestions. Their basic research paradigm permits the concurrent study of the biochemistry and behavior of alcoholic individuals prior to, during, and following a period of experimentally induced intoxication. Alcohol administration can be in programmed doses, or the subject can determine his own volume and frequency. The unique value of applying this model in studies of alcohol addiction is that the agent, alcohol, can be administered under controlled conditions to addicted subjects. The induced behavioral and biological changes can be measured through time as a function of alcohol administration and withdrawal. Under these conditions, the addicted subject serves as his own control; therefore it is possible to establish reliable baseline data and reduce one of the major problems in behavioral-biological research—the indeterminancy associated with interindividual variability.

Mendelson and Mello illustrate the use of their paradigm in the study of intoxication and withdrawal in alcoholic subjects; in biochemical assessments concerning the time course of changes of free fatty acid and serum triglyceride levels during 24 days of programmed alcohol intake; in classification of biochemical and physiological derangements in alcoholic patients in clinical practice; in dose-response relationships over an extended experimental period; in chronic ethanol ingestion and serum cortisol levels; in steroid level involving enzyme systems and alcohol metabolism; in sleep patterns during predrinking, drinking, and postdrinking phases; and in REM activities.

This paradigm can best be used to analyse those factors that combine to perpetuate and maintain drinking behavior once the syndrome of alcoholism is established. It seems logical that a similar paradigm could be devised in terms of etiological factors; in all likelihood, the perfection and implementation of the former would lead to the latter.

BEHAVIORAL SCIENCE BIAS AGAINST THE CONSTITUTIONAL APPROACH

Roger J. Williams, professor of chemistry at the University of Texas at Austin and consultant to the Clayton Foundations Biochemical Institute, Professor Jerry Hirsch, a psychologist at the University of Illinois, and H. J. Eysenck,[67] a British stimulus-response behaviorist psychologist, among others, have called attention to the neglect of biochemistry and genetics by many behavioral scientists. Professor Jerry Hirsch states that "the opinion makers of two generations have literally excommunicated heredity from the behavioral sciences." Roger J. Williams explains that the term *behavioral science* came into being several years ago as a result of the formulation of programs supported by the Ford Foundation and that the Ford Foundation has invited the biological sciences to stay out of the precinct of human behavior. H. J. Eysenck notes several barriers to the study and application of human genetics: (1) some democratic countries have let political ideology dictate the principles of behavioral science, e.g. the belief that man is born free and equal has led many to the erroneous conclusion that man has the same innate ability and personality potential, and that there are no limits to human perfectability; (2) religious beliefs have hampered the consideration of biochemical and genetic factors in human behavior, e.g. "freedom of the will"; (3) the false notion that genetic etiology leads to therapeutic nihilism; and (4) the anti-intellectual behavioristic opposition to "according heredity its proper place in the behavioral sciences" (under the aegis of Dr. John Broadus Watson, who has supplied the pattern assumed by so much of present-day thinking in psychology).

Current negative positions toward biochemical and genetic factors may reflect an academic fad, a strong equalitarian-humanitarian ethos, a radical deviation from former radical hereditary positions, and certainly above all, behavioristic opposition. Whatever their origin, the neglect of the study of heredity and biochemical factors in current behavioral science has produced a wide gap between biology and chemistry on the one hand, and psychology and sociology on the other.

Roger Williams, with justification, reminds us that each member of the human species possesses inborn differences based on his brain structure and on his vast mosaic of endocrine glands. Each of us has a distinctive set of drives for physical activity, for food, and for sexual expression. Taste and smell reactions frequently differ widely and are inherited. Each of us has a color vision all his own. He thinks that one excuse for excommunicating inheritance and biochemical factors from the behavioral sciences for two generations has been the fact that inheritance is recognized by careful scientists as being exceedingly complex and difficult to interpret. Only a few characteristics may be inherited through the operation of single genes. Estimates place the number of human genes at well in excess of 10,000. Many characteristics, those that differ in quantity, are ascribed to multiple genes of indefinite number and character. Recently, experiments with armadillos (who produce litters of four monozygous quadruplets) suggest that inheritance comes not by genes alone, but by cytoplasmic factors that help govern the size of organs and the cellular makeup of the central nervous system. Identical twins are not identical, except with respect to the genes in the nucleus of the egg cell from which they develop. This suggests that individual brain structures are made distinctive by the same mechanisms that make for differences in organ weights. The size, number, and distributions of neurons of normal brains vary greatly; this is biologically in line with the uniqueness of human minds.

Williams is not a therapeutic nihilist, nor does he argue that there is a one-to-one relationship between hereditary factors and specific deviant behaviors, such as crime, alcoholism, and drug addiction. He does claim that we may be able to recognize the unique leanings that are a part of each of us. Then we may see how, by adjusting the environment, these leanings can be turned toward ends that are socially constructive. When identified, each inherited factor may be influenced by an appropriate adjustment of the environment. He illustrates this thesis with alcoholism. He is convinced that inborn biochemical characteristics are basic to the disease, alcoholism, and that the application of knowledge about cellular nutrition will make it scientifically possible to prevent the disease and to correct the condition after its onset.

Williams[68] notes that rats have, as a part of their complete appestat system, a regulatory mechanism which governs alcohol consumption and that this device can be turned up or down like a thermostat by altering the nutrition of the animals. He hypothesizes that in human alcoholics, the entire appetite-regulation device may become defective (not just that portion which governs alcohol consumption), as is evidenced by the fact that alcoholics often show a strong aversion for food of any kind. He claims that he has demonstrated that abundantly good nutrition will prevent alcohol consumption in rats and humans and that good nutrition can abolish craving for alcohol by human as well as animal subjects (e.g. a nutritional supplement, glutamine, has proven in some cases to be of great benefit in abolishing the craving for alcohol). Williams points out that some confirmed alcoholics have lost their appetite for alcohol as a result of taking glutamine in their drinking water (with no knowledge that they were taking anything). Glutamine is claimed to be an unusual nutrient in that it is the only amino acid (derived from proteins) which readily passes the "blood brain barrier" and thus gets easily into the brain. Williams thinks this relatively tasteless substance is highly important in brain metabolism. Adding it to the diet decreases voluntary alcohol consumption in experimental animals.

Hirsch[69] calls for a behavior-genetic analysis of man's biological properties and an elucidation of their modus operandi in a socio-technological context; in other words, identification and (complex) behavior-genetic analysis of the phenotypic dimension of human variation. He advocates the "population" rather than "typological" approach, i.e. the consideration of entire genome at once; and he insists that we must turn to *family studies* rather than to broad spectrum studies of unrelated subjects. Hirsch proclaims that we must shift from insubstantial abstractions like learning, perception, and motivation to *concern with consanguinity relations* among the subjects we observe, i.e. among individuals of known ancestry.

Hirsch illustrates that (empirically) individual differences have been measured in the phenotypic expression of many traits and that, for some, observations have been conducted on the similarities and differences both within and between families. For example, Jost and Santog (1944) found that score similarity increased with genetic similarity on seven variables related to the autonomic nervous function: vasomotor persistence, salivary output, heart period, standing palmar conductance, volar skin conductance, respiration period, and pulse pressure (measured in children of three relationship categories—monozygotic twins, siblings, and unrelated individuals). Taste stimuli and auditory curves have been found to show high intrapair concordance among monozgotic twins; intrafamilial similarities, and significant differences among unrelated subjects. Individual differences in memory span, attention span, color blindness, and EEG rhythms have been measured. The study of EEG abnormalities demonstrates that they occur more frequently among persons whose parents had EEG abnormalities than among those without such parents. Many similarities have been found between schizophrenic patients and their parents. Hirsch cautions that we must (initially) stick to simple, rather than complex, behaviors in the identification and behavior-genetic analysis of the phenotypic dimensions of human variation. He concludes with the significant observation that the relative paucity of available data can more likely be attributed to lack of interest in family studies on the part of behavioral scientists rather than to its nonexistence.

The present authors think that many behavior scientists (especially sociologists) react negatively to behavior genetics on the basis of "hereditary" studies conducted in the 1920's when some family studies made rather radical claims for the hereditary factor. Many of these sociologists (and others) conduct their research, of whatever kind, on a *cardinal (false) assumption* that genetic differences among humans (group or individual) are relatively unimportant.

Hans Jurgen Eysenck[70] is quite intrepid in his leaping claim for the significant relationship between complex behaviors and genetic factors. His evidence, however, is indirect. Apart from his own laboratory studies which report that extroverts (psychopaths) are genetically determined (possess a distinctive autonomic nervous system), Eysenck analyzes a series of studies of twins, authored by different investigators in different countries, with a subject group of 225 pairs of twins (one of each pair a known criminal). Fraternal twins and identical twins utilized were in equal proportion. Eysenck says that the overall finding was that twice as many identical as fraternal twins were concordant. He also analyzes a series of twin studies (including some of the 225 pairs) including juvenile delinquents, children with behavior disorders, homosexuals, psychopaths, and alcoholics, which showed high concordance for identical twins as compared with fraternal twins. Some of the identical twins were reared apart, a factor which Eysenck thinks strengthens his hereditary contention. Perhaps Eysenck's claims for the hereditary factor are too great. Twin studies, however, are much more meaningful than was once thought. Twin studies lend strong indirect evidence for a genetic factor in human behavior, operating in an internal as well as external environment.

The preceding remarks on the behavioral science bias toward constitutional factors are not meant as a digression, but rather as a caveat to the student of alcoholism who negates, ignores, or overlooks human genetic variation. At the very minimum, future breakthrough in this area may prove to be fruitful adjuncts to other approaches. Some scholars maintain that all sociological theory rests ultimately on psychological theory. Still others think that psychological theory rests on a biological base. Are these thinkers guilty of reductionism? Maybe not.[71]

NOTES AND REFERENCES

1. Bleuler, Manfred: Familial and personal background of chronic alcoholics. In Diethelm, Oskar (Ed.): *The Etiology of Chronic Alcoholism*. Springfield, Thomas, 1955, pp. 110-166.
2. Bleuler, Manfred: *Ibid.*, p. 124. Although the data suggested the in-

fluence of heredity on alcoholism, further analysis suggested to Bleuler (p. 126) that "psychological and social factors must be considered even more than the possibility of heredity." The results of other studies on heredity and alcoholism are also presented.

3. Bleuler, Manfred: A comparative study of the constitutions of Swiss and American alcoholic patients. In Diethelm, Oskar (Ed.): *Ibid.*, pp. 167-178.

4. Jellinek, E. Morton: Heredity of the alcoholic. *Alcohol, Science and Society*. 1954, pp. 105-114.

5. Kinsey, Barry A.: *The Female Alcoholic*. Springfield, Thomas, 1955.

6. Moore, Robert A., and Ramseur, Freida: A study of the backgrounds of 100 hospitalized veterans with alcoholism. *Quarterly Journal of Studies on Alcohol*. *21*:51-67, March, 1960.

7. Kaij, Lennart: *Alcoholism in Twins: Studies on the Etiology and Sequels of Abuse of Alcohol*. Stockholm, Almquist and Wiksell, 1960. Three sets of triplets were included in the study, but for simplicity of discussion and analysis of data these were referred to as twin pairs.

8. Kaij, Lennart: *Ibid.*, p. 34

9. Kaij, Lennart: *Ibid.*, p. 38.

10. Partanen, Juha, Bruun, Kettil, and Markkanen, Tuoko: *Inheritance of Drinking Behavior*. Helsinki, The Finnish Foundation for Alcohol Studies, 1966. All multiple births were included, but for practical purposes of discussion and data analysis the term *twins* is used to cover all cases.

11. See Ward, Joe H., Jr., and Hook, Marian E.: Application of and hierarchial grouping procedure to a problem of grouping profiles. *Educational and Psychological Measurement, 23*:69-82, Spring, 1963. Quoted in Partanen, Bruun, and Markkanen: *op. cit.*, p. 45.

12. The exact criteria of addictive symptoms were not given therein. The classification is reported in Partanen, Juha: *Va Kijuomien Kayttatyypt* (A typology of drinkers). Social Research Institute of Alcohol Studies, Report No. 9, Helsinki, 1963. Quoted in Partanen, Bruun, and Markkanen: *op. cit.*, p. 45.

13. Eysenck, Hans Jurgen: *The Biological Basis of Personality*. Springfield, Thomas, 1967.

14. Amark, Curt: A study in alcoholism: Clinical, social-psychiatric and genetic investigations. *Acta Psychiatrica et Neurologica Scandinavica*, Supplement 70, 1951.

15. A discussion of Swedish beverage laws, Systems Companies, etc., is found in Amark, Curt: *Ibid.*, pp. 11-17.

16. Amark, Curt: *Ibid.*, p. 120.

17. Winokur, George, and Clayton, Paula J.: Family history studies, IV. Comparison of male and female alcoholics. *Quarterly Journal of Studies on Alcohol, 29*:885-891, December, 1968. Related studies quoted therein are: Winokur, George, and Pitts, F. N., Jr.: Affective

disorder, VI. A family history study of prevalence, sex differences and possible genetic factors. *Journal of Psychiatric Research, 3*:113-123, August, 1965; Pitts, Ferris N., Jr., and Winokur, George: Affective disorder, VII. Alcoholism and effective disorder. *Journal of Psychiatric Research, 4*:37-50, July, 1966; Winokur, George, and Clayton, Paula: Family history studies, I. Two types of affective disorder separated according to genetic and clinical factors. *Recent Advances in Biological Psychiatry, 9*:35-50, 1967.

18. See also Cruz-Coke, R., and Varela, A.: Inheritance of alcoholism: Its association with color blindness. *Lancet, 2*:1282-1284, December 10, 1966. For a discussion and review of twin studies and other research on the heritability of alcoholism see: Amark, Curt: *op. cit.*, pp. 4-5; Kaij, Lennart: *op. cit.;* Jellinek, E. Morton: *op. cit.;* Partanen, Juha, et al.: *op. cit.*, Ch. V; and Tahka, Viekko: *The Alcoholic Personality.* Helsinki, The Finnish Foundation for Alcohol Studies, 1966, pp. 23-25.

19. Roe, Anne: The adult adjustment of children of alcoholic parents raised in foster homes. *Quarterly Journal of Studies on Alcohol, 5*:378-393, December, 1944.

20. Roe, Anne: *Ibid.*, p. 393.

21. Lucero, Rubel Joseph, Jensen, Karl F., and Ramsey, Catherine: Alcoholism and teetotalism in blood relatives of abstaining alcoholics. *Quarterly Journal of Studies on Alcohol, 32*:183, March, 1971.

22. Jonsson, E., and Nilsson T.: Alcohol consumption in monozygotic and dizygotic pairs of twins. *Quarterly Journal of Studies on Alcohol, 31*:774, September, 1970.

23. Wolff, Peter H.: Ethnic differences in alcohol sensitivity. *Science, 175*:449-450, January 28, 1972.

24. McClearn, Gerald E., and Rogers, David A.: Differences in alcohol preference among inbred strains of mice. *Quarterly Journal of Studies on Alcohol, 20*, 691:695, December, 1959.

25. Rogers, David A., and McClearn, George E.: Mouse strain differences in preference for various concentrations of alcohol. *Quarterly Journal of Studies on Alcohol, 23*:26-35, March, 1962.

26. Rogers, David A., and McClearn, George E.: *Ibid.*, p. 33. Another recent study in this area on the heredity of mice as related to alcohol metabolism is Schlesinger, K., Bennett, E. L., and Hebert, Marie: Effects of genotype and prior consumption of alcohol on rates of ethanol 1-C^{14} metabolism in mice. *Quarterly Journal of Studies on Alcohol, 28*:231-235, June, 1967.

27. Thomas, Karla: Selection and avoidance of alcohol solutions by two strains of inbred mice and derived generations. *Quarterly Journal of Studies on Alcohol, 30*:849-861, December, 1969.

28. Eriksson, K.: The estimation of heritability for the self-selection of

alcohol in the albino rat. *Quarterly Journal of Studies on Alcohol, 31*:728-729, September, 1970.

29. Sheppard, J. R., Albersheim, P., and McClearn, G. E.: Enzyme activities and ethanol preference in mice. *Quarterly Journal of Studies on Alcohol, 31*:999, December, 1970.

30. Williams, Roger J.: *Alcoholism: The Nutritional Approach.* Austin, The University of Texas Press, 1959.

31. See also Williams, Roger J.: Biochemical Individuality and cellular nutrition. *Quarterly Journal of Studies on Alcohol, 20*:452-463, September, 1959.

32. Pelton, Richard B., Williams, Robert J., and Rogers, Lorne L.: Metabolic characteristics of alcoholics, I. Response to glucose stress. *Quarterly Journal of Studies on Alcohol, 12*:563-575, March, 1951.

33. Brady, Roscoe A., and Westerfield, W. W.: The effects of B complex vitamins on voluntary consumption of alcohol by rats. *Quarterly Journal of Studies on Alcohol, 7*:499-505, March, 1947.

34. Brady, Roscoe A., and Westerfield, W. W.: *Ibid.,* p. 497.

35. Mardones, Jorge: On the relationship between deficiency of B vitamins and alcohol intake in rats. *Quarterly Journal of Studies on Alcohol, 12*:563-575, December, 1951.

36. Brown, Russell V.: Vitamin deficiency and voluntary alcohol consumption in mice. *Quarterly Journal of Studies on Alcohol, 30*:592-597, September, 1969.

37. Brown, Russell V.: *Ibid.,* p. 596.

38. Smith, James J.: A medical approach to the problem drinker. *Quarterly Journal of Studies on Alcohol, 10*:251-257, December, 1949.

39. If a hereditary origin of the predisposition was not made explicit by an author, the work was included in this section rather than in *The Inherited Section.* If both hereditary and acquired origins were mentioned, it was placed in this section. It might be that some of these authors, unbeknownst to the present authors, in works not reviewed, have postulated hereditary factors. Some of the subcategories in this section were suggested by Jellinek, E. Morton: *The Disease Concept of Alcoholism.* New Haven, College & University Press, 1960, who has also reviewed biochemical studies dealing with alcoholism. Biochemical studies were also reviewed by Kalant, Harold: Some recent physiological and biochemical investigations on alcohol and alcoholism: A review. *Quarterly Journal of Studies on Alcohol, 20*:52-93, March, 1962. Another facet of the Constitutional Approach which deserves at least mention in a footnote is the metabolism of alcohol which has been dealt with, by (among others),: Isselbacher, Kurt J., and Greenberger, Norton J.: Metabolic effects of alcohol on the liver. *New England Journal of Medicine, 270*:351-356, February, 1964; and Metabolic effects of alcohol on the liver (Conclusion).

New England Journal of Medicine, 270:402-410, February, 1964; and by Mendelum, Jack: Ethanol 1-C^{14} metabolism in alcoholics and nonalcoholics. *Science, 159*:319-320, January, 1968.

40. See Selye, Hans: *The Stress of Life.* New York, McGraw-Hill, 1956.
41. Tintera, John W.: Office rehabilitation of the alcoholic. *New York State Journal of Medicine, 56*:3896-3902, December, 1956.
42. Tintera, John W., and Lovell, Harold W.: Endocrine treatment of alcoholism. *Geriatrics, 4*:274-280, September-October, 1949.
43. Goldfarb, Alvin I., and Berman, Sidney: Alcoholism as a psychosomatic disorder, I. Endocrine pathology of animals and man excessively exposed to alcohol: Its possible relation to behavioral pathology. *Quarterly Journal of Studies on Alcohol, 10*:415-427, December, 1949.
44. Kissin, Benjamin, and Hankoff, Leon: The acute effects of ethyl alcohol and chlorpromazine on certain physiological functions in alcoholics. *Quarterly Journal of Studies on Alcohol, 20*:480-492, September, 1959. See also Kissin, Benjamin, and Hankoff, Leon: The acute effects of ethyl alcohol on the Funkstein mecholyl response in male alcoholics. *Quarterly Journal of Studies on Alcohol, 20*:696-703, December, 1959.
45. Fleetwood, M. Friele: Biochemical experimental investigations of emotions. In Diethelm, Oskar (Ed.): *op. cit.*, pp. 43-109. This is a study others should attempt to replicate due to its far-reaching implications.
46. Lemere, Frederick: What causes alcoholism. *Journal of Clinical and Experimental Psychopathology, 17*:202-206, June, 1956.
47. Davis, Pauline A.: The effects of alcohol upon the electroencephalogram (brain waves). *Quarterly Journal of Studies on Alcohol, 1*:626-637, March, 1941.
48. Little, Samuel C., and McAvoy, Mercer: Electroencephalographic studies in alcoholism. *Quarterly Journal of Studies on Alcohol, 13*:9-15, March, 1952.
49. Tumarkin, Bernard, Wilson, Jay D., and Snyder, Gilbert: Cerebral atrophy due to alcoholism in young adults. *U. S. Armed Forces Medical Journal, 6*:67-74, January, 1955.
50. Skillicorn, S. A.: Presenile cerebellar ataxia in chronic alcoholics. *Neurology, 5*:527-534, August, 1955.
51. Rogers, Lorene L., and Gawineowski, A. H.: Metabolic characteristics of alcoholics, II. Serum copper concentrations in alcoholics. *Quarterly Journal of Studies on Alcohol, 20*:33-37, March, 1959.
52. Randolph, Theron G.: The descriptive features of food addiction: Addictive eating and drinking. *Quarterly Journal of Studies on Alcohol, 17*:198-224, June, 1956.
53. See, for example, Roebuck, Julian B., and Atlas, Robert H.: Chromosomes and the criminal. *Corrective Psychiatry and Journal of Social Therapy, 15*:103-117, Fall, 1969.

54. This point has also been made by Wexberg, Leopold: A critique of Physio-pathological theories on the etiology of alcoholism. *Quarterly Journal of Studies on Alcohol, 11*:113-118, March, 1950; and by Jellinek, E. Morton: *op. cit.*

55. Lester, David: Self-selection of alcohol by animals, human variation and the etiology of alcoholism: A critical review. *Quarterly Journal of Studies on Alcohol, 27*:395-438, September, 1966.

56. Lester, David: *Ibid.,* p. 415.

57. Lester, David: *Ibid.,* pp. 395-438.

58. Wexberg, Leopold: *op...cit.,* pp. 113-118.

59. Wexberg, Leopold: *op...cit.,* p. 117.

60. McCord, William, McCord, Joan, and Gudeman, John: *Origins of Alcoholism.* Stanford, Stanford University Press, 1960.

61. McCord, William, McCord, Joan, and Gudeman, John: *Ibid.,* p. 21.

62. McCord, William, McCord, Joan, and Gudeman, John: *Ibid.,* see pp. 1-28 for methodology.

63. McCord, William, McCord, Joan, and Gudeman, John: *Ibid.,* p. 28.

64. McCord, William, McCord, Joan, and Gudeman, John: *Ibid.,* pp. 49-50.

65. Jellinek, E. Morton: *op. cit.*

66. Mendelson, Jack H., and Mello, Nancy K.: A disease as an organism for biochemical research: Alcoholism. Ch. 20 in Mandell, Arnold J., and Mandell, Mary P. (Eds.): *Psychochemical Research in Man.* New York, Academic Press, 1969, pp. 379-403.

67. Williams, Roger J.: The biology of behavior. *Saturday Review,* January 30, 1971, pp. 17-19, 61; Williams, Roger J.: *You Are Extraordinary.* New York, Random House, 1967, pp. 108-142; Hirsch, Jerry: Behavior-genetic, or "experimental" analysis: The challenge of science vs the lure of technology. *American Psychologist, 22*:118-130, February, 1967; Eysenck, Hans Jurgen: *Crime and Personality.* Boston, Houghton-Mifflin, 1964, pp. 57-60; Eysenck, Hans Jurgen: *The Biological Basis of Personality.* Springfield, Thomas, 1967, pp. 3-33. The remaining discussion in this chapter is based primarily on these sources.

68. Williams, Roger J.: *op. cit.,* pp. 122-125.

69. Hirsch, Jerry: Behavior-genetic analysis. In Hirsch, Jerry (Ed.): *Behavior-Genetics Analysis.* New York, McGraw-Hill, 1967, Ch. 20, Epilogue, pp. 416-435.

70. Eysenck, Hans Jurgen: *op. cit.,* pp. 53-64; Eysenck, Hans Jurgen: *The Biological Basis of Personality, loc. sit.,* pp. 210-211.

71. McClearon, Gerald E.: Biology and the social and behavioral sciences. *Items, Social Science Research Council, 23*:33-37, September, 1969.

Chapter III

THE PSYCHOLOGICAL APPROACH

T HE PSYCHOLOGICAL APPROACH TO THE ETIOLOGY of alcholism comprises six types of theories and research.[1] While there is overlap, each emphasizes a different theoretical and/or methodological perspective. In a precursory sense, the six types evolved from three basic positions: factual studies in alcoholism (A), treatment attempts (C and D), and basic personality and/or learning theory (B, E, and F), as illustrated below:

A. *The alchohol effects orientation* deals with the effects of alcohol upon the individual.

B. *The reinforcement orientation* centers on psychological "learning" theories and experimental demonstrations of the reinforcing qualities of alcohol.

C. *The transactional orientation* emphasizes the interaction between the alcoholic and his environment.

D. *The psychoanalytic orientation* stresses personality dynamics based on Freudian and neo-Freudian principles.

E. *The field dependence orientation* deals with a relatively unusual method of attempting to delineate the personality of the alcoholic by studying the alcoholic's perceptual abilities.

F. *The alcoholic personality orientation* focuses on the personality traits and patterns related to alcoholism.

THE ALCOHOL EFFECTS ORIENTATION

One way to approach the question of the cause of alcoholism is to study the effects of alcohol and alcoholic beverages. The logic behind this perspective is quite simple. A person drinks alcoholic beverages because of the effects they produce. Find out what kinds of effects alcohol produces and one may better understand why people drink and why they become alcoholics.

The literature covers a large number of studies in this area involving numerous dependent variables. Generally, each study deals with only one or two dependent variables. Though there is overlapping, the following rough classification appears to fit and encompass extant studies.

1. Neurophysiological alcohol effects, e.g. brainwaves, cerebral dysfunctions, neural impairment, or disease.

2. Non-neurological physiological alcohol effects, e.g. endocrine gland functions, liver functions, blood chemistry, metabolism, body cell and tissue structure and function, enzymes, hormones, digestion, and respiration.

3. Psychological effects-response speed, e.g. reaction time, articulation, motor skills, auditory and visual skills.

4. Psychological effects-arousal level, e.g. euphoria, relaxation, sedation, inhibition, conflict behavior, stress, aggression, dreams, success.

5. Psychological effects—perception and cognition, e.g. hearing, vision, time perception, oral imagery, synesthesia, kinesthesia, mental lapses, attention and thinking processes, decision making, language, form perception and organization, space, color perception.

We selected for examination alcohol-effects studies of human beings, which involve study findings on euphoria, disinhibition, stress, tranquilization, aggression, self-concept, relaxation, arousal level, and anxiety stimulus.

General Works on the Effects of Alcohol

The main effect of alcohol on the body is its depressant action on the central nervous system.[2] Greenberg[3] outlined the effects of varying amounts of alcohol. In the average sized person, two or three ounces of whiskey in the body will produce 0.05 percent of alcohol in the blood. With this concentration of alcohol, the functions of the uppermost levels of the brain are depressed, resulting in the diminishing of judgment, inhibition, and restraint. The drinker feels that he is "sitting on top of the world." Because his normal inhibitions have vanished, he takes many personal and social liberties as prompted by impulse. He is long-winded and his self-critical abilities are lost. Five or six ounces of whiskey in the body results in a concentration of 0.10% alcohol in the blood. Functions of the lower motor area are dulled, and the individual sways perceptibly and his speech is slurred. At 0.20% alcohol (resulting from 10 ounces of whiskey), the entire motor area of the brain is affected and the individual requires assistance to walk or undress. A pint of whiskey in the body results in a concentration of 0.30% alcohol and, at this point, the drinker has little comprehension of what he sees, hears, or feels. At higher levels, a coma ensues, and at 0.60 or 0.70 percent, death results due to inability of the lower brain centers to control breathing and other vital processes.

Greenberg's general findings about the effects of alcohol are supported by others. Coleman[4] states that when a person is intoxicated, he typically experiences a sense of warmth, expansiveness, and well-being. In such a mood, "unpleasant realities are screened out and the drinker's feelings of self-esteem and adequacy rise . . . the drinker enters a generally pleasant world in which his worries are temporarily left behind." Coleman[5] opines that alcohol is used for at least five purposes: (1) to counter disappointment and hurt, e.g. a divorce or a broken love affair; (2) to bolster one's courage, e.g. acting a part in a play; (3) to alleviate feelings of isolation and loneliness (a reaction readily observable in bars); (4) to lower ethical restraints (thus enabling the individual to engage in infidelity or homosexual acts without feeling guilty); and (5) to blot out a sense of meaninglessness of one's existence (a common reaction among lonely, neglected, and frustrated housewives).

A few experiments involving human subjects demonstrate the disinhibiting effects of alcohol on verbal expressions of sexual and aggressive behavior in social drinking situations. The same dosage of alcohol may have diverse effects on different people because individuals vary in the types of responses inhibited, the strength of inhibitions, and variations in social conditions which probably (in part) operate to define and to control appropriate behavior.[6]

Research on the Effects of Alcohol Utilizing Normal Subjects

Descriptions of the effects of alcohol can be verified by any individual who has been intoxicated. However, two additional things are necessary: evidence of a more objective, empirical nature that alcohol has such effects, and evidence that these effects are operative among alcoholics. Greenberg and Carpenter[7] attempted to find out whether or not alcohol reduces emotional tension. They assumed that because the sympathetic nervous system controls electrical conductance of certain skin areas, conductance would be a sensitive measure of emotional activation. They conceived of the galvanic skin response (GSR) as a response to a stressful stimuli and an indication of emotional tension. The subjects were eight medical students who were neither abstainers nor problem drinkers. The experiment was divided into six sessions. The first and the last constituted control (no alcohol) sessions, while in the middle four sessions the subjects were given one of two drinks in one of two amounts. The drinks constituted of 12% alcohol Burgundy wine and a 12% (by volume) ethyl alcohol solution in water. The two amounts were 50 ml (2 ounces) and 350 ml (12 ounces). Each session was divided into a predrinking, drinking, and postdrinking period. In an attempt to maintain constant emotional level, the subjects were given a simple card-sorting task. The 50 ml of wine produced no change in basic skin conductance, while the 50 ml of alcohol solution produced a moderate reduction in skin conductance. The 350 ml dose of wine produced a marked reduction in skin conductance, while the 350 ml of alcohol solution caused no greater diminution than did the 50 ml solution.

The stress situation came in the postdrinking period. Roughly 30 minutes after the subject completed his drink (when the effect of the alcohol was presumed to be at a maximum), a 97 decibel electric horn was sounded without warning for 10 seconds. The 50 ml of wine and alcohol solution had only a small effect (5% and 8% reduction respectively) on the GSR induced by the horn. The 350 ml of wine reduced the GSR by 53 percent and the 350 ml alcohol solution reduced the GSR by 49 percent. The differential effects of the two drinks and two different amounts were attributed to rates of absorption for different beverages and to the different taste and gastrointestinal effects which may have, in and of themselves, been stressful situations.

A comparison of alcohol, meprobamate, and a placebo, by Lienert and Traxel,[8] shows that alcohol and the tranquilizer are equally effective in reducing (GSR) responses to disturbing verbal stimuli. Moreover, the subjects who had exhibited high emotionality, as assessed several weeks prior to the experimental session, were tranquilized by alcohol to a greater degree than those who had previously displayed low arousal.

Bennett, Bussard and Carpenter[9] desired to test the common observation that aggressive behavior is often brought on by intoxication. They present two theories which might explain the relation between alcohol and aggression. The disinhibition theory assumes that we are all aggressively motivated but that expression of aggression is checked by conscience and social restraints. The controlling effects are lessened by alcohol. Secondly, there is the assumption that alcohol enhances aggression directly. Alcohol may stimulate the organism in a way which energizes aggressive behavior.

The subjects (A) were 16 male graduate students. Their ostensible task was to teach other subjects (B) discrimination-learning tasks. When B made a correct response, A rewarded him with a signal light. When B made an incorrect response, A punished him by pushing one of two shock buttons, each of which supposedly delivered a different level of electroshock. The level of shock given was the level of aggression expressed. The experiment consisted of four sessions, one in which A received no alcohol and three in which he received .33, .67, and 1.00 ml of absolute alcohol per kg of body weight. Although the mean shock intensity administered rose over the seven blocks per session, the mean shock intensity was not significantly different for different levels of alcohol dose. The authors conclude that alcohol did not lead to aggression. A number of explanations for the failure of alcohol to elicit aggression were given. It was possible that the subjects "saw through" the experiment or that the amount of alcohol administered was not sufficient. One alternative theoretical explanation given was that it is alcohol as a libation rather than as drug that elicits aggressive behavior. Drinking usually occurs in an informal situation, and inbibing could be a cue (or excuse) for behavior that might be unacceptable at other times and places. Finally, it may be that imbibing, itself, is irrelevant. It may be that it is the social aspects of the drinking situation (the presence of many persons in an informal context) that enhances aggression.

Research on the Effects of Alcohol
Utilizing Alcoholic Subjects

Other investigators have studied alcoholics in an attempt to ascertain what effects the alcoholic seeks from alcohol and what effects alcohol does in fact have on the alcoholic.

Mulford and Miller[10] record an interview study of 1,185 persons selected through a quota sampling system to represent the adult population of Iowa. They utilized a scale of definitions of alcohol related to drinking behavior. Three of the items to which agreement indicated drinking for "extreme personal effects" were as follows: "Liquor helps me forget I am not the kind of person I really want to be; Liquor helps me get along better with other people; and Liquor helps me feel more satisfied with myself." Thirty-five persons were located who were presumed to be alcoholics. Seventy percent of the alcoholics defined alcohol in terms of personal effects, while only 21 percent of the other "heavy drinkers" and 12 percent of "all drinkers" defined it in this manner.

Kinsey[11] asked the 46 hospitalized female alcoholics in his study what effects they sought from alcohol. Thirty-four of these (or 74%) said that the desire to change or modify an undesirable self-image was the primary reason for drinking. Vanderpool[12] hypothesized that alcoholics drink to improve their self-concepts. He predicted that there would be more positive self-concepts expressed by alcoholics when they were drinking "optimally" (were satisfied and able to function, but not highly intoxicated) than when they were sober or partially satisfied. Fifty hospitalized males were given a moderate amount of the alcoholic beverage of their choice; they were then compared with 50 alcoholic controls matched as a group on age, education, and socioeconomic status. Self-concepts were measured by an adjective check-list and the Tennessee Self-concept Scale before and during the drinking period. The hypothesis was not supported, as the data showed that the self-concepts of the alcoholics did not improve during the drinking period; they were, in fact, more negative than the pre-drinking self-concepts.

Diethelm and Barr[13] studied 13 female and 10 male alcoholics who were given 60 to 70 cc of a 95% ethyl alcohol solution intravenously. After injection, the subjects were interviewed (in a nondirective manner) for 45 minutes. In an intoxicated state, the subjects showed a marked increase in emotional behavior, which included euphoria, elation, depression, resentment, anger, guilt, hostility, and (occasionally) anxiety.

Tamerin and Mendelson[14] studied four hospitalized males who had been alcoholics for 20 to 29 years. The first two weeks of the study involved baseline psychological assessment. The subjects were interviewed, and were given questionnaires about past drinking experiences and anticipated drinking experiences to come. All four men expected that intoxication would make them more relaxed, more comfortable, and less depressed. When the subjects were given alcohol, the initial effects were pleasurable as anticipated. They felt more relaxed, less inhibited, and generally elated. However, subsequent experiences during intoxication were generally more painful. The subjects showed guilt, remorse, self-deprecation, emotional lability, and protracted crying spells. This was interpreted to mean that intoxication brought on a weakening of psychic defenses, which brought out repressed memories and created depression and anxiety. Further drinking brought temporary relief, but when the immediate effects of alcohol wore off, the painful feelings returned with greater intensity. Assertiveness and aggressiveness increased during intoxication, but this was interpreted as "irritability," "childish demandingness," and "hypermasculine assertiveness." This last represented a defense against passive homosexual wishes which came closer to awareness with intoxication and had to be defended against. The marked increase in the capacity for closeness for members of both sexes emerged from behind previously maintained defenses. Intoxication was seen to have allowed expression of a regressive wish for intimacy with a nurturant figure.

The authors contended that their results indicated that anticipated pleasure enhancement or tension reduction were significant motivating factors in the *initiation* of a drinking episode. They concluded that the painful experiences following the initial elation were important factors in the *perpetuation* of the drinking episode.

Garfield and McBrearty[15] studied the arousal level and stimulus response in alcoholics after drinking. Their subjects, 27 hospitalized male alcoholics (mean age 43), were divided into three equal groups. Group one drank 0.5 ml of alcohol per kg of body weight in grapefruit juice; group two drank 1.0 ml of alcohol per kg; group three drank only grapefruit juice (drunk within 5 to 8 minutes). The patients were shown neutral and aversive stimuli prior to, and about 40 minutes after, drinking. The two sets of stimuli consisted of pictures of mutilated bodies of male victims of violent death (aversive) randomized among normal pictures of men (neutral). Basal skin conductance (three readings at one minute intervals) was measured before and after stimulus presentation, and before and after drinking. Galvanic skin response was recorded after each stimulus presentation. The mean blood alcohol concentration 40 minutes after drinking was 0.046 and 0.088 percent in groups one and two, respectively.

The basal skin conductance of all three groups increased after drinking ($p < .025$) but analysis revealed no significant effect of dose. The increase in group two was less than in group one, and that in group one greater than in group three. For all groups, the galvanic skin response was greater to the aversive than to the neutral stimuli ($p < .001$). The difference in responses to both stimuli was smaller after alcohol, and was directly related to the amount of dose. Additional analysis of the effect of dose on the predrinking and postdrinking ratio of responses to aversive and neutral stimuli disclosed a significant interaction ($p < .05$).

The authors concluded that alcohol consumption, or its anticipation, by alcoholics is an *anxiety stimulus* and that overall reactivity to stimuli in alcoholics is reduced by alcohol ingestion.

Studies on the Effects of Congeners

A new dimension has been added to the study of the effects of alcohol by the relatively recent concern with, and study of, congeners. Congeners are substances, other than ethanol, which occur in widely different proportions in various types of alcoholic beverages. Congeners include aldehydes, esters, ketones, ethers, and higher alcohols. Drinkers themselves have commonly observed that certain alcoholic beverages have different effects, both immediate as well as postdrinking, which may be attributable to the varying congener concentrations.[16] The congeners may have interaction effects with ethanol, or they may have effects completely independent of ethanol. The latter position has many similarities with the "food allergy" explanation of alcoholism presented by Randolph.

Teger et al.[17] tested the effects of alcoholic beverages and their congener content on risk taking. Risk taking was tested by use of the Kagen and Wallachis choice-dilemma questionnaire, which consists of 12 items. Each item requires the subjects to give advice to a hypothetical person who is faced with a difficult problem. The subject must decide whether to advise the person to make a risky or nonrisky decision. The items deal with a wide range of topics including health, politics, finance, career choice, and sports. The subjects were 36 male graduate students who were randomly assigned to one of two groups. In Group I, the subjects filled out the choice-dilemma questionnaire first, and were then given the first dose of alcoholic beverage. Three more doses were given at hourly intervals. Each dose contained 0.2 ml of ethanol per kg of body weight. One-half hour after the final dose, they were given the questionnaire again. The subjects in Group II were given four doses of alcohol, identical to those given the subjects in Group I. One-half hour after the fourth and final dose, they were given the questionnaire for the first time. Two and one-half hours later after their blood alcohol had dropped to .03 percent or lower, they were given the questionnaire again, with the explanation that the first questionnaire had been for practice only.

Within each group, subjects had been randomly assigned to receive one of three beverages. Some subjects received an 80 proof bourbon, to which four times the normal amount of bourbon congeners had been added. Other subjects received an 80 proof vodka, to which four times the normal amount of vodka congeners had been added. Even with the additional congeners added, the congener content for the vodka remained near zero. The remaining subjects received an 80 proof alcohol which was essentially congener-free.

A comparison of the performance of Group I (no alcohol) and Group II (alcohol) for the first test administration showed that drunk subjects were significantly riskier. Further analysis revealed that only those drunk on bourbon (the high-congener drink) had taken significantly more risk than sober subjects. The vodka and congener-free alcohol solutions produced nonsignificantly higher risk taking. Comparisons within Group II for the first administration of the questionnaire revealed that those drunk on bourbon were significantly riskier than those drunk on vodka and riskier (but not significantly so) than those drunk on congener-free alcohol. The vodka and alcohol subject-risk scores were not significantly different. The authors felt that their results indicated that people drunk on high-congener beverages took greater risks than those drunk on low-congener beverages. They concluded that congeners are partially responsible for the condition loosely referred to as "drunkenness" by the general public.

Nathan et al.[18] studied eight white male volunteers (four in each of two studies) who had come to a correctional institution to "dry out" after a lengthly drinking spree. The observations took place in a closed, controlled human laboratory. The observations involved two studies. In both there were four subjects, and the studies differed only in the order in which beverages were made available to the subjects in an 18-day drinking period. In Study I, subjects could drink only 43% ethanol for the first nine days and only bourbon (43% alcohol) the second nine days. In Study II, the subjects drank only bourbon the first nine days and vodka (40% alcohol) the second nine days. The bourbon was highest in congener content, containing almost 40 times as much congener content as the vodka and roughly 50 times as much congener content as the ethanol. The subjects could obtain the beverages in an operant-type situation. In addition to physical and physiological measures, a 330-item Behavioral Inventory Scale (BI), a Word Sociogram (WS), a Mood Adjective Checklist (MACL), and the Wittenborn Psychiatric Rating Scales (WPRS) were used.

Analysis of the operant-response data revealed that no subject showed a consistent pattern of preference for either high- or low-congener beverages. The BI and WS did not reveal any consistent differences in behavior as a function of congener content. The MACL did not reveal mood differences as a function of congener level, and the WPRS similarly failed to find differences that could be attributed to congener differences. In terms of the physiological measures, the authors concluded that "congeners in the amounts found in alcoholic beverages do not have a measurable effect on the functioning of the central nervous system."

Murphree et al.[19] analyzed the EEG's of eight men and two women who were light to moderate social drinkers. The subjects were given doses of bourbon, "superbourbon" (containing eight times the normal amount of congeners), or an orange juice placebo. On the basis of previous work, they concluded that no significant differences in blood alcohol concentration (as measured by Breathalyzer) occurred after doses of any drink containing equal amounts of ethanol, but differing amounts of congeners. In terms of EEG, the superbourbon produced an entirely different effect than that of the other beverages. The most distinguishing effect of the superbourbon occurred in the parietals. The authors concluded that there were similarities between the effects of the superbourbon and barbiturates that might somehow be related to the congener content of the alcoholic beverage.

THE REINFORCEMENT ORIENTATION

The theories in this category are often described as psychological learning theories. Investigators theorize that something is learned or some kind of behavior perpetuated because it is reinforced. These theorists mostly agree that the alcoholic drinks because of the effects alcohol produces, and designate these effects reinforcement. Thus, if one finds out how alcohol is reinforcing, and why, then perhaps alcoholism can be understood.

According to Conger,[20] the basic assumption of a reinforcement theory of learning is that the learning of an association between a stimulus and a response requires the presence of some sort of reward or reinforcement. Reinforcement, in turn, is defined in terms of drive reduction. Thus, if making a certain response in the presence of a cue or stimulus leads to a reduction in the strength of a drive (the latter being a state of tension resulting from an unsatisfied need), the individual will be more likely to repeat that response when confronted with the same or similar stimulus situations on subsequent occasions.

Dollard and Miller[21] theorize that alcohol is reinforcing because it results in a reduction of fear, conflict, and anxiety. Kingham[22] presents a learning theory of alcoholism. The alcoholic is a person with an unconscious desire to escape reality; this desire is symptomatic of a cycloid personality, featuring avoidance of, or discomfort with, anything but an "average" mood. For such a person to become an alcoholic, a number of conditions must be met. First, the "blitz" drinking pattern (a drinking "binge" which is rapid and inexorable) must be available as a potential response. Secondly, the "blitz" response must become dominant possibly through trial and error. For example, a person may become a member of a group which competes to see who can drink the most, or he may be exposed to unusual stress conditions (e.g. wartime) in which alcohol is specifically used to escape reality. Alternately, the dominance of the blitz response can be built up insidiously over a number of years. For a response to become dominant, it must be reinforced. Any reinforcement situation can be described in terms of the folowing paradigm:

$$\text{Drive} \rightarrow \text{Cue} \rightarrow \text{Response} \rightarrow \text{Reinforcement.}$$

In the case of the alcoholic:

Drive　　　　　　= Disturbance of homeostatic condition
Cue　　　　　　　= Alcoholic beverage
Response　　　　= Blitz drinking pattern
Reinforcement = Return of homeostasis

Fear, anger, frustration, loneliness, depression, or other emotional states are considered disturbances of homeostasis. The alcoholic beverage provides the cue for the blitz drinking response. The drinking response is reinforced because it alleviates the unpleasant psychic state and restores homeostasis.

The alcoholic drinking pattern is further strengthened and developed through transfer of the response to other situations. For example, the person who used alcohol initially to reduce feelings of depression may later use alcohol to reduce feelings of rejection or loneliness. The response gains additional strength by being reinforced in additional situations. The goal gradient principle can also account for additional strengthening of the response. Responses nearest the goal or reinforcement situation are strengthened the most, while those progressively distant from the goal are strengthened less and less. For the alcoholic, those aspects of drinking behavior which are farthest from the goal of intoxicated oblivion tend to disappear.

Conger[23] suggested that the drinking response is learned because it leads to a reduction in drive. The inspiration for Conger's studies came from the work of Masserman and Yum.[24] These investigators trained cats (to work) to open a box to obtain food. Later in the experiment, when the cats opened the box, they were made "neurotic" by being subjected to electric shocks or blasts of air. This caused the cats to avoid the situation, and they stopped working for food. With the administration of alcohol, they began working again for the food. (Smart [1965] further confirmed the anxiety-mitigating effects of alcohol.)[25] Conger reasoned that the situation in which the cats were placed contained elements of an approach-avoidance conflict situation. Conger designed three experiments to determine if alcohol could produce a reduction in the fear drive, motivating avoidance in an approach-avoidance situation.

In the first experiment, ten rats were trained to approach the distinctively lighted end of a straight-line alley to secure food. There were 50 of these approach trails. Next, they were given avoidance training by being subjected to an electric shock at the food goal. Finally, the rats were given injections of alcohol or water. Those injected with alcohol ran up to get the food, while those injected with water would not approach the goal. Having concluded, on the basis of the first experiment, that alcohol resolved the approach-avoidance conflict, Conger designed a second experiment, in order to determine more clearly how alcohol affected each of the two competing tendencies. More specifically, he wanted to know if alcohol strengthened the approach response, weakened the avoidance response, or produced some complex interactive pattern. The results indicated to Conger that the primary reason for the resolution of the approach-avoidance conflict in the first experiment was the reduction of the avoidance response. A third experiment was designed to test the possibility that effects of alcohol were confounded with a change in the animal's condition; that is, it was logically possible that the decreases in the avoidance response might be wholly or partially due to other changes in the animals' condition rather than being solely due to the effects of "inebriation." On the basis of this final experiment, Conger concluded that "inebriation" itself was at least partly responsible for the results of previous experiments.

Bandura maintains that excessive alcohol consumption (alcoholism) is maintained through positive reinforcement resulting from the central depressant and anesthetic properties of alcohol.

Individuals who are repeatedly subjected to environmental stress are consequently more prone to drink anesthetic quantities of alcohol than those individuals who experience less stress and for whom, therefore, alcohol has only weak reinforcing value. Moreover, for many, excessive drinking may primarily serve to relieve the aversive effects of boredom.[26]

If it is assumed that the drinking response is learned because it is reinforced, then how can drinking be learned, when it often leads to social punishment rather than reward. Conger wisely addressed himself to this question and concluded there were two possible answers. First, there is the learning principle of the gradient of reinforcement. According to this principle, immediate reinforcements are more effective than delayed ones. Thus, the immediate reduction in anxiety may more than compensate for the punitive attitude of others later on. The second factor which must be taken into account is the amount of drive. If the drive level is high enough, the drive-reducing effects of alcohol may outweigh the competing social punishment. Conger's position in another context is explained later in this chapter.

Freed[27] utilized 80 hungry rats who were trained to run a straight 15-foot long runway to obtain food. Later the rats were given an electric shock near the food goal to induce an avoidance response and create an approach-avoidance conflict. The conflict situation was considered established when a rat met the criterion of three consecutive one-minute trails in which the animal was not shocked and did not eat. After reaching the criterion, the rats were given one of four interperitoneal injections: 2.5, 5.0, or 7.5 grams of alcohol in a water and dextrose solution or an equitonic control solution of dextrose and water.

Blood alcohol concentration (BAC) was determined and had a roughly linear relationship with amount injected. Analysis of BAC revealed four modal clusters corresponding roughly to the one-control and three-alcohol doses. None of the control rats resolved the conflict by eating within the ten one-minute trials set as the criterion. On the other hand, 14 of the 60 alcohol-treated animals resolved the conflict. Of these 14 rats, two had been given the lowest alcohol dose, seven the intermediate, and five the highest dose. In terms of BAC, the two highest clusters (0.07%-0.14%

and 0.15%-0.26%) each had six rats resolving the conflict, while the 0.01%-0.06% BAC group had only two rats resolving the conflict. Freed contended that his results lent support to the body of literature reporting the anxiety and conflict-reducing effects of alcohol.[28] In a similar study, Freed[29] found results which were again suggestive of the possible mitigating effects of alcohol upon conflict. In each case, alcohol-treated rats showed a slightly greater degree of conflict resolution than their controls.[30]

Brown[31] placed 19 mice in a "stress" situation by spinning them for five minutes at 78 rpm in a cage mounted on a phonograph turntable. The mice were subjected to spinning once a day for two weeks. Before, during, and after spinning, the mice had a choice of water or a 5% ethyl alcohol solution. The mice showed a significant proportional increase in alcohol consumption during spinning and a decline in consumption during the post-spinning period to a level below that of a pre-spinning period.

Brown, in a second study, housed 20 mice individually and 20 in groups of four, and spun them for 20 minutes once a day for two weeks. The individually housed mice showed increased alcohol consumption during spinning, and decreased consumption (to a new low) after spinning. Mice housed in groups did not increase their alcohol consumption during spinning. Brown suggested that grouping of mice was some sort of protection against the stress effects of spinning.[32] Another explanation mentioned by Brown was that of Thiessen and Rogers,[33] who suggested that adrenal activation due to the stress effects of grouping may reduce alcohol consumption.

Casey[34] studied the relative intake of water and an alcohol solution as a function of aversive shocks programmed according to a variable interval schedule. Under these conditions of uncertainty, the animals drank larger amounts of alcohol for the period of stress, but the greatest increments in voluntary alcohol consumption occurred during the following month, after the shocks had been stopped. In a second group of animals provided with a free choice of water or a solution of reserpine (a drug with long-delayed effects), the same experimental manipulations failed to increase the attraction of reserpine. These different findings suggest that the relatively rapid absorption of alcohol, and the concomitant reduction in aversive arousal, may partly contribute to its (alcohol's) effectiveness as a positive reinforcer under conditions of aversive stimulation.

Gowdy and Klaase[35] followed the lead of Adamson and Black,[36] who suggested that voluntary alcohol consumption is directly related to an internal tension dimension. This dimension, in turn, is reflected in differences in performance. Rats with high internal tension should consume more alcohol. The alcohol, by reducing tension, would be reinforcing. Rats with low tension levels would find alcohol less reinforcing and should consume less. In an attempt to separate rats by level of tension, an avoidance learning test was set up. Presumably, the high-tension animals would learn the avoidance response (or condition) more quickly.

Before being placed in the learning situation, the rats were given their choice of tap water or a 10% ethyl alcohol solution. The high tension rats (so designated by their ease of learning in the subsequent learning situation) should be those that consume the most alcohol.

After determining the liquid preferences of the rats, Gowdy and Klaase placed them in the experimental learning setting, consisting of two shuttle boxes separated by a low barrier. The grid floor in each box could be electrified independently. A buzzer was used as a conditioned stimulus. Five seconds after the buzzer began, the grid floor was electrified. The shock continued until the rat jumped over the barrier to the other compartment. A rat was considered to have learned the avoidance response if he successfully avoided the shock on six consecutive trials. Eighty-five of the 101 rats tested met the learning criteria within 140 trials. The correlation between alcohol consumption and subsequent learning ability (number of trials to criterion) was .036, which was nonsignificant. Their results failed to support contentions about the tension reducing (hence reinforcing) effects of alcohol.

Senter and Sinclair[37] suggested that if the potential alcoholic is viewed as having a chronic drive state due to persistent anxiety or stress, and if it is further assumed that he used alcohol to reduce this drive state, then almost any of the traditional learning theories would predict that the act of consuming alcohol would become functionally autonomous and eventually achieve goal properties itself. Therefore, an alcoholic's affinity for alcohol might be regarded as a type of approach behavior toward a secondary goal (alcohol) which had acquired incentive value by its association with primary drive reduction. Senter and Sinclair utilized 40 rats in an attempt to gain support for their theoretical viewpoint. Twenty of the rats were placed on a thiamine-deficient diet for three weeks. Ten of these rats (Group I) continued on the thiamine-deficient diet for three more weeks (the "association period") but had thiamine available ad libitum in a 7% alcohol solution. This concentration of thiamine was chosen so that the rats would be forced to consume 20 ml of alcohol solution daily to meet their minimum requirement of thiamine. Another 10 rats (Group II) were put on a regular diet including thiamine during the association period, and had a choice of a 7% alcohol solution (without thiamine) and water. The other 20 rats were on a normal diet for the first three weeks. In the three-week association period, ten of these rats (Group III) had a

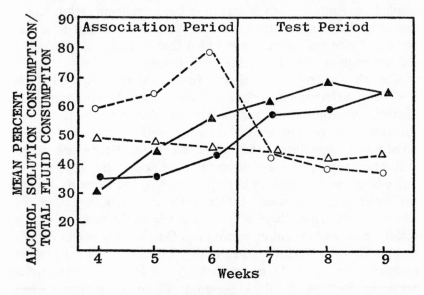

LEGEND

Group I = o---o   Group II = △---△
Group III = ●---●   Group IV = ▲---▲

Figure I. Mean alcohol solution consumption (by volume) during association and test periods.

Adapted from R. J. Sentner and J. D. Sinclair: Thiamine-induced alcohol consumption in rats. *Quarterly Journal of Studies on Alcohol*, 29:430, June, 1968.

normal diet and had a choice of the alcohol-thiamine solution or water. During the association period, the final ten rats (Group IV) had a normal diet, and a choice of water and a 7% alcohol (no thiamine) solution. In the final three weeks (the test period), all rats had a normal diet and a choice of water or alcohol (without thiamine). The alcohol consumption by week and period for all groups is plotted in Figure 1. As expected, during the association period, the rats in Group I consumed markedly larger amounts of alcohol to obtain thiamine. During the test period, however, Group I consumed the lowest amount of alcohol. Group II (which also had been on a thiamine deficient diet) also showed almost as little alcohol consumption as Group I.

In the test period, the total liquid intake for the two groups on thiamine-deficient diets (Group I and II) was significantly lower than that of Groups III and IV. This suggested that thiamine deprivation (irrespective of other conditions) leads to a decrease in alcohol consumption, which may have been strong enough to mask any secondary reinforcing value that the alcohol might have acquired. Senter and Sinclair concluded that in their study, alcohol did not acquire secondary reinforcing properties.

Keehn[38] adopted a very similar theoretical viewpoint but took a slightly different methodological approach. He reinforced the alcohol consumption of four hungry rats with food. Later, when the rats were offered alcohol and saccharine solution, without constraint or conditions, they chose the latter. Keehn concluded that when appropriate experimental conditions were applied, the animals ingested alcohol in large proportions, but when these contingencies were removed, the animals exhibited no taste for alcohol at all. Thus, there was no evidence of the taste or of any effects of alcohol becoming reinforcing. On the basis of this experiment with rats, Keehn suggested that alcoholism in man might sometimes be similarly maintained by reinforcing contingencies set up inadvertently by the community. There are occasions when it is not alcohol per se that maintains excessive drinking, but other environmental contingencies that have gone unobserved.

Probably the most provocative, and perhaps the most plausible, reinforcement theory of alcoholism to date is Bandura's "social learning theory."[39] Research data (some of which appears above) indicates that excessive drinking is maintained through positive reinforcement deriving from the depressant and anesthetic properties of alcohol on people in stressful situations. Protracted and excessive use of alcohol produces alterations in the metabolic system which provide the basis for a "second maintaining mechanism" that is independent of the original functional value of alcohol, i.e. the withdrawal of alcohol causes aversive physiological reactions, such as tremulousness, nausea, vomiting, and other withdrawal symptoms. Following physical dependence on alcohol, the individual is compelled to consume large amounts of alcohol to allay withdrawal symptoms and to prevent their recurrence. The consumption of alcohol in these circumstances quickly alleviates physiologically generated aversive stimulation; therefore, drinking behavior is automatically and continuously reinforced. Following addiction, the alcoholic's time and resource are devoted to maintaining a persistently high level of intoxication.

Bandura recognizes that aversion reduction and other positive reinforcements which accompany social drinking may account for the maintenance of inebriety, but that an adequate theory of alcoholism must include additional social-learning variables, since most people who suffer stressful experiences do not become alcoholics. He disagrees with those theorists who postulate internal determinants as a link here (e.g. some form of personality aberration) and points to the pre-alcoholic social learning of drinking behavior as the key in the development of alcoholism. Though social-learning variables take several forms, at the most general level they are reflected in the cultural norms that define the reinforcement contingencies associated with the use of alcohol. Cultural and subgroup mores are transmitted through the modeling of socializing agents. Members of a particular group or class do not have the same learning experiences. The relationship of stress to alcoholism is perhaps strongest among alcoholics who are members of subcultural groups that negatively sanction drinking. Stressful situations elicit a wide variety of behaviors. Alcoholics are people who have acquired, through "differential reinforcement" and modeling experiences, alcohol consumption as a widely generalized dominant response to aversive stimulation.

Bandura's thesis that alcoholism often arises in rewarding social interactions in which drinking serves an instrumental rather than a reinforcing function is supported by a number of studies utilizing operant techniques originally developed by B. F. Skinner. According to the operant conditioning theory, behavior which is immediately reinforced tends to be repeated, while behavior which is rarely reinforced tends to be extinguished. Since addictive drinking appears to emerge gradually over a period of many years, operant conditioning theory has important implications for the better understanding of alcoholism.

Cahalan[40] analyzed several different kinds of studies that support operant conditioning theory: Levy (1958) demonstrated that alcohol becomes habituating (reinforcing) when it economically solves a large variety of the individual's problems in a specific way and when, as a result of excessive drinking, there is a breakdown of social functioning which can be pacified only by further drinking. Ferster, Neuenberger, and Levitt (1962) attempted to explain the twin paradoxes that permit addictive drinkers to persist in drinking in the face of heavy social disapproval which inevitably follows heavy drinking, and also permit obese people to continue to overeat even though the long-term consequences of this action are obviously aversive. In both cases, short-term pleasure from eating and drinking provides immediate reinforcement which outweighs (in terms of motivation) later difficulties associated with obesity and hangovers and other symptoms of alcoholism. Conger (1956) implied that persistence and excess of drinking are a consequence of a gradient of reinforcement, including the anxiety-reducing effects of continued drinking to postpone anxiety from thinking about the resulting punishment for drinking. Knight (1937) considered the "essential" versus "reactive" alcoholic. The "essential" demands immediate gratification, whatever the environmental circumstances; the "reactive" alcoholic drinks heavily because of temporary environmental influences. Knupfer (1968), in a quantitative San Francisco survey, found an association between psychosomatic complaints and problem drinking, and between smoking, eating, and problem drinking. Allan F. Williams (1965), in experimental studies with college men who answered anxiety-depression questions before, during, and at the end of cocktail parties, found that the problem drinkers were self-critical and tended to endorse adjectives suggestive of neurosis. He also found that while anxiety and depression decreased significantly at low levels of alcohol consumption, anxiety and depression tended to increase at high levels of consumption. Lastly, Reinert (1968) summarized the operant conditioning and social-psychological interactionist position in an article entitled, "The Concept of Alcoholism as a Bad Habit." Addiction involves the discovery that alcohol can serve several important functions, e.g. gives pleasure, reduce pain and fear, raise self-esteem, or provide a socially recognized identity. Ultimately, the use of alcohol becomes inextricably tied to a variety of common social situations or emotional states in a similar way that the use of tobacco does for those who cannot stop smoking.

THE TRANSACTIONAL ORIENTATION

Investigators studying the effects of alcohol on the individual and the stress-reducing aspects of alcoholics have generally concentrated on the reinforcing effects of alcohol on the individual. Alcoholism is related to the effects that alcohol has on intrapsychic structures and processes. Alcohol is reinforcing because it relieves the individual's inner tensions or resolves his conflicts. Alcohol may inhibit higher brain centers, lessening normal controls, or it may relieve stress or drive by acting on lower brain centers. This paradigm accepts alcoholism as a personality state which a person carries around with him until he is cured.[41] In contrast to this more traditional S-O-R (stimulus-organism-response) paradigm, which attributes the control of behavior (R) to an internal mental apparatus (O), and consequently seeks the causes of behavior through analysis of intrapsychic processes and structures, is the more recent S-R-S^R (stimulus-response-reinforcement) paradigm. This paradigm centers on the transactions going on between an organism and its environment. It focuses upon the environmental conditions which precede (S) and follow (S^R) the operant behavior (R) of an organism. This behavior analysis considers the causes of behavior separately from the nature of consciousness. Like transactional analysis, it seeks the causes of behavior in interpersonal transactions rather than in intrapsychic processes.[42]

This latter perspective suggests that it is not the direct effects of alcohol on the individual which are reinforcing, but the effects or consequences of being drunk (or being an alcoholic) that are reinforcing. Keehn,[43] after failing to find evidence for the conclusive and persistent reinforcing properties of alcohol, suggested that it is not necessarily alcohol per se that maintains excessive drinking, but reinforcing contingencies set up by the community, i.e. the interpersonal transactions brought on by the use of alcohol which provide the reinforcement. He contended that more emphasis should be placed on the positive reinforcing consequences of drinking that are *not* provided by alcohol itself. Keehn realized the difficulty of applying this approach to the solitary drinker (who would not be able to "transact" with others). The problem of the solitary drinker was solved by reference to the concept of the reinforcement schedule. To be maintained, a response need not be reinforced at every emission. Possible social reinforcements for the solitary drinker are the occasions on which he is taken to the hospital or those when he describes his condition to sympathetic listeners in clinics and social agencies. Relatedly, the drinker's solitary drinking pattern does not emerge all at once. He exhibits a gradual progression from social to solitary drinking, from a high- to a low-density schedule of social reinforcement.[44]

Keehn[45] demonstrated with several animal studies the circumstances under which punishment could enhance, rather than reduce, the probability of emission of a punished response. After early training, the experimental animals were reinforced in the presence of punishment and not reinforced in its absence. This resulted in the establishment of a stimulus as a discriminative stimulus for a response. By analogy, he claimed that an individual's (solitary and/or destructive) excessive drinking behavior can come under similar discriminative stimulus control. He also demonstrated that drinking acquired through positive social reinforcement might in the long run be maintained by negative reinforcement more or less alone. This could be the case, he claims, with the long-term alcoholic, who has developed a dependence on alcohol. Overall, Keehn tried to show how *social transactions* could function to generate and maintain solitary drinking by reference to the phenomena of reinforcement schedules, discriminative functions of punishment, multiple-schedule control, and behavioral byproducts of intermittent reinforcement.

Steiner[46] made a radical, detailed, and highly controversial attempt to unravel the transactions between the alcoholic and others in his environment which lead to and maintain alcoholism. The pharmacological properties and effects of alcohol have little meaning for him. The reinforcement for alcoholic behavior comes with what is termed the "interpersonal payoff." Steiner challenged the conventional medical view of alcoholism as an illness. He maintained that, for *some* alcoholics, at least, the illness concept is inappropriate. The existence of physiological addiction is not denied but is seen as the end result of alcoholic behavior, not its cause.

Steiner adopted the frame of reference presented by Berne in his book *Games People Play*,[47] a position similar to that of Alfred Adler, though neither Berne nor Steiner acknowledges Adler as a precursor. The transactional or game-playing perspective can be applied to almost any type of human behavior. Basic to this perspective are the concepts of "life script" and "game." The life script is a life plan which a person assumes in childhood and becomes the blueprint for future behavior. The life script is based on one's self-concept or identity (especially about one's worth) and the worth of significant others. A game is a sequence of transactions between two or more persons with a "payoff" as the ulterior motive. The game is a repetitive behavior pattern engaged in to promote the script. The game leads to a payoff for one or more of the players. The payoff comes in the form of psychological, social, or biological satisfactions which are often defenses against unpleasant stimuli.

Steiner contends that appropriate transactional responses (or payoffs) from others are at the root of alcoholism. Alcoholism is the result of alcoholic game playing. The transactional analysis perspective suggests that an alcoholic stranded on a desert island with a large supply of alcohol will stop drinking, because drinking is only part of the transactional situation. Without other persons to transact with, the need for alcohol will disappear. As Keehn suggested, this perspective is contrasted with the more traditional view that might predict that since the alcoholic's need for alcohol is due to an illness, the marooned alcoholic would still continue to drink.

Steiner evolved his view on alcoholism from an examination of 500 alcoholics seen at the Center for Special Problems (a county outpatient alcoholism and drug-addiction clinic in San Francisco) and 50 alcoholic patients treated intensively both at the center and in private practice. Steiner claimed that the majority of these alcoholics would have been classified by Jellinek's typology as either gamma or delta alcoholics. The examination and treatment of these cases led Steiner to two major points: (1) alcoholics engage in at least three distinct, repetitive, interpersonal behavior sequences (games), and (2) the ulterior motive of alcoholic behavior is the production of certain interpersonal payoffs. Alcohol is incidental to this activity.

The alcoholic's theme or life script is a subtle variation of "you are no good, I am no good." Namely, "I am no good and I know it, but you are no good either, and since you don't seem to be aware of it, I am going to expose you." In short, the alcoholic, by masterful roleplaying, exposes the weaknesses of others by "luring" and "hooking" them into one of the following alcoholic game roles: "foolish patsy," "rageful persecutor," "impotent rescuer," or perhaps just another alcoholic.

Steiner found that his alcoholics played one of three different games, depending upon their different personality inadequacies. He did not maintain that all alcoholics utilized these games—only the ones he had observed. On occasion, the alcoholic's significant others (other players in the game) also receive a payoff. In all three games, the alcoholic puts himself in a disapproved position, permitting those who disapprove of him to appear ostensibly virtuous and blameless. The alcoholic's ulterior purpose is to reveal that the other players are actually no good either. He contrives to confuse all involved about their real roles and motives.

Game Type I: Aggressive or "Drunk and Proud of it" (D and P)

His central theme is "you're good, I'm bad; try and stop me." This is a three-role game between the alcoholic and another player who generally alternates between the roles of persecutor and patsy. There is no rescuer in this game, because the alcoholic manages to make a fairly adequate adjustment in his occupational and social roles, and because he doesn't desire a rescuer. He is primarily interested in infuriating significant others and in making them appear impotent and foolish. The D and P player seldom drinks at home. He usually engages in unacceptable behavior (under the influence) such as extramartial relationships, in order to get caught, and chastised, and to place his wife in either the role of a patsy (forgiving wife) or the role of a persecutor (nagging and unforgiving wife). He rarely seeks therapy (a rescuer), and should he be forced into therapy, he casts the therapist into the role of a patsy.

Usually the D and P player is rebelling against an overprotective parent or dominating spouse, or both. He plays the alcoholic game in order to obtain guilt-free expression of aggression. The game permits an internal expression of anger with an external avoidance of blame for anger.

Game Type II: Psychosocial Self-damage or "Lush"

This game is frequently played by middle-aged suburban wives, white-collar employees, and aging male homosexuals. The game is a response to sexual deprivation. The thesis is, "I'm crazy (depressed), you can make me feel better (cure me) (ha, ha)." It is played with a partner who does not give sexual satisfaction. As long as the game is played, the partner may appear blameless and go unexposed. The partner in this case may switch (because of guilt feelings) from persecutor to rescuer. The game is usually three-handed: the alcoholic, the wife as persecutor or rescuer, and the therapist (who may play rescuer or patsy). The "connection," a minor player, stands ready to sell alcohol to the alcoholic. Steiner assigns the term "lush" to this type of alcoholic who is making a plea for sexual gratification. Under usual circumstances, the partner does not give sexual satisfaction, so the player settles for the attention that he receives when "rescued." The lush is saying, "nobody loves me." He plays the alcoholic game to avoid his own inadequacies.

Game Type III: Tissue Self-destruction or "Wino"

The script of this player is "I am sick (try and avoid that), you're well (ha, ha)." The wino player is orally deprived and plays for keeps in dead earnest. There are two players: "It" (the alcoholic), and "connections." "It," by putting his survival on the line (drinking to the point of physical and mental destruction), forces others, called connections (soup kitchens, jails, clinics, hospitals, etc.), to take care of him. When the player places himself in such an untenable position in order to get help, he is saying that people in power positions who really could help him are not O.K. They wait until he is nearly dead before they help. The police, courts, judges, and correctional personnel who might handle him with understanding and compassion are all connections. The activities of these connections satisfy the player's oral needs.

Steiner pointed out that alcoholic games possess certain characteristics that make for their persistence. They provide players with a full-time structured activity. Many players may play without great danger of being exposed, e.g. the rescuer plays what appears to be a humanitarian role, and it is rarely obvious that he is (frequently) as interested in keeping the alcoholic drunk as is the alcoholic himself. Players are always available from skid row to the therapist's office.

The D and P player does not become a lush or wino, because he is not willing to sacrifice his health. Alcohol per se is of no great interest to him. Alcohol is a vehicle through and by which he angers others with his game. A self-destructive script is not part of his life style. Some lushes become winos, some do not. The transition from lush to wino depends on the life script of the lush, i.e. the degree of self-destructive tendencies.

THE PSYCHOANALYTIC ORIENTATION

One of the primary foci of the psychoanalytic perspective is the origin and dynamics of psychological aberration. It is thus not surprising that psychoanalysts (and those with similar perspectives) have dealt with alcoholism.

Regression, Oral Passivity, and Alcoholism

Many psychoanalytic writers associate alcoholism with oral passivity and regression. Fenichel,[48] in his review and synthesis of psychoanalytic works, classed alcoholics with morphine addicts and other drug addicts because of their (claimed) basic personality similarities. All such persons use the effects of the drugs "to satisfy the archaic oral longing which is a sexual longing, a need for security, and a need for the maintenance of self-esteem simultaneously."[49] Thus, all addicts may be characterized by their oral and narcissistic premorbid personalties. They have never estimated object relationships very highly, and objects are nothing but deliverers of supplies. Addicts are interested solely in their own gratification; they are intolerant of tension, and their drug of choice offers an escape. Those persons for whom the effect of the drug has a specific significance become addicts. For them it means fulfillment or hope of fulfillment "of a deep and primitive desire more urgently felt by them than are sexual or other instinctual longings by normal persons."[50] Genital organization breaks up and regression begins. The various points of fixation determine which field of infantile sexuality comes to the fore; in the end, the libido remains an unorganized amorphous erotic tension energy.[51]

According to Fenichel, the specific elation from alcohol is characterized by the fact that inhibitions and limiting considerations of reality are removed from consciousness before the instinctual impulses are, so that a person who does not dare to perform instinctual acts may gain both satisfaction and relief with the help of alcohol. The superego is defined as the part of the mind that is soluble in alcohol. Therefore, alcohol has always been extolled for its power to banish care. To those intoxicated, obstacles appear smaller and wish fulfillments nearer because of diminished inhibitions. Some people when inebriated withdraw from reality to pleasurable daydreams.[52] There are a few conditions that are specific to alcoholics. The difficult family constellations that alcoholics come from create specific oral frustrations in childhood. These frustrations in turn lead to oral fixations.

Menninger[53] views alcohol as an artificial coping device to relieve stress. Alcohol is a symbol of the primal food (mother's milk). When one adds to this the chemical effects of alcohol (a diminishing sharpness of reality-testing, and an elevation of the general feeling tone), one can understand why alcoholic drinks are commonly employed as an adjuster of minor disturbances in equilibrium. Alcohol is habit forming. Larger and larger doses are required. In the self-administered "treatment" (use of alcohol), the individual has the satisfaction of thinking that he has done something by and for himself without recourse to dependency upon the mother (or her substitute). Denied the mother's nipple, one can always substitute one's thumb. There is only a short step from the thumb to other objects, one of which is alcohol.

The syndrome of addiction is seen as a character deformity in which narcotization is incorporated as a necessity. Alcoholism is an artificial regression, a chemically induced escape from reality. Symptom patterns, instituted as emerging devices to insure survival, may become incorporated into the character structure. They may be treasured for obscure reasons after the original need for them has disappeared and become the "ego-tolerated" traits. Alcoholism is conceptualized as an example of "acting out" aspects of episodes of earlier life without being able to remember them.

Kastl[54] conceptualized alcohol intoxication as a "regressed" state in which changes in self-awareness affect motility and modes of thought occur. More specifically, he hypothesized that alcohol intoxication induces some shift to the primary process mode of thought, which should be manifest in a preference for drive-related stimuli and for unconventional, subjectively structured stimuli.

Kastl's subjects were 16 male medical students. All were tested four times, once with no alcohol, then with 0.33, 0.67, and 1.00 ml of absolute alcohol per kg of body weight. Under each condition, a number of postcard-size reproductions of art works were shown, and the subjects were asked which they preferred. If there was a shift to the primary process mode of thought, drive-related fantasies should increase, and subjects experiencing such fantasies should prefer drive-related art. The subjects were also expected to prefer abstract, subjective art over conventionally structured art. Thirty paintings selected as indicators of drives (10 oral, 10 sexual, 10 aggressive) were paired with 10 neutral paintings. Similarly 15 "abstract" and 15 "fantastic" paintings were paired with 30 neutral paintings. Unfortunately for the hypothesis, preference for drive-related or unstructured art did *not* change with alcohol dose.

Bertrand and Masling[55] noted the psychoanalytic theories connecting oral fixation and alcoholism; they hypothesized that, if such theories are relevant, alcoholics should give more oral-dependent responses on the Rorschach test than a control group of non-alcoholics. They did not feel that alcoholics would give more oral-sadistic responses. These subjects included 40 white hospitalized males, none of whom had a primary diagnosis of alcoholism, but all of whom had been classified as being strongly dependent upon alcohol as a means of coping with their problems. The control subjects were white males in the same psychiatric unit who were either total abstainers or light social drinkers. The groups were matched on age, years of education, primary diagnosis, and Wechsler Adult Intelligence Scale scores.

Each subject was given an individual Rorschach, but only the free-association responses were analyzed. Response subcategories which were scored as oral-dependent included references to foods, gifts and givers, and "needing help"; subcategories scored as oral-sadistic included destruction and aggression references.

The test results, with identification removed, were scored independently by two judges. As predicted, the alcohol-dependent subjects gave more oral-dependent responses. The two groups did not differ in overall use of oral-sadistic responses. Bertrand and Masling contended that their results supported clinical observations connecting alcoholism and oral dependency. They also noted striking similarities in the response patterns of the alcohol-dependent subjects and those of a predominantly female population of obese Israelis tested in a previous study.[56] Although no direct evidence was available, they felt that it was unlikely that the Israeli sample contained any alcoholics. They concluded:[57] "The similarity between alcoholic and obese Rorschach performance may be related to early deprivation of oral gratification in infancy and subsequent fixation as suggested by psychoanalysis."

Wolowitz and Barker[58] report that some of the effects of intoxication could be described as a sense of being pleasantly filled, along with a mild sense of warmth and glow. These effects were seen to be similar to the psychoanalytic description of the oral-passive state. These authors attempted to test the hypothesis that alcoholism involves a regression to the oral-passive state. Their focus was on foods. They theorized that during the oral-passive period of infancy, eating forms the main focus of the infant's gratificatory experiences. Associated with this period is a diet which tends to be wet rather than dry, soft rather than hard, bland rather than spiced, sweet rather than sour or bitter or salty, rich rather than thin in consistency, smooth rather than rough, and which requires sucking and swallowing rather than chewing or biting.[59]

If the alcoholic has regressed to an oral-passive state, then he might be expected to prefer foods characteristic of that phase of

infancy. In order to measure preference for these food characteristics, a Food Preference Inventory (FPI) was constructed. It was
a forced-choice inventory, and subjects were asked which of the two
foods they preferred. A higher FPI score indicated preference for
food thought to be preferred by infants in the oral-passive phase.

In the first study, 30 self-committed alcoholics were compared
with 30 men from a YMCA club. The alcoholics had a higher FPI
score. In a second study, an extended family, some of whose members were alcoholics, was studied. Of the 23 family members (all
blood relations or spouses) there were seven male and seven
female alcoholics and nine nonalcoholic controls (six women, three
men). The alcoholic family members had significantly higher FPI
scores. Next, the mean FPI scores of all 23 family members were
compared with the means of five control groups: (1) 62 gastrointestinal patients without ulcers, (2) 23 male psychiatric patients,
(3) 25 college students, (4) 29 college students, (5) 16 female
YWCA club members. The family members had significantly
higher FPI scores.

Walowitz and Barker hold that their results support clinical
observations of the alcoholic as a passive dependent, similar to the
infant in the early oral stage of development in search of an escape
from stimuli.[60] The escape is partially and temporarily achieved
through excessive drinking, which, in addition to its familar function of reducing painful psychic states (e.g. guilt, anxiety, inhibition
and conflict), enables the drinker to experience de-differentiation
and narcissistic fulfillment. He achieves a momentary sensation of
restful equilibrium with his environment, thereby recreating the
earlier quality of passive gratification.

Latent Homosexuality and Alcoholism

A number of authors writing in the psychoanalytic framework
have attempted to causally associate alcoholism to latent homosexuality.[61] There is little empirical support for this correlation.
Fenichel[62] claimed that for alcoholic males, the infantile frustrations leading to oral fixation resulted in a turning away from the
frustrating mother to the father, i.e. to more or less repressed
homosexual tendencies. Latent homosexuality is thus a concomitant
result of the conditions conducive to alcoholism.

Machover et al.[63] conceptualized the relationship between alcoholism and infantile experiences (and homosexuality) in terms of an overindulgent mother who stimulates an intense oral libidinization whose demands cannot be met. Traumatic weaning then forces the child to seek supplies from his father. The father's emotional coldness impels him to force the child into independence which, in light of the father's essential ambivalence and his defensiveness against the threat of the child's competition, must be experienced as rejection and deprecation. The child is left with intense needs for oral indulgence and with deep feelings of inferiority, expressed particularly in puberty, in his envy of masculine potency as exemplified by his father. Compulsive drinking is then seen as an effort to allay anxiety over masculine inadequacy, and as a means of masculine assertion.[64] Overt homosexuality is not an inevitable development for the alcoholic. The alcoholic's homosexuality is latent, residing in feelings of masculine inadequacy and in drives toward overcoming it through submission to strong father figures.[65]

Although recognizing the differences between overt and latent homosexuality, Machover et al.[66] attempted to evaluate this theoretical framework by utilizing a criterion group of 23 practicing, male, volunteer, homosexuals. The responses of the homosexuals on the Rorschach and Machover Figure Drawing Test (MFDT) were used to construct scales indicative of male homosexuality. The homosexuals were also given the MMPI Mf scale. Also utilized were two alcoholic groups and a control group. The first alcoholic group consisted of 23 unremitted alcoholics (still drinking, but tested while sober). The second consisted of 23 alcoholics in remission. The control group consisted of 23 males from a variety of sources. All groups (including the criterion group) were fairly even on age. The alcoholic and control groups were also matched on ethnic background. No data was available on the ethnic backgrounds of the homosexuals. The homosexuals had somewhat higher IQ's and education.

The scores of all alcoholics on the Rorschach homosexuality scale were higher than those of controls, but the difference did not reach statistical significance. The unremitted alcoholics showed *less* homosexual content than the controls, while the remitted alcoholics showed significantly more such content than controls. For the MFDT homosexuality scale, the combined alcoholics again had significantly higher scores than controls. The unremitted alcoholics had only slightly higher scores than the controls. The remitted alcoholics had significantly higher scores than controls. For both the Rorschach and MFDT, the remitted alcoholics had significantly higher scores than the unremitted alcoholics. For the MMPI Mf scale, the homosexuals scored highest, the controls lowest. As before, the remitted alcoholics scored significantly higher than controls, while there was no significant difference between unremitted alcoholics and controls. The difference between remitted and unremitted alcoholics was not significant.

The authors admitted that the relationship between alcoholism and homosexuality could not be unqualifiedly accepted due to the widely different performance of the two alcoholic groups. They conjectured that the differences between the two alcoholic groups might be attributable to one of two factors: the unremitted alcoholics had lower scores because of more rigid global defenses against homosexuality, or because there were a large number of individuals in the unremitted group with no substantial pressures toward homosexuality.

Other Formulations

Chordorkoff[67] assumed that alcoholics are individuals whose ego functions are deficient. Parental-environmental or constitutional factors make it impossible for many persons to develop the need or means of establishing object relations or attachments. In an effort to adapt, the prealcoholic relates to his own body in a characteristic way. His ego takes his body as an object which is readily available and to which it can relate with a measure of security. There are two features that differentiate the alcoholic from others with similar problems. In the alcoholic, the ego-body relationship lacks stability and the alcoholic feels a need to provide himself with some way of acknowledging the maintenance of the ego-body relationship. Alcohol intoxication serves to produce physiological changes which the individual experiences as assurance of the continuance of the ego-body relationship. Thus, the alcoholic uses the effects of alcohol for security and as a substitute for external object attachments. Chordorkoff presented brief, inconclusive clinical notes on five cases to "verify his views."

Karl Menninger[68] has made a number of statements about alcoholism. He maintains that alcoholics have a powerful urge to destroy themselves because of guilt and a need for punishment caused by personally unacceptable aggressive wishes. Alcoholism performs two psychological functions: it is a form of gradual self-destruction, satisfying the need for punishment; and, at the same time, it is a mechanism used to avert or escape an even greater form of self-destruction. He claims that the excessive use of alcohol may result from attempts to control aggressive impulses by displacement to the body.[69] Alcohol addiction and other compulsive narcotizations illustrate a method of partial suicide. Alcoholism represents self-destruction through an attack on the body purporting to be a relief of pain.

A study by Tahka[70] of 50 Swedish alcoholics being treated at an outpatient clinic gives impressionistic support for Menninger's position. Tahka concluded, on the basis of clinical interviews, Rorschach tests, and interviews with relatives of alcoholic patients, that self-punishment was one of the main psychodynamic functions of drinking.

Levy[71] observed a large number of patients with all degrees of drinking problems. Taking a basically psychoanalytic perspective, he impressionistically outlines eight psychodynamic functions of alcohol. These eight functions illustrate many early psychoanalytic views, as well as those espoused by contemporary Freudian writers:

1. *The discharge function.* Alcohol diminishes the effectiveness of repressing forces. It blunts anxiety signals and feelings of guilt and shame, and consequently allows for the expression of impulses and dissociated ego states. Alcohol diminishes the need of the ego for logical consistency, synthesis, and unambivalence. Therefore, impulses and modes of action which do not fit in with the person's overall picture of himself and others can be discharged.

2. *The narcotizing function.* The function of alcohol is to produce temporary or constant narcosis, so as to impede any internal or external stimuli from reaching the conscious ego.

3. *Symbolic functions.* The act of drinking, the perception of the immediate organic effect, the perception of the long-range toxic effects, and the perception of the interpersonal effects tend to become involved with potent symbolic meaning.

4. *The "infantomimetic" function.* The important effect of alcohol is the re-creation of various infantile modes of experiencing, not the stimulation or use of the mouth. Tension reduction through sucking and swallowing is only one element, and not of primary importance among the habituating symbolic factors.

5. *Masochistic functions.* Alcohol can serve a variety of masochistic needs. For example, a hangover is an obvious form of self-punishment. For others, alcoholic stupor represents a self-punitive death.

6. *Hostility.* The act of drinking can allow for subtle expression of hostility in a variety of ways. For some drinkers, drunkenness serves as a negativistic affirmation of the self, the retreat to a realm where nobody can influence them.

7. *Homosexuality.* Levy noted the common contention that alcohol helps to discharge, sublimate, and deny homosexual strivings. He concluded that transient-overt homosexual contacts found among his patients reflected a lack of concern with, and perception of, the nature of the sexual object. He interpreted this type of sexuality to be autoerotic and related to the patient's need to re-create infantile modes of experience.

8. *Identification and identity.* For many patients with parents who were pathologic drinkers, alcohol was used as a device to help solve parental identification problems. Further, becoming an alcoholic helped give the individual definite identity and role.

THE FIELD DEPENDENCE ORIENTATION

The projective and nonprojective personality tests are the best known and most widely used instruments through which attempts are made to understand personality. A somewhat different method that has also been used with a wide range of personality types, including alcoholics, is that of Witkin et al.[72] Their basic premise is that personality influences perception; thus personality can be understood by examining modes of perception. The perceptual function they studied was extent of dependence on the prevailing visual field (field dependence). Generally, a field-dependent individual is one who is dependent upon the visual field in which the stimuli occur in making judgments about (perceiving) the stimuli. The three most widely used tests of field-dependence are the embedded-figure test (EFT), the rod-and-frame test (RFT), and the body-adjustment test (BAT).[73]

The EFT stimuli consist of a series of 24 complex geometric designs. Embedded in each complex design is a simple figure which the subject must locate as quickly as possible. The subject's score is the total amount of time he takes to locate the simple figures in the 24 complex designs. The longer the subject takes to find the simple embedded figures, the more field-dependent is his perception.

In the RFT, the subject is seated in a totally darkened room. The only objects visible are a luminous rod surrounded by a luminous square frame. The rod and the frame are always presented in tilted positions, either to the left or the right. The subject's task is to adjust the rod to the vertical while the frame remains in its initial position of tilt. For eight trials, the subject's chair is tilted to the left; for eight trials, it is tilted to the right; and on eight trials the subject sits perfectly erect. The subject's score for the test is the sum of degrees of deviation of the rod from the true vertical for the 24 determinations. Larger scores reflect greater field-dependence.

In the BAT, the subject is seated in a chair within a small, specially constructed room. Both the room and chair can be tilted (independently or together) to the left or right. At the beginning of each of six trials, chair and room are tilted to pre-set position. The subject's task is to adjust the chair (and thus his body) to the true vertical position, while the surrounding room remains tilted. The score for the rest is the sum of degrees of deviation of the chair from the upright on the six trials; larger scores reflect greater field-dependence.

In each of the three tests, the task is to separate an object (a geometric figure in the EFT, a rod in the RFT, or the body in the BAT) from an organized field. Extent of field-dependence is reflected in the relative ease of, or ability in, separating object from field.

Witkin et al.[74] utilized the Rorschach, TAT, Figure Drawing Test, interviews, and case histories in delineating the personality correlates of field-dependence-independence. They concluded[75] that: Field-dependent persons tend to be characterized by passivity in dealing with the environment; by unfamiliarity with and fear of their own impulses, together with poor control over them; and by the possession of a relatively primitive, undifferentiated body image. Independent or analytical perceptual performers, in contrast, tend to be characterized by activity and independence in relation to the environment. They have closer communication with, and better control of, their own impulses. Finally, they possess a relatively high self-esteem and a more differentiated mature body image.

Zwerling and Rosenbaum[76] compared the field-dependence-independence responses of 23 alcoholics (with two or more years of sobriety) with those of a control group of college students. The procedure utilized was that outlined by Witkin et al. The alcoholics and controls were presented with three sets of tasks—the EFT, RFT, and BAT.

In the RFT and EFT, the alcoholics showed significantly more field-dependence; in the BAT, the alcoholics were more field-independent than the controls. The results were consistent among the alcoholics, despite the range of psychiatric-diagnostic entities included in the group. The authors felt that the alcoholics possessed a personality somewhere between that of completely field-dependent and field-independent persons. The alcoholics were seen to have progressed to the point of developing distinct body boundaries, although not a well-defined body concept. Further, they had not achieved a level of self-differentiation necessary for a completely field-independent orientation.

Zwerling and Rosenbaum concluded that alcoholics manifest a pervasive passive-dependent attitude, coupled with a primitive, insulating narcissism through which the response (in the BAT) is due to preoccupation with the body and its sensations more than it is to simple resistance to the field.

Witkin, Karp, and Goodenough[77] used the EFT, RFT, and BAT in three separate studies. In the first, they compared 20 alcoholics with 51 college men and found that the former were more field-dependent. In a second study, 30 male alcoholics were compared with 30 controls matched on age, education, and ethno-religious background. Again, the alcoholics were found to be more field-dependent. Finally, 20 male alcoholics were matched on age with 20 male nonalcoholic psychiatric patients. The alcoholics were more field-dependent.

These authors hold that field-dependence is a manifestation of a *general* personality constellation of dependence, passivity, and poor self-differentiation, and *not* a characteristic specific only to alcoholics. They postulate that this mode of perceiving occurs in consistent association with alcoholism, because people with such a personality-type commonly adopt alcoholism as a way out of their difficulties. They expect that other clinical groups also characterized by passivity, such as cases of obesity and ulcer patients, would also show field-dependence. They cite an unpublished study by Gordon[78] which indicates that ulcer patients are, in fact, markedly field-dependent.

Karp et al.[79] reviewed much of the pre-1965 literature in alcoholism and field-dependence and concluded that the studies generally showed that male and female alcoholics are markedly field-dependent in their perception and tend to have global concepts of their bodies. These characteristics have been conceived as a manifestation of a limitedly developed differentiation. Other manifestations of limited differentiation which have been found to be associated with field-dependence and global body concepts are a poorly developed sense of separate identity and a tendency to use nonspecific defenses, such as primitive denial and massive repression.

Karp wisely pointed out the two possible interpretations of the connection between characteristics inferred from field-dependence and alcoholism. Field-dependence may be the result of the physical deterioration brought on by alcoholism, or it may be a factor predisposing to alcoholism. He recommended a prediction study in which assessment of differentiation is made prior to the onset of alcoholism. In lieu of such a study, he attempted to test the following hypothesis: if field-dependence (limited differentiation) is a consequence of alcoholism, then field-dependence might be greater in the intoxicated state than in the sober state. The subjects were 22 male alcoholics. Field-dependence was tested under two types of conditions. Subjects were tested in the "dry condition" in which they received no alcohol, and in the "wet condition" in which they received a cocktail consisting of fruit juice and 1 ml of absolute alcohol per 100 grams of body weight. The battery of tests consisted of the EFT, the RFT, and the BAT. There was no evidence that alcohol had any effect on performance in the BAT or RFT. In the EFT, subjects required significantly more time to locate the embedded figures after the ingestion of alcohol than before. Because the measure of field dependence in the EFT is time taken to locate the embedded figures, the author thought that it might be the decreased ability to concentrate on the task brought on by alcohol ingestion that was responsible for the differences rather than alcohol-induced changes in perceptual ability. The author found that the extent of field-dependence in alcoholics is not different when they are intoxicated than when they are sober.

Karp concluded that the finding that the extent of field-dependence was not altered by alcohol ingestion does not provide direct support for the view that the marked field-dependence associated with alcoholism antedates the onset of drinking behavior. However, by reducing the plausibility of one alternative hypothesis (that field-dependence is a consequence of alcoholism), more credence is lent to the position that field dependence is somehow causally related to alcoholism.

Smith and Carpenter[80] also reported that none of four separate doses of alcohol had significant effects on field-dependence-independence. More importantly, however, their results demonstrated a relationship between perceptual performance (and the associated personality traits) and rate of alcohol absorption into the bloodstream.

Sixteen males who described themselves as moderate drinkers were given the RFT. Eight were found to be markedly field-dependent. The remaining eight did not meet the criteria of field-independence but were more field-dependent than the others. These eight were designated "middles." Each subject was tested four times, with at least one day between each session. At each session a subject was given one of four drinks: one containing no alcohol, or one of three containing 0.33, 0.67, or 1.00 ml of absolute alcohol per kilogram of body weight. Blood alcohol concentration (BAC) was ascertained by use of a Breathalyzer. The subjects were requested not to eat within four hours of the testing session and were required to drink the entire amount of beverage in 15 minutes. BAC was measured four times for each dose: before drinking, and at 40, 65, and 90 minutes after starting to drink.

The results evinced that quite different functions were needed to represent the BAC curves of the two groups over time. Generally, the results disclosed that, at any point, the middles had absorbed more alcohol into the blood than had the field-independent subjects. At the highest alcohol dose, differences were the greatest and were statistically significant.

THE ALCOHOLIC PERSONALITY ORIENTATION

An inspection of the etiological psychological-psychiatric literature exposes two contrasting points of view.[81] On the one hand, numerous investigators see alcoholism as a unique and distinct psychiatric entity. Alcoholics possess a specific personality type predisposed to alcoholism. In brief, all alcoholics are assumed to have similar basic personality characteristics. Many investigators have tried to isolate these "common personality characteristics," and their study results are usually presented in terms of clinical and psychological test findings. On the other hand, some other investigators posit a typology of alcoholics, i.e. they attempt to correlate types of personality with certain types of alcoholics. Another group of researchers (or clinicians) view alcoholism as a symptom rather than as a disease entity (e.g. the result of emotional maladjustment or some form of psychopathology). Generally, this "symptom group" classifies alcoholics in terms of conceptional psychiatric nosologies; therefore, they are included in the typological school, for purposes at hand.[82] Most of these latter formulations treat alcoholism as a symptom of a neurosis,[83] and some few equate alcoholism with psychosis.

Many authors in the above two broad groups find many similar, superficial characteristics of the alcoholic—emotional lability; escape use of alcohol from conflicts, deterioration and regression; dependence on others for psychological and economic support; difficulty in handling strong effect. The two camps differ, however, on the psychopathology and personality dynamics of the alcoholic.[84]

Though sometimes hard to classify, there are a number of scholars who take the position that the elusive search for an alcoholic personality type is like pursuing the Holy Grail. They accuse the personality searchers of psychological reductionism. The aforementioned interactionist, Alfred Bandura, represents this school of thought.

The Alcoholic as a Specific Personality Type

Catanzaro[85] reviewed a number of studies and reported 13 general personality characteristics of alcoholics: high level of anxiety in interpersonal relations, emotional immaturity, ambivalence toward authority, low frustration tolerance, grandiosity, low self-esteem, feelings of isolation, perfectionism, guilt, angry overdependency, compulsiveness, sex-role confusion, and inability to express angry feelings adequately.

Klebanoff[86] analyzed the Thematic Apperception test results of 17 hospitalized alcoholics. He found that, in contrast to an unspecified control group, the primary characteristics of alcoholics were passivity, introversion, and strong feelings of inadequacy and insecurity. The alcoholics also showed a lack of aggressive tendencies which Klebanoff attributed to their tendency to internalize hostility.

Tahka[87] researched 50 Swedish male alcoholics attending the Outpatient Clinic for Alcoholics at St. Eriks Hospital in Stockholm. All subjects were interviewed (nondirective, clinical) several times (at least 8.5 hours per person), and each was given the Rorschach test (before the interview). The Rorschach results of the alcoholics were compared with those of a matched, control sample of 50 Finnish males without alcoholism or any manifest psychiatric disorders.

Compared with the controls, the alcoholics showed highly statistically significant differences in two Rorschach items, significant differences in eight items, and almost-significant differences in sixteen items. Alcoholics, more frequently than nonalcoholics, had various deficiencies in ego structure. They had poor impulse control and a low degree of differentiation and autonomy, coupled with various defense mechanisms. Among the alcoholics there were signs of dynamically active, oral-receptive needs, as well as severely restricting egos with inhibition of aggressive impulses and independent judgments. The author does not claim that he found any alcohol pattern in the Rorschach test capable of being used for diagnosing alcoholism. On the other hand, he did report a higher frequency of oral-narcissistic needs among alcoholics when compared to nonalcoholics.

The Rorschach and interview materials revealed the alcoholic personality picture to have a close resemblance to an oral character disorder. Tahka also reported that the alcoholics showed a premorbid personality picture characterized by passivity, mother-fixation, ambivalent object relationship, a poorly developed sense of masculine indentity, pronounced inhibitions of aggressive and sexual impulses with a tendency toward guilt feelings and inferiority, a relative lack of initiative and tenacity, and high frequencies of neurotic symptoms.

The alcoholics' histories were more frequently marked by a combination of an excessively infantilizing maternal influence and an insufficient opportunity to identify with a father figure. The main psychodynamic functions of drinking among the alcoholics were satisfaction for orally determined needs, discharge of aggressive tensions along with self-punishment, and a substitute for object relations. Tahka concluded that men (like his alcoholics) with early fixations and highly ambivalent relationships with their mothers, early damaged self-esteem, defective masculine identification, and predominantly maternal superegos, with inhibition of sexual and aggressive impulses, are predisposed to the development of alcoholism. This specific developmental history and personality may not necessarily lead to alcoholism, but, according to Tahka, might constitute an indispensable prerequisite for it.

Zwerling and Rosenbaum[88] studied 46 alcoholics, all of whom were given a number of psychological tests. Psychiatric histories were obtained in five hours of anamnestic interview per subject. The most significant psychiatric finding was the consistent presence of five descriptive-dynamic states which suggested a basic character disorder underlying the varied psychopathological features of the subjects. The alcoholics were found to be:

1. *Basically schizoid.* They showed a sense of estrangement or isolation from people. The subjects who were overtly outgoing were seen to be putting on a facade, covering a pervasive emotional detachment from people.

2. *Depressed, with feelings of futility, hopelessness, and sadness.* This behavior ranged from sporadic expressions of worthlessness to suicide attempts.

3. *Dependent.* This was reflected in an irrational dependence upon external agents for security and care.

4. *Hostile.* At times, they would display an overwhelming amount of chronic rage.

5. *Sexually immature, with serious problems of masculine identification.* Behavior ranged from markedly reduced heterosexual behavior to active homosexuality.

Zwerling and Rosenbaum concluded that the basic character disorder they discovered was a necessary, but not sufficient, condition for the development of alcoholism. Variations in cultural attitudes toward drinking were seen to be the crucial co-variable. The authors asserted that although alcoholism may be found in the setting of any clinical-diagnostic state, the addictive process develops in a specific character matrix common to all alcoholics.

Buhler and Lefever[89] attempted to find whether alcoholics have certain physical or psychological characteristics in common which would justify the construct "alcoholic personality." Their experimental group included 100 urban alcoholic patients (23 women, 77 men) referred by hospitals and private physicians. Sixty patients were referred to Buhler, a psychologist, from the Neuro-psychiatric Division of the Minneapolis General Hospital; seventeen were referred from the Psychopathic Division of the Los Angeles County General Hospital. Twenty-three private patients were referred to the authors by Minneapolis and Los Angeles physicians and by the Alcoholics Anonymous Association. This group of mixed alcoholics had an average age of 38 and enjoyed relatively high education and occupational levels. The total mixed group of 100 alcoholics (experimental group) was compared with 30 normals, 70 mixed psychoneurotics, and 30 mixed psychopaths (selection procedure for these controls is unknown). The greatest qualitative and quantitative differences were found in comparisons of alcoholics and normals; the smallest differences occurred in comparisons of alcoholics and psychopaths. The total group of mixed alcoholics ranked between psychoneurotics and psychopaths, although nearer the latter.

In all comparisons of the alcoholics with the psychopaths and other nonclinical groups, the chief statistical finding was the incapacity of the alcoholic group to stand strain. More than any other group, the alcoholics were less able to withstand strain and tension, to endure and persist under the impact of difficulties. The alcoholics shared these incapacities with the psychopaths and, like them, lacked the trait of inner directivity, i.e. resourcefulness in setting up goals and following means toward the goals.

In contrast to the psychopaths, the alcoholics suffered from anxieties and guilt feelings in regard to themselves. They were introspective and rational, but conflictive in their interests. Though ambitious, they were unable to withstand strain and pressure. Since they lacked both the resourcefulness for setting up goals and the persistence in obtaining them, they fell short of their expectations and resorted to wishful thinking or frustration. Their awareness, coupled with the incapacity to overcome sluggishness of mind, caused anxieties which lead to escape-drinking, according to Buhler and Lefever.

The experimental group was also found to have much in common with a group called organics (epileptics and nonpsychotic organics). Buhler and Lefever observed that alcoholics (even from different clinical groups) have certain basic personality characteristics in common. They theorized that this "alcoholic pattern" might result in part from certain physical dispositions rather than from a primarily psychogenic development. The alcoholic personality (they found) could be referred to as a mixed type, psychopathic-neurotic. This type is explained by subjective dynamic description, rather than by objective Rorschach test-item comparisons.

A more objective approach utilizing modern statistical procedures was taken by MacAndrew,[90] who compared the MMPI responses of 300 male alcoholics and 300 male nonalcoholic psychiatric outpatients. The alcoholics were being treated at a clinic in the same building as the psychiatric outpatients. Each group was divided into a standarization group (N = 200) and a cross-validation group (N = 100). Item analysis of the MMPI responses yielded 51 items, which differentiated the two groups at the .01 level of significance (chi-square). The two items with the highest chi-square values dealt directly with drinking practices (MMPI numbers 215 and 460). Because of theoretical considerations, these two items were removed, leaving 49 items. Analysis of these 49 items in the two validation groups revealed that they could be used to correctly classify 81.5 percent of the combined cross-validation sample. In a subsequent study,[91] MacAndrew factor-analyzed the responses of the 200 male alcoholics in the standarization group to the 49 items which had differentiated them from the nonalcoholic psychiatric outpatients.

Thirteen factors were delineated which supposedly represent the differences between male alcoholics and male nonalcoholic outpatients (the numbers in parentheses are the numbers of the MMPI items which had loadings greater than .33 on that factor):

1. *Interpersonal adroitness.* Alcoholics were found to be more likely to be outgoing ad interpersonally competent (482, 37, 309).

2. *Ability to concentrate.* Alcoholics were less likely to complain either of difficulties in concentration or of a lack of self-confidence (335, 356, 86).

3. *Lack of sexual preoccupation.* Alcoholics were less likely to claim that they frequently dreamed of, or worried about, "sex matters" (320, 179, 149).

4. *Difficulties in school.* Alcoholics were more likely to profess having been disciplinary problems in school (56, 118, 419).

5. *Freedom from parental control.* Alcoholics were more likely to claim having been independent and free from family rule (235).

6. *Female identification.* Alcoholics were more likely to claim a closer childhood attachment to a woman than to a man, and they more frequently claimed to suffer for their prior misdeeds (562, 94).

7. *Lived wrong kind of life.* Alcoholics were more likely to profess a generalized dissatisfaction with what they had made of their lives (61, 378).

8. *Religiosity and guilt.* Alcoholics were more likely to profess agreement with religious doctrine, but voiced a theology not of redemption, but of resentment (483, 413, 488, 507).

9. *Self-responsibility for one's own troubles.* Alcoholics were more prone to claim knowledge of the source of their difficulties (127).

10. *Chronic deterioration.* Alcoholics were more likely to admit having trouble with the law. They more frequently mentioned coughing up blood (294, 130).

11. *Blackouts.* Alcoholics were more frequently reported having blank spells and possession of evil spirits (156, 251, 27).

12. *Bodily complaints*. Alcoholics were more likely to claim proneness to somatized anxiety, and less frequently complained of bodily pains (263, 186, 243).

13. *Unnamed*. Alcoholics more frequently reflect a general boredom and disdain for the proprieties of everyday life (120, 116, 446).

MacAndrew concluded: "While the present results are scarcely sufficient to foreclose the argument, the existence and nature of these several dimensions of differential self-representation are clearly contrary to the assumption that alcoholics are simply 'neurotics-who-also-happen-to-drink-too-much.' "[92]

Several studies have attempted to differentiate alcoholics from nonalcoholics, utilizing various scales derived from the Minnesota Multiphasic Personality Inventory. The MacAndrew scale remains a better choice (than any of the others that have been derived from the MMPI) for screening patients in an alcoholic unit. Though not designed to do so, the MacAndrew scale of alcoholism has been used to differentiate (in a rough sense) alcoholic and non-alcoholic patients. We need a scale of MMPI items specifically validated for differentiating alcoholic patients and nonalcoholic psychiatric patients.[93]

The Typological Approach

Parthington and Johnson[94] arrived at a personality typology of alcoholics in a study of 186 male first admissions to the Alcoholic and Drug Addiction Research Foundation outpatient clinic in Londan (Ontario), Canada, during 1965. This sample was drawn from a lower- to middle-class population. Some (approximately 40%) were referred by physicians and agencies. The others were self-referred. The sample's average educational level was grade 10, with the majority having completed grades 8 to 12. Approximately 60 percent were employed; half were either married or lived in stable common-law relationships. The average age was 41 years and ranged from 23 to 58.

The study was based on the assumption that there was no such thing as an alcoholic personality type. The authors conjectured that investigators interested in identifying the alcoholic personality would be misled if they assumed intragroup homogeneity (using a mean personality profile to characterize a group of alcoholics). The means would fail to indicate the presence of distinct types in a study sample, and would also conceal all significant individual variation. The specific purpose of the study was to provide an experimental test of the assumption (found in much of the literature on alcoholism) that alcoholics are homogeneous with respect to variables other than uncontrolled drinking behavior. To this end, an objective method for identifying personality types was developed (a modified form of Differential Personality Inventory, DPI), composed of 371 true-false items, sampling 18 pathological and personality constructs. The DPI was applied to profiles of alcoholics within a cross-validation design. Additional data included demographic indices, verbal intelligence (Quick Tests), life history materials, medical examination results, and psychiatric clinical judgments. Standardized questionnaires, intake diagnostic interviews by psychiatrists, and psychiatric-therapeutic ratings (via interviews) were also utilized. Clinical judgments were made on the basis of a 5-point scale denoting degree of self-understanding, motivation for treatment, and prognosis. The Straus-Bacon Social Stability scale was used to determine social stability. Neuroticism, personality disturbance and sociopathic behavior tendencies were determined by a symptom-pattern procedure developed for epidemiological research.

Initially, DPI personality profiles for all the alcoholics were established. Then a modal-matching classification procedure was applied to the condensed DPI personality profiles, which resulted in the delineation of "five distinct, stable and replicable personality types." Finally, a multiple discriminant function analysis was carried out to enhance understanding and to facilitate interpretation of the personality structure of the five types. This involved a number of other items, including life history materials and clinical characteristics. Finally, these types included the DPI personality traits, as well as demographic, clinical, and life history materials; however, and importantly, the combined materials were clearly demarcated as to source. The results of the multiple discriminant function analysis indicated that the types were separable in terms of these variables as well as DPI items.

Type I (20% of the total sample). Their average DPI profile

was characterized by low Response Style (desirability and defensiveness) and high Antisocial (socially defiant attitudes, hostility, cynicism, rebelliousness) and Thought Disturbance (neurotic disorganization, depression, irritability, impulsivity, somatic complaints, familial discord, psychotic tendencies) components. These patients were not concerned with what others thought about them and were prone to behave in a rebellious antisocial manner. They were emotionally unstable and cognitively disorganized. They were relatively young, with poor employment records, and had been in serious trouble as a consequence of drinking. Psychiatric ratings characterized these patients as the most socially unstable, most chronically depressed and anxious, and most aggressive and antisocial. Finally, they were not interested in the treatment process.

Type II (19% of the total sample). Their DPI profile was marked by moderately low Antisocial, and moderately high Thought Disturbance components. These patients usually conformed, but at times tended to lose emotional and cognitive control. They had high verbal intelligence, experienced marital difficulties, and had milder behavior problems when drinking than had other groups. They were more favorably disposed toward abstinence and toward the treatment process than any other type, and they evinced greater insight into their problems than any other group.

Type III (10% of the total sample). Their DPI profile showed a great elevation of Neuroticism, including hypochondriasis, health concern, shallow affect, and headache proneness. They were older, less verbally intelligent, and less educated than the other types. Though they had relatively stable employment records, acceptable living accommodations, and reasonable marital status, they drank more steadily than the other types. Psychiatric data showed them to possess the least amount of self-understanding, even though they were the most socially stable group, with the fewest symptoms of basic personality disturbance.

Type IV (23% of the total sample). Their average DPI profile had a high elevation on the Response Style Component, and low elevation on all other components. These patients were judged to be *either* highly stable and healthy *or* deceivers. They claimed the highest level of education and admitted to the fewest serious consequences due to drinking when compared with all other types. The psychiatrist rated them lowest on manifest expression of antisocial tendencies. The authors assumed that these patients were responding defensively, as a result of a pervasive need for social approval.

Type V (28% of total sample). Their DPI profile was approximately average compared with the other types except for a moderately low Thought Disorder Component. These patients were typical of the remainder of the sample in terms of Stylistic Responding, Antisocial Tendencies, and Neuroticism, but were less cognitively and emotionally upset. Life history data indicated that this type reported greater satisfaction with their relationships than did other types. The psychiatrist reported fewer neurotic symptoms among them. Negatively, members of this type reported higher frequencies of drinking episodes and greater average amounts of alcohol consumed per drinking occasion than did any other type.

Parthington and Johnson concluded that their findings revealed unequivocal evidence of several alcoholic personality types, and that on this basis, the quest for a "cure" of alcoholism, according to the traditional medical model (pure-type alcoholic), should be discontinued. According to them, treatment efforts should be diversified and applied to personality types, rather than to the nosological group, "alcoholics". Parthington and Johnson further concluded that they had demonstrated a more objective method of typing alcoholics than had been used before. They claimed that a 93% level of confirmed classifications were yielded by the procedure of modal-matching and that this level exceeds what might be expected of clinical-judgment procedures alone.

Sherfey,[95] in a qualitative, psychopathological typological attempt, analyzed the psychiatric case history materials of 161 chronic alcoholics (72 women, 89 men) treated at the Payne Whitney Clinic. These cases were selected from 455 records chosen at random from the clinic's record room (during a treatment interval from 1932 to 1949), on the basis of completeness and preciseness of case history and clinical materials. Follow-up letters were posted to patients and their relatives for additional information; follow-up interviews were obtained in 16 of these cases.

Sherfey reported (on the basis of case-history analysis from the clinical records) that the cases fell into two general sections, depending on the underlying psychopathology and character structure: (1) cases belonging to recognized diagnostic entities, i.e. cases where excessive drinking was a symptom within a well-defined psychopathologic or physical disease syndrome; (2) cases that did not belong to any usual diagnostic entity, and in which excessive drinking was the outstanding clinical feature.

Group I (69 cases) was broken down into the following categories:

a. *Paranoid schizophrenia* (14 cases, 8.7%). These cases were marked by early pathological drinking (average age of about 22) and a violent acting-out pattern of behavior. There was a high incidence of mental illness, especially schizophrenia, in the family histories.

b. *Manic-depressive reactions* (11 cases, 6.8%). The onset of heavy drinking and the occurence of mental disease coincided. Excessive drinking was usually engaged in during the manic phases. Of five follow-up reports available, two claimed recovery after two or more years. A high incidence of mental illness, particularly manic-depressive disease, was reported in these family histories, in addition to a high incidence of chronic alcoholism.

c. *Poorly organized asocial psychopathic personalities* (11 cases, 6.8%, all males). These patients were reported to be classic psychopaths and chronic alcoholics, since adolescence or the early twenties. Psychopathic behavior was ever-present, but more obvious and flagrant during intoxicated periods.

d. *Poorly organized, psychoneurotic psychopathic personalities* (15 cases, 9.3%, all females). These cases were diagnosed as neurotics and psychopaths; they exhibited mixed symptoms of both. The consciences were strong, but there was almost complete inability to live up to them; the result was guilt feelings. The total personality was immature. Acting-out behavior, particularly in the sexual sphere, was notable. They had abnormal EEG's. There was a high incidence of mental illness and chronic alcoholism in their family histories.

e. *Epilepsy and epileptoid reactions* (7 cases, 4.3%). All of these cases had some kind of neural disorder; two had epilepsy, two were diagnosed as epileptic equivalents (dizzy spells, amnesic episodes, etc.). The remainder showed epileptoid psychopathology, including convulsions, abnormal EEG's, and antisocial behavior. In all cases, alcoholism commenced either at the same time of the neural disorder or soon thereafter. Three of seven cases showed family histories of mental illnesses; four of seven had alcoholism in their family histories.

f. *Brain Damage* (5 cases, 3%). Intoxication periods in these cases were marked by severe emotional reactions, rage reactions, homicidal threats, assaultiveness, and self-mutilation. Convulsions during periods of intoxication were frequent. One subject had encephalitis; three had suffered head injuries and exemplified psychopathic patterns and convulsions; one had neurosyphilis.

Group II (92 cases), without usual diagnostic categories (character disorders), was broken down as follows:

a. *Rigidly organized obsessive-compulsive personalities* (22 male cases, 13.6%). This group was middle-aged, successful, rigid, hypochondriacal, fearful, and perfectionistic. Mental difficulties, loss of professional status, lessening of sexual powers, and fear of the aging process often triggered their excessive drinking. In younger years, they were heavy, but socially controlled, drinkers. In later years, when intoxicated, they lost their usual neurotic defenses. They responded to treatment readily and rapidly.

b. *Rigidly organized neurotic personalties with paranoid features* (17 cases, 10%). These women were in conflict because of a lack of early positive identifications. They could neither accept a feminine role nor succeed in a masculine one. Resentment was their strongest underlying emotion. Sexually frigid, they suffered from unfulfilled sexual tension. Alcoholism usually began with marriage or with attempts at heterosexual adjustment. Marital histories were replete with difficulties and discord involving husbands and children. Situational crisis situations brought on heavy drinking. During periods of intoxication, they acted erotically toward men and women. Family histories demonstrated high incidences of mental illnesses and alcoholism.

c. *Poorly organized, inadequate psychoneurotic personalities* (30 male cases, 18.6%). This group characterized those most frequently attended to as typical alcoholics. They were passive, dependent, and immature, with neurotic character structures marked by strong dependency needs. They were inadequate and most frequently failures in all undertakings. Despite average or above intelligence, they failed early in life and became alcoholics in their twenties. They had oral traits and blunted affect. They sought excessive approval from others, expected too much of others, and frequently married aggressive, dominating, or motherly women. Drinking began early and was often resorted to in order to relieve self-consciousness, tension, and fear of failure. Actual failures resulted in frequent and heavy drinking bouts. Their behavior while intoxicated was rarely of the acting-out type; it was rather of a retreatist nature, characterized by depression, self-pity, self-castigation, and crying. The incidence of mental illness and of alcoholism was high in their family histories.

d. *Dependent psychoneurotic personalties accompanied by depression and tension* (12 female cases, 7.4%). These group members suffered from dependent, passive needs and exemplified reactions of depression, tension, anxiety, and feelings of rejection and loneliness. They were feminine, but immature, with strong needs for love, protection, and companionship. They tended to be self-righteous, with high moral standards. They were devoted to loved ones, including husbands and children, but were over-protective and fearful. Mood swings were in reaction to life situations, and their heavy drinking was tied to situations in which their dependency needs were not met. Alcohol was used to relieve tension and to permit the acting-out and verbalization of their passivity demands. They drank to "stop thinking." Frequent and severe hangovers were followed by remorse and guilt. Family histories indicated a high incidence of alcoholism, but a low incidence of mental illness.

e. *Middle- and late-life depressions* (11 cases, 5 males, 6 females, 6.8%). These subjects were abstainers or average social drinkers before the middle or late years. Prior to the point of excessive drinking, they seemed to have been well adjusted. Excessive drinking was associated with late difficulties, such as threatened economic and professional insecurity, physical illness, business reverses, death of spouse, disappointment in children, impotency. Excessive drinking accompanied dramatic loss of defenses and emotional control, e.g. extreme elation and/or depression, public scenes, suicidal tendencies. Cardiac conditions and cerebral arteriosclerosis frequently complicated the reaction to alcohol. Family histories showed a low incidence of mental illness. Alcoholism was frequently found in the family histories of the females, but not in those of the males.

Sherfey concluded that chronic alcoholism in the cases studied was a symptom of different illnesses. Alcoholism did not exist without previous personality defects predating the drinking pattern. She does admit that otherwise normal alcoholics might be found outside hospital practice, but thinks they would be rare. She stressed psychogenic rather than constitutional factors, and thought that the direct psychological influence of the relatives on the children explained the high incidence of alcoholics in her sample family histories. In general, the cases indicated that patients used alcohol in a neurotic way. The behavior during intoxication was an attempt to escape inadequacies; to ward off unpleasant emotions; to verbalize or act out neurotic needs; to express repressed or suppressed emotion. Therefore, observation of intoxicative behavior patterns leads to understanding the alcoholics' underlying problems. Unexpressed resentment was reported to be the most frequent underlying emotion of alcoholics. Accepting the validity of Sherfey's findings, a constitutionalist could make a strong case for organic and/or genetic—rather than psychogenic—etiology, since many of her cases suffered from organic and mental disease, and since mental disease and alcoholism were frequently found in these family histories.

Sherfey's typological attempt is representative of many psychiatric classifications in the past (and some current ones) that are based on clinical observations and case histories, without precise categories and quantitative support.

A more recent study by DeVito et al.[96] further illustrates a psychopathological typology. On the basis of psychiatric diagnoses made on 200 men (mean age 39) at the Loyola-Hines Alcoholism Treatment Unit and 100 males (mean age 40) at Chicago's Alcoholic Treatment Center, utilizing interviews, clinical observations, and four psychological tests, four diagnostic groups were differentiated: (1) an acting-out prone group (58%), which includes passive-aggressive, explosive-hysterical and antisocial personalities; (2) a depression prone group (22%) comprised of obsessive-compulsive and asthenic personalities; (3) an ego disintegration prone group (13%) including paranoid, schizoid, and inadequate personalities; and (4) an overt breakdown group (8%) made up of neurotics, psychotics, and sexual deviants. The first group drank to facilitate acting-out behavior; the depression group drank to offset despondency; the ego-disintegration group drank to quell anxiety; and the breakdown group drank to modulate neurotic, psychotic, or sexual deviant symptomatology.

Goldstein[97] recently attempted to validate Jellinek's former typology of five basic types of alcoholics by means of the MMPI. A methodology attempting to adjust for power and error problems of MMPI scales used to identify alcoholics was employed. A re-standardization of all MMPI scales was made. In comparing two multivariate grouping techniques on the clinical and validity scales of the MMPI, the correlational cluster analysis was discovered to be superior to computation of distance functions followed by the application of the hierarchial grouping procedure. The subjects were 497 hospitalized alcoholics. Actual studies of the MMPI records of over 200 of these were used for standardization. Of these, 111 fitted four types: 46 belonged to type I, Jellinek's alpha alcoholics (people who poorly controlled anger); 38 belonged to type II, Jellinek's gamma alcoholics (severe alcoholism with somatic complaints); 22 belonged to type III, Jellinek's beta alcoholics (long history of frequent hospitalization and many losing attempts at abstinence); and 4 belonged to type IV, Jellinek's epsilon alcoholics (drug addiction as well as alcoholism). There were no cases corresponding to the delta alcoholic. MMPI records of 251 alcoholics were used in the cross-validation study. Of these, 106 corresponded to the four types (34, 44, 22, and 6 respectively).

Perhaps the most explicit and discerning work representing the "symptom group" classifiers is that of Rosen.[98] Theoretically, Rosen attempted to account for the development of the "alcoholic symptom" within the heterogeneous alcoholic group. He reasoned that the intemperate use of alcohol might be dependent on the fortuitous availability of sufficient quantities of alcohol to neurotic persons whose emotional conflicts and anxiety are at the same optimal level. The neurotic might use alcohol initially as a tranquilizer during the period of high anxiety and high conflict. The effect of the alcohol may then lead to an elimination or reduction of neurotic tension. The alcoholic may then enter a circular process of anxiety; ingestion of alcohol to quiet the anxiety, then the resulting guilt, leading to further anxiety. As the alcoholic process continues, the alcoholic experiences an increasing difficulty in tolerating internal stress and emotional discomfort. In the middle stages of the alcoholic process, the alcoholic requires analgesic quantities of alcohol, in order to withstand the normal day-to-day stress of life. In the late stages of alcoholism, the personality configuration observed might be the result of the toxic effects of the chronic excessive ingestion of alcohol, a condition to a degree independent of the original etiological factors accounting for drinking in the first place. Etiological factors probably vary with different stages in the alcoholic process.

Rosen also takes up the question of the non-neurotic individual who becomes an alcoholic only after many years of heavy alcoholic consumption. He thinks physiological factors or physiological vulnerability may be the answer here. Alcoholism might develop in the physiologically vulnerable persons suffering from a psychoneurotic conflict who is living in a social and cultural milieu that permits the intemperate use of alcohol. Alcoholism might also occur after protracted use while one or more of the other factors diminish in importance. He contended that the variation in causation may be the essential difference between the primary alcoholic (with psychoneurotic disposition) and the secondary alcoholic (without psychological precursors).

Rosen viewed alcoholism as a symptom associated with other psychiatric problems and not as a specific disease entity. A major concern of his present study was to account for the conflicting findings in many investigations describing psychological test differences between alcoholics and nonalcoholics. He assumed that the described differences were more likely to be a result of sample error (e.g. noncomparability) than of real differences in personality between alcoholics and persons with other psychiatric disorders.

Rosen hypothesized that general unselected psychiatric outpatients would not differ from general unselected alcoholic outpatients when drawn from similar populations. Moreover, he hypothesized that alcoholic patients would display the same range and spectrum of psychiatric symptoms as other psychiatric patients when selected from comparable populations. He gave the MMPI to the following groups: 78 male patients from an alcoholism clinic (consecutive admissions); 35 psychiatric outpatient males (consecutive admissions); 17 male skid-row alcoholics who had volunteered for a psychotherapeutic program on skid row (these were older than the first two groups and had lower academic and vocational achievements); 64 nonpsychotic alcoholics from a state mental hospital; and two samples of females (25 patients from an alcoholic clinic and 56 patients from a psychiatric clinic). With the exception of the skid row alcoholics, the groups were similar in reference to age, education, vocation, residence.

Rosen's results show that there was great similarity in personality profile between the male alcoholic-clinic patients and the male psychiatric-clinic patients. The alcoholic-clinic patients differed from the psychiatric-clinic patients primarily in terms of the expression of asocial or antisocial impulses or attitudes as measured by the psychopathic deviate scale. These groups, as well as the skid-row alcoholics, differed from the hospitalized alcoholics on most of the scales. The two women's groups were different from that of the males, but were similar to each other. Scores of alcoholic women were lower than those of women in the psychiatric clinic.

On the MMPI, alcoholic women as a group exhibited less pathology than the women psychiatric outpatients. A consistent difference between the alcoholic and nonalcoholic sample was the higher score by the former on the psychopathic deviate scale. While the alcoholic group and the skid-row alcoholics both scored somewhat higher than the psychiatric clinic outpatients on the psychasthenia and schizophrenia scales as well as on the hypochondriasis and F scales, the total shape and form of the profiles was similar in all three groups. The form of the profiles of the psychiatric clinic and the form of the alcoholic clinic groups were more similar to one another than either profile form of the alcoholic outpatient groups was to that of the hospitalized alcoholics. The main difference between the two samples and the psychiatric clinic sample was the greater degree of difficulty of the alcoholic sample in the areas of social regulation. They also had a lower level of anxiety than the psychiatric clinic sample. The higher Pd score in the alcoholic groups was interpreted not only as a result of problems of authority, but also an indication of the difficulties that alcoholics experienced in the community as a result of being intoxicated (e.g. the alcoholic was more frequently arrested).

Rosen concluded that when one selects alcoholics with similar motivation and needs to conform, one finds that they do not differ significantly from psychiatric outpatients. Alcoholism is not a primary disorder. Alcoholics do not form a homogeneous group, and are not so different from other psychiatric patients as to require a unique diagnostic designation. In short, Rosen's alcoholics did vary from his nonalcoholics in one respect—the alcoholics had a psychoneurotic character structure, along with a greater-than-average amount of impulsive acting-out and rebellious feelings toward authority (mixed neurotic and psychopathic). Certainly this marks a significant difference. Some scholars are quick to point out that Rosen's findings (overall) make the search for identifiable personality characteristics among alcoholics unrewarding. They appear to forget that Rosen compared alcoholics with another abnormal group, not with normals. It is quite likely that alcoholics share some personality aberrations with psychiatric-clinic patients. Alcoholics might also suffer from mental aberrations of one kind or another.

COMMENTS ON THE PSYCHOLOGICAL APPROACH

The Orientations

The Alcoholic Effects Orientation

The alcohol effects orientation is perhaps the most straightforward. The psychophysiological effects of alcohol have been well studied, but their relationship to the etiology of alcoholism remains unanswered. We need alcohol-effects studies at the various stages in the process of alcoholism. Jellinek has demonstrated that there are phases of alcohol addiction;[99] therefore, neither the alcoholic's original reasons for drinking nor his observed behavior during the early drinking stage will necessarily explain why he drinks at a later drinking stage. Tamerin and Mendelson[100] noted that the motivating factors involved in the initiation of a drinking episode were not the same as those involved in the perpetuation of the episode. The probability that the alcoholic or prealcoholic utilizes alcohol for different drinking stages needs further investigation. Certainly we need to find out more about the alcoholic's differential effects of his drinking (on emotional state and behavior) at the various stages throughout his drinking career. There is some evidence to support the view that alcoholics drink in different ways when involved in different social situations. We also need to know why some so-called escape-drinkers choose alcohol rather than some other drug.[101] The choice of alcohol as a means of escape might be closely related to social attitudes toward drinking or to deeper psychological factors, or both.

MacAndrew and Edgerton have challenged the conventional view of alcoholic effects,[102] i.e. that alcohol is a disinhibiter as well as an impairer of sensorimotor skills and that alcohol alters the character of social comportment. They agree that alcohol impairs sensorimotor skills but deny that alcohol is a disinhibiter which alters social comportment. They question the American Medical Association's position that alcohol produces changes in comportment by impairing the higher brain functions leading to the "loss of inhibition," among other things. In brief, they claim that alcohol does not depress the powers of judgment by weakening inhibitions. These authors present their analysis of drinking customs in five societies (the Camba, Aritama, Ifaluk, Takashima, and a Mixtec Indian barrio) in which they report the absence of any "disinhibiting" effects of alcohol. In these cultures, the inhibitions that are normally in effect are reported to remain in effect even when their members are heavily intoxicated. They claim that drunken persons in these societies (and in others like them) may stagger, speak thickly, and become stuporous, without any corresponding display of behavior in which they would not ordinarily indulge.

MacAndrew and Edgerton contend that alcohol does not impair normally operative controls; that the drunk does not become a creature of impulse; and that alcohol is not a "superego solvent," because of its toxic action. They conclude that their data (from different drinking practices in different cultures) document the inadequacy of the conventional understanding of alcohol effects on human conduct and thinking. They offer instead a radical social-psychological formulation. The way people comport themselves when they are drunk and how they feel when drunk is not determined by alcohol's toxic assault upon the seat of moral judgment and conscience, but by society's definition of the situation of drunkenness and what society imparts to its membership about the state of drunkenness. Even should we find that alcohol disinhibits the will, the society will still channel the "disinhibiting behavior"; veto it; control it. These provocative but questionable conclusions were based primarily on (historical) ethnological observations on Indians in Canada. Indians learned how to act and feel when intoxicated by observing and imitating white drinkers (trappers, soldiers, merchants, and roustabouts). Many of their drinking models were debauched.

MacAndrew and Edgerton have probably overdrawn their case, since there is a plethora of evidence from the clinical and pharmacological literature that shows alcohol's disinhibiting effect. Their data, though at times conflicting, indicate that different personality types (though not defined as such) react differently to the effects of alcohol when drinking within the same cultural context. The important caveat to remember is that MacAndrew and Edgerton dealt with the alcohol effects on drinkers and not on alcoholics. Their findings confirm the need for additional cross-cultural studies on alcohol effects, and the further study of culture's role in "telling" the drinker how to feel, act, and react while drinking. *Alcohol*, however, remains a drug with fairly specific effects and may never be equated with *water!* Casanovas knew a long time before Ogden Nash that "Candy is dandy but liquor is quicker." Nash succinctly and poetically recorded the very vital point for posterity.

Reinforcement Theories

Reinforcement of learning theories hold that alcoholism (alcoholic behavior) provides certain rewards, both positive and negative. In contemporary reinforcement theory, little or no attention is paid to the etiology of alcoholism per se. The stimulus-response psychologist concentrates on discovering the conditions under which alcohol or its effects are reinforcing. Interpreted in this way, the reinforcement approach implies that, under the appropriate circumstances, anyone could become an alcoholic.

Many of the studies in this area have been conducted with sub-humans, and (as have many biochemical studies) any inferences drawn from them to humans must be cautionary. Lester[103] maintained that researchers who do not examine the blood alcohol content of their experimental animals may not claim that alcohol was ingested in large enough quantities to produce stress-reducing effects. He said that more emphasis should be placed on the personality and physiological condition of the individual. Kingham[104] has taken a step in this direction. Severely maladjusted people who absorb alcohol into the bloodstream rapidly are probably more likely to find alcohol reinforcing and, therefore, learn "alcoholism" as a response than are others without these characteristics. Perhaps alcohol would not be reinforcing for some individuals, under any circumstances, because of their physiological makeup. *This does not negate reinforcement.* What it does is suggest that future reinforcement theories (to be etiologically useful) must be more explicit in terms of *specifying what conditions are necessary for alcohol or its effects to be reinforcing.*

Albert Bandura's aforementioned "social learning theory" meets these criticisms more adequately than any other reinforcement theory to date. It could be argued that this theory is interdisciplinary, since it requires the articulation (not mixing) of several frames of reference, and therefore dictates research at different levels of analysis. It provides contingency allowances for such diverse elements as stress reduction, biochemical factors, and social reinforcement. The authors think that it represents the most objective and testable theory on alcoholism found in the reinforcement literature and probably in the literature period.

The Transactional Orientation

The transactional orientation is relatively new, and many difficulties inherent in this essentially analytic approach have yet to be explored. This type of analysis focuses attention on the social environment of the alcoholic, the claimed crucial element in the causation of alcoholism. J. D. Keehn and Albert Bandura, both stimulus-response psychologists, have stressed the social milieu of the alcoholic. Keehn's position is similar to Bandura's social learning hypothesis. Both agree that alcoholic behavior is maintained by reinforcement, but Keehn emphasizes the reinforcing social environment more heavily than Bandura. The point of disagreement between the two is in terms of what specific events are reinforcing. However, there is no reason to assume that alcoholic behavior in all individuals must be maintained by the same type of reinforcer; e.g. in two alcoholics, alcoholic behavior may be maintained by two entirely different reinforcers or by a combination of different reinforcers.

Steiner's approach in transactional analysis is a radical departure from traditional stimulus-response psychology, and is based on a psychoanalytical stance. There have been many criticisms of Steiner's application of transactional analysis to alcoholism and its treatment.[105] Machover,[106] for example, contends that Steiner's analysis is an oversimplification and that alcoholic patients are not voluntaristic game players. Many other criticisms defend the conventional view of alcoholism as an illness. Steiner is frequently charged with treating sick people as if they were not sick. Steiner's methodology is based on subjective clinical interview materials and, unfortunately, is most unclear. He gives no explanation as to why an individual specifically chooses alcoholism as a means of promoting a life script. Hypothetically granting the existence of Steiner's life scripts, it appears that they could be promoted by a number of other means or vehicles excluding alcohol. There is little evidence, if any, to support the position that alcoholics or non-alcoholics might not possess several life scripts, differing at various life stages. Steiner has presented an interesting, if not unique, line of analysis, although in its current form it is simplistic. Hopefully, he will provide an empirical methodology for his thesis. He[107] has suggested a control experiment to test his propositions. Certainly this is a step in the right direction.

Alcoholic game-playing modeled on the transactional analysis paradigm, however, may be questioned on yet another dimension. Alcoholism has been defined by society as destructive behavior, and there is evidence to support that this is the case in a physiological sense. We must not construe this to mean that the individual alcoholic necessarily seeks alcoholism as being destructive. If the individual does not see alcoholism as destructive to himself, then those theories which emphasize the self-punitive effects of alcoholism (e.g., Steiner's transactional analysis thesis) are probably in error.

Psychoanalytic (Dynamic) Approaches

Psychoanalytic or similar dynamic approaches are probably the most controversial and the least empirically supported of the myriad etiological works on alcoholism. The sparseness of empirical etiological works within the dynamic mold is related to the difficulties in operationalizing dynamic theoretical concepts. Many dynamic writers seem content to demonstrate their postulates through and by limited qualitative, illustrative case histories. Past attempts to operationalize dynamic concepts have frequently led to methodological problems, which have rendered replication studies difficult. Frequently, the sampling techniques employed (if any) in the selection of case histories are not designated; adequate (if any) control groups are infrequently employed. Another difficulty with this approach (at least for the nonanalyst) is the frequency with which similar personality syndromes and aberrations may or may not lead to alcoholism. Frequently, similar personality syndromes predispose to all kinds of deviant behaviors, sometimes including and sometimes excluding, alcoholism.

Blum's[108] criticisms of psychoanalytic works on alcoholism appear appropriate; she states that (1) the patients seen by psychoanalysts are probably not representative of all alcoholics; (2) most psychoanalysts neglect important sociocultural factors; and (3) there are probably no consistent criteria applied by psychoanalysts in assigning a diagnosis of alcoholism. This last criticism is not confined to psychoanalysis.

Field Dependence Theory

Field dependence theory involves the concept that perceptual organization is somewhat governed by or related to an individual's personality characteristics. Actually, it represents an indirect method to assess personality. Insofar as people who become alcoholic can be characterized as having a distinct personality, their responses to such perceptual tasks as the FET, RFT, and BAT could be used in estimating the likelihood that they would become alcoholics. However, there is the possibility that the alcoholics' responses to the operationalized perceptual tasks are a result of the use of alcohol, rather than being indicators of any underlying psychogenic personality type. This alternative explanation is supported by the significant and highly important results of Smith and Carpenter,[109] who found that a critical variable in alcoholism is the individual's rate of absorption of alcohol into the blood stream. These results show that some biological factors are involved in the making of alcoholics. We need many more studies of this type.

Personality Theories

Personality theories of alcoholism have been (and are) criticized on the basis of our lack of evidence for a single, distinct, personality type associated with alcoholism. Sutherland, Schroeder, and Tordella[110] reviewed almost 40 studies on the alcoholic personality published up until 1949; they discovered that the methods of study were inadequate, and that the alcoholic had not been shown to be distinct type of personality. Syme[111] reviewed 26 studies in the literature from 1949 to 1957 and reported: "The sort of empirical evidence presented to substantiate theoretical notions falls far short of scientific requirements. Methods and procedures are often questionable; moreover, when they are adequate the results obtained often contradict the findings of other competent investigators . . . [Thus] there is no warrant for concluding that persons of one personality type are more likely to become alcoholic than another type."

Current critics, including psychologists, of the personality approach to alcoholism, agree in great part with Sutherland and Syme. The basic flaw in personality theories is their lack of specificity.[112] Many characteristics found among alcoholics, e.g. disturbed parent-child relationships, dependency problems, and internal and/or external stress leading to escapism, are also found among nonalcoholic psychiatric patients. An acceptable personality theory must hypothesize one or more variables that are found among alcoholics, but not among other maladjusted persons.[113]

The evidence that no unique, specific personality traits predispose an individual to alcoholism does not preclude further research of the relationship between personality variables and alcoholism. At a minimum, it has been established that alcoholics as a group suffer more frequently from personality aberrations of one kind or another than do (nondeviant) nonalcoholics. Assuredly, this finding warrants continued personality research. Perhaps, in reference to ex post facto studies, the typological approach in the area of personality study has proved the most rewarding, e.g. Jellinek's work.

No mater what type of psychological approach is used with alcoholics, there is always the possibility that the discriminating characteristics delineated are caused (or influenced) by alcoholism itself. Do the theoretical explanations about the alcoholic's current drinking also account for his initial drinking? Most studies dealing with the personality factors involved in the causation of alcoholism have been ex post facto studies. The psychodynamic functions of alcoholism may change over time. There is no assurance that the personality pattern which the alcoholic presents to the researcher or clinician is the pattern that initially predisposed the individual to alcoholism. Future longitudinal studies may reveal etiological relationships between particular types of personalities and particular types of alcoholics; an example of such study might be a typology of alcoholics in terms of drinking patterns (and behavior while intoxicated) as well as reactions to alcohol (alcohol effects). *The personality syndromes involved* will probably be based on cultural, psychological, and biological foundations. Hopefully, longitudinal studies will enable us to solve the problem of cause and effect.

Two longitudinal studies providing psychological data are available. Jones,[114] in an unpublished study, followed up normal, public school children over a 30-plus-year period. She described problem drinkers as adults as attention seeking, aggressive and acting out, socially extroverted, lacking impulse control, resentful of authority, and lacking feelings for others. They also possessed power-seeking and self-destructive impulses. The problem drinkers as children were more tense, had less satisfactions and had fewer ways of solving life problems than normals. The second, that of McCord et al., is very significant and requires a separate analysis.

McCord's Social-Psychological Personality Paradigm

McCord's[115] data (previously noted in Chapter I) negated many psychoanalytical theories of alcoholism. He arrived at prealcoholic and postalcoholic personality types, primarily through and by behavior patterns rather than projective or objective personality tests. He found that boys who showed oral tendencies (e.g. thumb-sucking after infancy, excessive smoking at an early age, eating orgies, playing with the mouth) did not tend (statistically) to become alcoholic more frequently than boys who lacked these tendencies; boys who were markedly feminine (e.g. played with dolls, sometimes wore dresses, frequently expressed wishes that they had been girls) and were presumably with latent homosexual tendencies did not have a greater tendency to alcoholism than boys markedly masculine; boys conditioned by strong maternal encouragement of dependency (e.g. mother welcomed babyish behavior, rewarded boys for hanging on to her petticoat) did not become alcoholics more frequently than boys who were relatively independent of their mothers; restrictive mothers (e.g. sheltered boys from adversity, selected their friends and activities, curtailed independence) produced a lower proportion of alcoholic sons than did less restrictive mothers. McCord concluded that subjects with marked suicidal tendencies *may* have been more likely to become alcoholic than boys without suicidal tendencies and that boys with strong, consciously expressed inferiority feelings were significantly less likely to become addicted than those who would not express inferiority feelings (those expressing very self-confident and moderately self-confident feelings).[116]

McCord[117] claims that his data lend more support to the theory of Robert White in *The Abnormal Personality* than to any other psychological position. Though White holds that no one set of motives inclines an individual to alcoholism, he affixes special importance to two personality traits; a desire for maternal love and an urge to be aggressive. White depicts the person who is most likely to become alcoholic as follows:

> There is a *repressed* but still active craving for loving maternal care. There is also a very strong aggressive need, *suppressed* by circum-stances to the extent that it comes to expression only in verbal form. Alcohol does a lot for these two needs. It permits the young man to act as aggressively as he really feels, without forcing him to assume full responsibility for his actions. It permits him to gratify his depen-dent cravings without forcing his sober consciousness to become aware of them. Alcohol thus allows him to satisfy strong needs with-

out disturbing the neurotic protective organization that ordinarily keeps them in check.[118]

McCord's[119] paradigm for alcoholism is based primarily on "under the roof" interrelationships between prealcoholic boys (N=29) and their parents. His prealcoholic boys were faced with predisposing stressful influences (environmental and neurological) which led to anxiety stemming from an internal conflict between strong dependency needs and equally strong desires for independence. Heightened dependency needs resulted in dependency conflict (via mother-son relationships). The boys grew up with a confused self-concept ("role confusion") due to faulty relationships with inadequate fathers and mothers.

Alcoholics in childhood were *apparently* self-contained compared to the nondeviants (nonalcoholics and noncriminals). They were more likely to have been outwardly self-confident, undisturbed by abnormal fears, indifferent toward their siblings and disapproving of their mothers. They were also more aggressive and anxious than the nondeviants. In childhood, the alcoholics exhibited apparent fearlessness, self-sufficiency, and aggressiveness which in our society are regarded as being masculine.[120] McCord assumes that this overemphasis on masculinity was a facade to cover up feminine dependent tendencies (resulting from unfulfilled and erotic dependency needs expected and desired from parents) that were unwanted and distasteful to the boys. Since the American culture eschews male dependency needs, the boys were faced with individual, as well as social, pressures to repress their dependency feelings and actions. Despite the masculine facade, dependency needs persisted into adulthood, where they were further suppressed. The confused young men encountered a dilemma; if they lived up to the masculine role, i.e. satisfied the dependent needs of others (wives, children) and denied dependent satisfactions to themselves, they would suffer continual repression. If, on the other hand, they strived for open satisfaction of their heightened dependency needs, they would have to give up the cultural male role along with an individual masculine self-image.

At some point in young adulthood, these prealcoholic males learned that alcohol (an *alternate solution* to marrying a strong, domineering mother type and wallowing in childhood dependency needs, joining the army, entering a monastary, going to jail or prison at regular intervals, etc.) could provide them with a compromise solution to their "conscious or unconscious dilemma." Through and by excessive drinking, generally (and erroneously) regarded as masculine behavior, they might think that they could satisfy their dependent desires and maintain their slim grip on a masculine self-image at one and the same time. McCord ties together his causation chain by pointing out that males psychologically similar to his alcoholic subjects, males who underwent similar social pressures, males who had no alternate solutions to drinking, and males who grew up with no prescriptions against drinking would likely become alcoholics.[121]

McCord's adult male alcoholics (experimental sample varied in number from 61 to 82) differed from his nondeviants (control group) in several ways: they were significantly more likely to have been irregularly employed; nonparticipants in formal community organizations; more likely to have rejected their sons; to have played a passive role in their families or have been dictators; to have been involved in strong conflict with their family; to have disciplined their sons in an erratically punitive or lax manner; more likely to have felt victimized by society; to have demonstrated feelings of grandiosity, in being hedonistic above all else, in being intensely aggressive, and being openly dependent. He claims that these differences indicate that alcoholic men are distinguishable from adult nondeviant men (in his sample 158 nonalcoholics and noncriminals) in their relations to society and their families, and in their personalities. McCord's alcoholic syndrome, therefore, includes attitudes, feelings, values, behavior patterns, and what we generally classify as personality traits. This, of course, constitutes a heady mixture with which some psychologists would quibble, on the basis that McCord has mixed up several levels of analysis. On the other hand, an alcoholic syndrome (should it exist) would not have to conform to any current psychological or psychiatric syndrome.[122]

McCord has done methodologically what has never been done before or since. He carefully studied a sample of prealcoholics in childhood and adulthood, and compared them with a sample of adult alcoholics (also carefully studied in childhood and adulthood). The adult alcoholics felt victimized by their society; the prealcoholics appeared to be self-confident. The adult alcoholics were frequently intensely dependent; the prealcoholics stressed their independence, whereas the adult alcoholics avoided group activities and expressed feelings of grandiosity. Neither of these last two traits differentiated the prealcoholic from the nonalcoholic children. Both groups were aggressive, and both rejected their immediate families. Finally, McCord arrived at his "alcoholism-prone character," "pattern of personality characteristics," or "alcoholic syndrome" from comparisons of these two sample sources.

We think that McCord has made a very significant contribution to the literature of the alcoholic's personality type by attempting to (empirically) articulate the sociological and psychological levels of analysis. Unfortunately, he did not strongly pursue neurological, genetic, and chemical relationships to alcoholism. This, of course, was impossible in the case of his sample's childhoods. Hopefully, some future longitudinal study will do just this. McCord has suggested (objectively) an alcoholic personality syndrome, at the least. At the most, he has postulated an etiological theoretical paradigm (predisposing factors, heightened dependency, role confusion, destruction of self-image, alcoholism) which appears logical and plausible. Future longitudinal, replication studies are needed to confirm, negate, or modify his provocative and intriguing model. We must keep in mind that McCord's restricted number of cases in various sample groups precluded highly significant statisical comparisons at several points throughout his study. Hopefully, future longitudinal studies will utilize large samples for both experimental and control groups.

Whatever the specialist's orientation toward psychological, physiological, or sociological explanations of alcoholism, many scholars sooner or later turn to social-psychological interactionist conclusions. We think this "healthy" movement is evident in Albert Bandura's reinforcement and social learning theory. Additional studies in Chapter IV further mark the social-psychological approach.

SUMMARY STATEMENT

The general theme best characterizing the psychological approach to alcoholism is one depicting the alcoholic as an escapist—alcohol being the means of escape. The type of personality most frequently associated with alcoholism is a passive-dependent one. The combination of these perspectives suggest that the alcoholics are basically dependent personalities who have turned to alcohol as a means of escape from internal or external stress.

NOTES AND REFERENCES

1. Some of the components of this frame of reference were suggested by: Pittman, David J.: *Alcoholism: An Interdisciplinary Approach*. Springfield, Thomas, 1959; and Jellinek, E. Morton: *The Disease Concept of Alcoholism*. New Haven, College & University Press, 1960. The six types are not meant to include *all* aspects of psychological theory and research.

2. Greenberg, Leon A.: Intoxication and alcoholism: Psychological factors. *The Annals of the American Academy of Political and Social Science, 315*:22-30, January, 1958. Other works by Greenberg on the effects of alcohol are: Alcohol in the body. In McCarthy, Raymond G. (Ed.): *Drinking and Intoxication: Selected Readings in Social Attitudes and Controls*. New Haven, College & University Press, 1959, pp. 7-12; The concentration of alcohol in the blood and its significance. In *Alcohol, Science and Society*. New Haven, *Quarterly Journal of Studies on Alcohol*, 1945, pp. 45-58; Alcohol and emotional behavior. In Lucia, Salvatore P. (Ed.): *Alcohol and Civilization*. New York, McGraw-Hill, 1963, pp. 109-121. See also: Haggard, Howard W.: The physiological effects of large and small amounts of alcohol. In *Alcohol, Science and Society, op. cit.*, pp. 59-72; Jellinek, E. Morton: Effects of small amounts of alcohol on psychological functions. In *Alcohol, Science and Society, Ibid.*, pp. 83-94; Carpenter, John A.: The effects of alcohol on some psychological processes. *Quarterly Journal of Studies on Alcohol, 23*:274-314, June, 1962; Nash, H.: *Alcohol and Caffeine: A Study of Their Psychological Effects*. Springfield, Thomas, 1962; Lysansky, Edith S.: *Psychological Effects in Drinking and Intoxication: Selected Readings and Social Attitudes and Controls*, pp. 18-25; the pre-1940 literature was extensively covered by Jellinek, E. Morton, and McFarland, R. A.: An analysis of psychological experiments on the effects of alcohol. *Quarterly Journal of Studies on Alcohol, 1*:272-371, September, 1940. For a technical explanation of the effects of ethanol on the deep cerebral structures, see Segal, B. M., Kushnarev, V. M., Unakov, G., and Misionzhrik, E. U.: Alcoholism and disruption of the activity of deep cerebral structures. *Quarterly Journal of Studies on Alcohol, 31*:587-601, September, 1970.

3. Greenberg, Leon A.: Intoxication and alcoholism: physiological factors, *op. cit.*, pp. 22-30.

4. Coleman, James C.: *Abnormal Psychology and Modern Life.* Chicago, Scott-Foresman, 1964, pp. 421-422.

5. Coleman, James C.: *Ibid.,* p. 471.

6. Brunn, Ketill: Significance of role and norms in the small group for individual behavioral changes while drinking. *Quarterly Journal of Studies on Alcohol, 20*:54-64, March, 1959; Clark, Rusell A., and Sensibar, Minda R.: The relationship between symbolic and manifest projections of sexuality with some incidental correlates. *Journal of Abnormal and Social Psychology, 50*:327-334, May, 1955.

7. Greenberg, Leon A., and Carpenter, John A.: The effect of alcoholic beverages on skin conductance and emotional tension: Wine, whisky and alcohol. *Quarterly Journal of Studies on Alcohol, 18*:190-211, June, 1957.

8. Lienert, G. A., and Traxel, W.: The effects of meprobomate and alcohol on galvinic skin response. *Journal of Psychology, 48*:329-334, 1959.

9. Bennett, Richard M., Bussard, Arnold H., and Carpenter, John A.: Alcohol and human physical aggression. *Quarterly Journal of Studies on Alcohol, 30*:870-976, December, 1969.

10. Mulford, Harold A., and Miller, Donald E.: Drinking in Iowa, IV. Preoccupation with alcohol and definitions of alcohol, heavy drinking and trouble due to drinking. *Quarterly Journal of Studies on Alcohol, 21*:279-291, June, 1960; and Drinking in Iowa, V. Drinking and alcohol drinking. *Quarterly Journal of Studies on Alcohol, 21*:483-499, September, 1960.

11. Kinsey, Barry A.: *The Female Alcoholic.* Springfield, Thomas, 1966.

12. Vanderpool, James A.: Alcoholism and the self-concept. *Quarterly Journal of Studies on Alcohol, 30*:59-77, March, 1969.

13. Diethelm, Oskar, and Barr, Rosalie, M.: Psychotherapeutic interviews and alcohol intoxication. *Quarterly Journal of Studies on Alcohol, 23*:243-251, June, 1962.

14. Tamerin, John S., and Mendelson, Jack H.: The psychodynamics of chronic inebriation: Observations of alcoholics during the process of drinking in an experimental group setting. *American Journal of Psychiatry, 125*:886-899, January, 1969. See also McNamee, H. Brian, Mello, Nancy, and Mendelson, Jack H: Experimental analysis of drinking patterns of alcoholics: Concurrent psychiatric observations. *American Journal of Psychiatry, 124*:1063-1069, February, 1968.

15. Garfield, Z. H., and McBrearty, J. F.: Arousal level and stimulus response in alcoholics after drinking. *Quarterly Journal of Studies on Alcohol, 31*:1008, December, 1970; Garfield, Z. H.: Effect of alcohol ingestion by alcoholics on arousal level and stimulus response: An explanatory study. Ph.D. dissertation, Temple Univer-

sity, 1968. (University Microfilm No. 69-14,085.) Source of abstract: Diss. Abst. 30: B-1375-1376, 1969.

16. The discussion of congeners is from Greenberg, Leon A.: Introduction. *Quarterly Journal of Studies on Alcohol*, Supplement 5:1-5, May, 1970. This Supplement to the *Quarterly Journal of Studies on Alcohol* deals exclusively with studies on congeners and their effects on men and animals. The hangover is that facet of drinking behavior that is most often purported to be influenced by the congener content of the beverage. Chapman reviewed much of the literature in this area and found, in an empirical study, that those drunk on vodka (low on congener content) had less acute hangovers than those drunk on bourbon (high on congener content). See Chapman, Loring F.: Experimental induction of hangover. *Quarterly Journal of Studies on Alcohol*, Supplement 5:67-86, May, 1970. See Randolph for food allergy explanation; Randolph, Theron G.: The descriptive features of food addiction: Addictive eating and drinking. *Quarterly Journal of Studies on Alcohol*, *17*:198-224, June, 1956. Randolph's viewpoint was discussed briefly above in Chapter II.

17. Teger, Allan I., Katkin, Edward S., and Pruitt, Dean G.: Effects of alcoholic beverages and their congener content on level and style of risk taking. *Journal of Personality and Social Psychology*, *11*:170-175, February, 1969.

18. Nathan, Peter E., Zare, Nancy C., Ferneau, Ernest W., Jr., and Lowenstein, Leah M.: Effects of congener differences in alcoholic beverages on the behavior of alcoholics. *Quarterly Journal of Studies on Alcohol*, Supplement 5:87-100, May, 1970.

19. Murphree, Henry B., Schultz, Robert E., and Jusko, Allan G.: Effects of high congener intake by human subjects on the EEG. *Quarterly Journal of Studies on Alcohol*, Supplement 5:50-61, May, 1970.

20. Conger, John J.: Reinforcement theory and the dynamics of alcoholism. *Quarterly Journal of Studies on Alcohol*, *17*:296, June, 1956. See also Conger, John J.: The effects of alcohol on conflict behavior in the albino rat. *Quarterly Journal of Studies on Alcohol*, *12*:1-29, March, 1951.

21. Dollard, John, and Miller, Neal E.: *Personality and Psychotherapy.* New York, McGraw-Hill, 1950, pp. 185-187.

22. Kingham, Richard J.: Alcoholism and reinforcement theory of learning. *Quarterly Journal of Studies on Alcohol*, *19*:320-330, June, 1958.

23. Conger, John J.: The effects of alcohol on conflict behavior in the albino rat, *op. cit.*, pp. 1-29.

24. Masserman, Jules H., and Yum, K. S.: An analysis of the influence of alcohol on experimental neuroses in cats. *Psychosomatic Medicine*, *8*:36-52, January-February, 1946.

25. Smart, Reginald G.: Effects of alcohol on conflict and avoidance be-

havior. *Quarterly Journal of Studies on Alcohol, 26*:187-205, June, 1965.

26. Bandura, Albert: *Principles of Behavior Modification.* New York, Holt, Rinehart & Winston, 1969, p. 533.
27. Freed, Earl X.: The effect of alcohol upon approach-avoidance conflict on the white rat. *Quarterly Journal of Studies on Alcohol, 28*:236-254, June, 1967.
28. Freed, Earl X.: *Ibid.,* p. 248.
29. Freed, Earl X.: The effect of self-intoxication upon approach-avoidance conflict in the rat. *Quarterly Journal of Studies on Alcohol, 29*:323-329, June, 1968.
30. Freed, Earl X.: *Ibid.,* p. 327.
31. Brown, Russell V.: Effects of stress on voluntary alcohol consumption in mice. *Quarterly Journal of Studies on Alcohol, 29*:49-53, March, 1968.
32. Brown, Russell V.: *op. cit.* pp. 49-53.
33. Thiessen, D. D., and Rogers, David A.: Alcohol injection, grouping and voluntary alcohol consumption of inbreed strains of mice. *Quarterly Journal of Studies on Alcohol, 26*:378-383, September, 1956.
34. Casey, A.: The effect of stress on the consumption of alcohol and reserpine. *Quarterly Journal of Studies on Alcohol, 21*:208-216, June, 1960.
35. Gowdey, C. W., and Klaase, Jacobus: Voluntary alcohol consumption and avoidance learning by rats; Lack of correlation. *Quarterly Journal of Studies on Alcohol, 30*:336-344, June, 1969.
36. Adamson, Robert, and Black, Roger: Volitional drinking and avoidance learning in the white rat. *Journal of Comparative Physiological Psychology, 52*:734-736, December, 1959, quoted in Gowdey, C. W., and Klaase, Jacobus: *op. cit.,* pp. 415-427.
37. Senter, Roberick J., and Sinclair, J. D.: Thiamin induced alcohol consumption in rats. *Quarterly Journal of Studies on Alcohol, 29*:337-341, June, 1968.
38. Keehn, J. D.: Voluntary consumption of alcohol by rats. *Quarterly Journal of Studies on Alcohol, 30*:320-329, June, 1969. See also Keehn, J. D., et al.: Use of the reinforcement survey schedule with alcoholics. *Quarterly Journal of Studies on Alcohol, 31*:602-615, September, 1970, illustrating that alcohol to some alcoholics is no more (or in some cases less) reinforcing than other reinforcers.
39. Bandura, Albert: *op. cit.,* pp. 533-537.
40. Cahalan, Don: *Problem Drinkers.* San Francisco, Jossey-Bass, 1970, pp. 71-74; Levy, Robert I.: The psychodynamic functions of alcohol. *Quarterly Journal of Studies on Alcohol, 19*:649-659, December, 1968: Ferster, C. B., Nurnberger, J. I., and Levitt, E. B.: The control of eating, *The Journal of Mathetics, 1*:87-109, 1962;

Conger, J. J.: Reinforcement theory and the dynamics of alcoholism. *Quarterly Journal of Studies an Alcohol, 17*:296-305, June, 1956; Knight R. P.: The dynamics and treatment of chronic alcohol addiction. *Bulletin of the Menninger Clinic, 1*:233-250, 1937; Knupfer, Genevieve: The epidemiology of problem drinking. *American Journal of Public Health, 57*:973-986, August, 1967; Williams, Allan F.: Social drinking, anxiety, and depression. *Journal of Personality and Social Psychology, 3*:689-693, June, 1965; and Reinert, R. E.: The concept of alcoholism as a bad habit. *Bulletin of the Menninger Clinic, 32*:25-46, January, 1968.

41. Keehn, J. D.: Reinforcement of alcoholism: Schedule control of solitary drinking. *Quarterly Journal of Studies on Alcohol, 31*:28-39, March, 1970. The discussion in this and the following paragraphs owes much to this article by Keehn. The Transactional Orientation is perhaps more strictly social-psychologcal than psychological. No provision was made, however, for a social-psychological approach, and thus such works were placed in either psychological or sociological chapters.

42. Keehn, J. D.: *Ibid.,* p. 38. Keehn termed the approach he discussed "behavior analysis." His behavior analysis is similar to Berne's transactional type analysis, but takes a more psychological learning theory perspective. Because of the similarities, Keehn's discussion is included here rather than in the Reinforcement Orientation section.

43. Keehn, J. D.: Voluntary consumption of alcohol by rats, *op. cit.,* p. 324.

44. Keehn, J. D.: Reinforcement of alcoholism: Schedule control of solitary drinking, *op. cit.,* pp. 35-39.

45. Keehn, J. D.: *Ibid.,* pp. 29-31. See also Culter, Henry S. G., Schwaab, Eugene L., Jr., and Nathan, Peter E.: Effects of alcohol on its utility for alcoholics and nonalcoholics. *Quarterly Journal of Studies on Alcohol, 31*:369-378, June, 1970.

46. Steiner, Claude M.: The alcoholic game. *Quarterly Journal of Studies on Alcohol, 30*:920-938, December, 1969. The theoretical base for the discussion that follows was derived from this article. Although transactional analysis is a therapy technique, it is based, as are other therapy techniques, on etiological assumptions. For a brief and concise explanation of the transactional analysis game-playing model, see McCormick, Paul, and Campos, Leonard: *Introduce Yourself to Transactional Analysis,* Stockton, San Joaquin TA Study Group, April, 1967.

47. Berne, Eric: *Games People Play.* New York, Grove Press, 1964.

48. Fenichel, Otto: *The Psychoanalytic Theory of Neuroses.* New York, W. W. Norton, 1945. For a discussion of fixation and the oral stage of psychosexual development and related concepts see Freud, Sigmund: Psychoanalytic notes upon an autobiographical account of

a case of paranoia (dementia paranoides), tr. by Riviere, Joan, in Jones, Ernest (Ed.): *Sigmund Freud: Collected Papers, 3.* New York, Basic Books, 1959, pp. 390-412; and *An Outline of Psychoanalysis,* tr. by Strachey, J., New York, W. W. Norton, 1949 (especially chapter 3). An excellent review of psychoanalytic works on alcoholism is Blum, E. M.: Psychoanalytic views on alcoholism. *Quarterly Journal of Studies on Alcohol,* 27:259-299, June, 1966.

49. Fenichel, Otto: *Ibid.,* p. 376.
50. Fenichel, Otto: *Ibid.,* p. 376.
51. Fenichel, Otto: *Ibid.,* p. 377.
52. Fenichel, Otto: *Ibid.,* p. 479.
53. Menninger, Karl: *The Vital Balance.* New York, Viking Press, 1963.
54. Kastl, Albert J.: Changes in ego functioning under alcohol. *Quarterly Journal of Studies on Alcohol,* 30:371-383, June, 1969.
55. Bertrand, Sharon, and Masling, Joseph: Oral imagery and alcoholism. *Journal of Abnormal Psychology,* 74:50-53, February, 1969.
56. Masling, Joseph, and Rabie, Lillie: Obesity, level of aspiration, and Rorschach and TAT measures of oral dependence. *Journal of Consulting Psychology,* 31:233-239, June, 1967.
57. Bertrand, Sharon, and Masling, Joseph: *op. cit.,* p. 53.
58. Wolowitz, Howard M., and Barker, Michael J.: Alcoholism and oral passivity. *Quarterly Journal of Studies on Alcohol,* 29:592-597, September, 1968.
59. Wolowitz, Howard M., and Barker, Michael J.: *Ibid.,* p. 593.
60. Wolowitz, Howard M., and Barker, Michael J.: *Ibid.,* p. 597.
61. See Tahka, Veikko: *The Alcoholic Personality: A Clinical Study.* Helsinki, The Finnish Foundation for Alcohol Studies, 1966, p. 35. Some of Freud's discussions of homosexuality are found in Freud, Sigmund: *Leonardo Da Vinci: A Psychosexual Study of an Infantile Reminiscence,* tr. by Brill, A. A. New York, Moffat, Yard, n.d.; and Certain neurotic mechanisms in jealousy, paranoia and homosexuality, tr. by Riviere, Joan, in Jones, Ernest (Ed.): *Sigmund Freud: Collected Papers, 2.* New York, Basic Books, 1959, pp. 232-243.
62. Fenichel, Otto: *op. cit.,* p. 379.
63. Machover, Soloman, Russo, Frank S., Machover, Karen, and Plumeau, Francis: Clinical and objective studies of personality variables in alcoholism, III. An objective study of homosexuality in alcoholism. *Quarterly Journal of Studies on Alcohol,* 20:528-542, September, 1959..
64. Machover, Soloman, Russo, Frank S., Machover, Karen, and Plumeau, Francis: *Ibid.,* p. 528.
65. Machover, Soloman, Russo, Frank S., Machover, Karen, and Plumeau, Francis: *Ibid.,* p. 529.
66. Machover, Soloman, Russo, Frank S., Machover, Karen, and Plumeau,

Francis: *Ibid.,* pp. 528-542.
67. Chordorkoff, Bernard: Alcoholism and ego function. *Quarterly Journal of Studies on Alcohol,* 25:292-299, June, 1964.
68. Menninger, Karl: *Man Against Himself.* New York, Harcourt Brace, 1938.
69. Menninger, Karl: *The Vital Balance, op. cit.,* pp. 136, 184, 286.
70. Tahka, Veikko: *op. cit.,* pp. 181, 184, 229.
71. Levy, Robert I.: The psychodynamic functions of alcohol. *Quarterly Journal of Studies on Alcohol,* 19:649-659, December, 1958.
72. Witkin, Herman A., Karp, Stephen A., and Goodenough, Donald R.: *Personality Through Perception.* New York, Harper & Brothers, 1954.
73. The description of the three tests and the paragraph immediately following are from Karp, Stephen A., Witkin, Herman A., and Goodenough, Donald R.: Alcoholism and psychological differentiation: Effects of alcohol on field dependence. *Journal of Abnormal Psychology,* 70:262-265, August, 1965.
74. Witkin, Herman A., Karp, Stephen A., and Goodenough, Donald R.: *Personality Through Perception, op. cit.*
75. Witkin, Herman A., Karp, Stephen A., and Goodenough, Donald R.: *Ibid.,* p. 469.
76. Zwerling, Israel, and Rosenbaum, Milton: Alcoholic addiction and personality. In Arieti, S. (Ed.): *American Handbook of Psychiatry.* New York, Basic Books, 1959, pp. 624-644.
77. Witkin, Herman A., Karp, Stephen A., and Goodenough, Donald R.: Dependence in alcoholics. *Quarterly Journal of Studies on Alcohol,* 29:493-504, September, 1959.
78. Witkin, Herman A., Karp, Stephen A., and Goodenough, Donald R.: *Ibid.,* p. 503. This study as cited by Witkin, Karp, and Goodenough is from Gordon, B.: An experimental study of dependence-independence in social and laboratory setting. Ph.D. dissertation, University of Southern California, Los Angeles, 1953.
79. Karp, Stephen A., Witkin, Herman A., and Goodenough, Donald R.: *op. cit.,* pp. 262-265. See also Goldstein, Gerald, and Shelly, Carolyn H.: Field dependence and cognitive, perceptual and motor skills in alcoholics. *Quarterly Journal of Studies on Alcohol,* 32:29-40, March, 1971. They concluded from a study sample of 50 male alcoholics, drawn at random from participants in the alcoholism treatment program at the Topeka Veterans Administration Hospital, that alcoholics tended to be field dependent; that field dependence was a factor relatively independent from other tests of cognitive functioning in alcoholics; and that their alcoholics showed normal language and memory functions, but impaired psychomotor dexterity and speed. Moreover, their findings indicated that alcoholics contain more individuals with mild intellectual impairment than would be

found in a comparable group of nonalcoholics. Patterns among their 50 male alcoholics resembled those often found in elderly persons; therefore, field dependence with their cases was equated with a premature aging process (presumably resulting from alcoholism).

80. Smith, George M., and Carpenter, John A.: Alcohol absorbtion and field dependence. *Quarterly Journal of Studies on Alcohol, 30*:15-20, March, 1969.

81. Other views of the literature note these two contrasting points of view. See Gibbins, Robert J.: *Chronic Alcoholism and Alcohol Addiction: A Survey of Current Literature.* Toronto, University of Toronto Press, 1953; Armstrong, John D.: The search for the alcoholic personality. *Annals of the American Academy of Political and Social Sciences, 315*:40-47, January, 1958: and Rosen, Alexander C.: A comparative study of alcoholics and psychiatric patients with the MMPI. *Quarterly Journal of Studies on Alcohol, 21*:253-266, June, 1960.

82. See Jellinek, E. Morton: *The Disease Concept of Alcoholism, op. cit.,* pp. 27-28, for a review of studies and theories suggesting that alcoholism is a symptom rather than a specific disease entity; and Tahka, Veikko: *op. cit.,* for a discussion of typologies of alcoholics. While this dichotomy in the second viewpoint may be superfluous, it will be mentioned to facilitate presentation. Other studies that may be of interest are: Horn, John L., and Wonberg, Kenneth W.: Symptom patterns related to the excessive use of alcohol. *Quarterly Journal of Studies on Alcohol, 30*:35-38, March, 1969; and Machover, Soloman, and Russo, Frank S.: Clinical and objective studies of personality variables in alcoholism, I. Clinical investigation of the "alcoholic personality." *Quarterly Journal of Studies on Alcohol, 20*:505-519, September, 1959.

83. Additional discussions of this approach are found in Jellinek, E. Morton: *The Disease Concept of Alcoholism, op. cit.,* p. 28; Heredity of the alcoholic, in *Alcohol, Science and Society.* New Haven, *Quarterly Journal of Studies on Alcohol,* 1945, pp. 105-114; Tahka, Veikko: *op. cit.,* Amark, Curt: A study in alcoholism: Clinical social-psychiatric and genetic investigations. *Acta Psychiatrica et Neurologica Scandanavica Supplement, 70*:1951; Freed, Earl X.: Alcoholism and manic depressive disorders, some perspectives. *Quarterly Journal of Studies on Alcohol, 31*:62-89, March, 1970; and Pitts, Ferris N., Jr., and Winokur, George: Affective disorder, VII. Alcoholism and affective disorder. *Journal of Psychiatric Research, 4*:37-50, July, 1966.

84. See Rosen, Alexander C.: *op. cit.,* pp. 253-266.

85. Catanzaro, Ronald J.: Psychiatric aspects of alcoholism, in Pittman, David J. (Ed.): *Alcoholism.* New York, Harper & Row, 1967.

pp. 31-44.

86. Klebanoff, Seymour G.: Personality factors in symptomatic chronic alcoholism as indicated by the thematic apperception test. *Journal of Consulting Psychology, 11*:111-119, May-June, 1949.

87. Tahka, Veikko: *op. cit.,* pp. 115-117.

88. Zwerling, Israel, and Rosenbaum, Milton: *op. cit.,* pp. 624-644.

89. Buhler, Charlotte, and Lefever, D. Welty: A Rorschach study on the psychological characteristics of alcoholics. *Quarterly Journal of Studies on Alcohol, 8*:197-260, September, 1947.

90. MacAndrew, Craig: The differentiation of male alcoholic outpatients from nonalcoholic psychiatric outpatients by means of MMPI. *Quarterly Journal of Studies on Alcohol, 26*:237-246, June, 1965. MacAndrew's alcoholism scale has been evaluated by Uecker, Albert E.: Differentiating male alcoholics from other psychiatric inpatients. *Quarterly Journal of Studies on Alcohol, 31*:379-383, June, 1970. A more recent MMPI alcoholism scale is that of Rhodes, Robert J.: The alcoholism scale. *Journal of Clinical Psychology, 26*:188-191, April, 1969. A number of MMPI profiles of alcoholics are reviewed in Lanyon, Richard I.: *A Handbook of MMPI Profiles.* Minneapolis, University of Minnesota Press, 1968. See also Rohan, William P., Tatro, Richard, and Rotman, S. R.: MMPI changes in alcoholics during hospitalization. *Quarterly Journal of Studies on Alcohol, 30*:389-400, June, 1969. A bibliography of MMPI studies on alcoholism and drug addiction is found in Butcher, James Neal (Ed.): *MMPI: Research and Clinical Applications.* New York, McGraw-Hill, 1969, pp. 360-361.

91. MacAndrew, Craig: Self-reports of male alcoholics: A dimensional analysis of certain differences from nonalcoholic male psychiatric outpatients. *Quarterly Journal of Studies on Alcohol, 28*:43-57, March, 1967.

92. MacAndrew, Craig: *Ibid.,* p. 57.

93. Uecker, Albert E.: *op. cit.*

94. Parthington, John T., and Johnson, F. Gordon: Personality types among alcoholics. *Quarterly Journal of Studies on Alcohol, 30*:21-33, March, 1969.

95. Sherfey, Mary J.: Psychopathology and character structure in chronic alcoholism, in Diethelm, W. Oskar (Ed.): *The Etiology of Chronic Alcoholism.* Springfield, Thomas, 1955, pp. 16-42.

96. DeVito, R. A., Flaherty, L. A., and Mozdzierz, G. J.: Toward a psychodynamic theory of alcoholism. *Quarterly Journal of Studies on Alcohol, 31*:1009, December, 1970.

97. Goldstein, Steven George: The identification, description and multivariate classification of alcoholics by means of the Minnesota Multiphasic Personality Inventory. Ph.D. dissertation, Purdue Uni-

versity, 1968 (University Microfilms No. 68-12,555).
98. Rosen, Alexander C.: *op. cit.*, pp. 253-266.
99. Jellinek, E. Morton: Phases of alcohol addiction. *Quarterly Journal of Studies on Alcohol, 13*:673-684, 1952.
100. Tamerin, John S., and Mendelson, Jack H.: The psychodynamics of chronic inebriation: Observations of alcoholics during the process of drinking in an experimental group setting. *American Journal of Psychiatry, 125*:886-899, January, 1969.
101. This is not to suggest that this problem has been ignored. See Trice, Harrison M.: *Alcoholism in America*. New York, McGraw-Hill, 1962, pp. 80-90; Meerlo, Joost A. M.: Artificial ecstasy, in Podolsky, E. (Ed.): *Encyclopedia of Aberrations*. New York, Philosophical Library, 1953; Tahka, Veikko: *op. cit.*, pp. 38-40; Mueller, Edward E.: Personality and social factors in the addiction prone alcoholic. *Corrective Psychiatry and Journal of Social Therapy, 15*:28-37, Spring, 1969; Chessick, Richard D., Loff, David H., and Price, Hazel G.: The Alcoholic-narcotic addict. *Quarterly Journal of Studies on Alcohol, 22*:261-268, June, 1961; and Bier, William C.: *Problems in Addiction: Alcohol and Drug Addiction*. New York, Fordham University Press, 1962.
102. MacAndrew, Craig, and Edgerton, Robert: *Drunken Comportment*. Chicago, Aldine, 1969, pp. 165-173.
103. Lester, David: Self-selection of alcohol by animals, human variation and the etiology of alcoholism: A critical review. *Quarterly Journal of Studies on Alcohol, 27*:395-438, September, 1966.
104. Kingham, Richard J.: Alcoholism and the Reinforcement theory of learning. *Quarterly Journal of Studies on Alcohol, 19*:320-330, June, 1958.
105. Doreshtov, Ben J.: Therapy for the nondiseased: Comment on "The Alcoholic Game." *Quarterly Journal of Studies on Alcohol, 30*:939-941, December, 1969; Osmond, Humphrey: Blood sports? Comment on "The Alcoholic Game." *Quarterly Journal of Studies on Alcohol, 30*:945-948, December, 1969; Edwards, Griffith: Comment on "The Alcoholic Game." *Quarterly Journal of Studies on Alcohol, 30*:948-951, December, 1969; Pattison, E. Mansell: Comment on "The Alcoholic Game." *Quarterly Journal of Studies on Alcohol, 30*:953-956, December, 1969.
106. Machover, Solomon: Comment on "The Alcoholic Game." *Quarterly Journal of Studies on Alcohol, 30*:941-944, December, 1969.
107. Steiner, Claude M.: *op. cit.*, p. 922.
108. Blum, Eva Marie: Psychoanalytic views on alcoholism. *Quarterly Journal of Studies on Alcohol, 27*:259-299, June, 1966.
109. Smith, George M., and Carpenter, John A.: Alcohol absorption and field dependence. *Quarterly Journal of Studies on Alcohol, 30*:15-20, March, 1969.

110. Sutherland, Edwin H., Shroeder, H. G., and Tordella, C. L.: Personality traits and the alcoholic: A critique of existing studies. *Quarterly Journal of Studies on Alcohol, 11*:547-561, December, 1965.

111. Syme, Leonard: Personality characteristics of the alcoholic. *Quarterly Journal of Studies on Alcohol, 18*:288-320, June, 1957.

112. Buss, Arnold H.: *Psychopathology.* New York, John Wiley & Sons, 1966, p. 446. Buss also presented Button's theoretical statement.

113. Button, Allen D.: The genesis and development of alcoholism: An empirically based schema. *Quarterly Journal of Studies on Alcohol, 17*:671-675, December, 1956.

114. Jones, Mary: unpublished study (1965) quoted in Blum, Richard H.: Mind-altering drugs and dangerous behavior: Alcohol. *Task Force Report Drunkenness.* Publications of the President's Commission on Law Enforcement and Administration of Justice. Washington, U. S. Government Printing Office, 1967, pp. 29-49.

115. McCord, William, McCord, Joan, and Gudeman, John: *Origins of Alcoholism.* Stanford, Cal., Stanford University Press, 1960, pp. 140-163.

116. McCord, William, McCord, Joan, and Gudeman, John: *Ibid.,* pp. 28-35.

117. McCord, William, McCord, Joan, and Gudeman, John: *Ibid.,* pp. 34-35.

118. White, Robert: *The Abnormal Personality.* New York, Ronald Press, 1948, p. 147.

119. McCord, William, McCord, Joan, and Gudeman, John: *op. cit.,* pp. 125-142,

120. McCord, William, McCord, Joan, and Gudeman, John: *Ibid.,* pp. 139-141.

121. McCord, William, McCord, Joan, and Gudeman, John: *Ibid.,* pp. 151-153.

122. McCord, William, McCord, Joan, and Gudeman, John: *Ibid.,* pp. 133-142.

Chapter IV

THE SOCIOLOGICAL APPROACH
TO ALCOHOLISM

T HE CURRENT PREEMINENCE OF THE SOCIOLOGICAL approach to
alcoholism and to problem drinking stems from at least three
empirical happenings:

1. The failure to find a unique personality type or a unique
psychiatric nosological group associated with alcoholism.

2. The importance of both sociological and social-psychological
variables in alcoholism and problem drinking as reported (a) by a
number of descriptive studies on drinking behavior and (b) by a
number of studies of the association of sociocultural factors in
alcoholism (including a few longitudinal studies).

3. The development of operant conditioning theory, and its
implications for the understanding of alcoholism and problem
drinking. The process of addiction has been found to involve cognitive process, involving anticipatory and perceptual process, as well
as learning of both neural and other bodily tissues. Furthermore,
it has been demonstrated that the reinforcing properties of alcohol
must be augmented by social-psychological and/or cultural factors,
in order to culminate in heavy drinking.

For purposes at hand, we are primarily interested in the second
happening. Cahalan, Cisin, and Crossley,[1] in the first national
probability sample on American drinking practices (*American
Drinking Practices*), confirm that, "Whether a person drinks at
all is primarily a sociological and anthropological variable rather
than a psychological one." This is evident from the great differences in the incidence of drinking by sex, age, social status,
ethnicity, degree of urbanization, and religion—all of which are
sociological or demographic variables. On the other hand, they
demonstrate that certain measures of personality are useful in
explaining some of the variations in heavy drinking.

Cahalan, Cisin and Crossley, in their comparison of abstainers

139

and heavy drinkers in the 1964-1965 national survey, discovered a relationship between psychological and sociocultural characteristics, in relation to problem drinking. In comparing abstainers and heavy drinkers, they found that "the choice of means of artificial escape from one's daily problems is dependent upon the culture's permissiveness concerning specific substances for specific groups, but that a person's abuse of a substance (alcohol, drug, food) is also dependent upon his personality and his immediate environment."[2]

Scholars pronouncing the social-psychological position, generally (explicitly or implicitly) posit a model including sociological variables (in the nature of social structural and/or demographic independent variables) and social-psychological intervening variables as operating between the independent and sociological variables and drinking behavior. Obviously, the problem of classification again looms. We will concentrate on social and social-psychological studies, generally including at least two levels of analysis.

According to Dr. Barry Kinsey,[3] the assumption that there are some relationships between social structure and alcoholism rates is the basic premise underlying all sociological approaches to inebriety. In general, sociologists and anthropologists treat social structure at three levels. Some writers postulate hypotheses which apply to all cultures or societies, the "supra-cultural orientation." Others formulate hypotheses that apply to one culture, related cultures, or to comparisons between specific cultures, the "specific-cultures orientation." Still others concern themselves with institutions (e.g. the family and religion) or with sociological or demographic variables (e.g. age, sex, degree of urbanization, religion, ethnicity, and social status—or socioeconomic class). This final perspective designates the "sub-structural orientation."

It is important to note that in contrast to the constitutional or psychological approaches to alcoholism, sociological approaches do not attempt to explain why an individual becomes an alcoholic. As Kinsey affirms, sociologists (in the strictest sense of the term) are interested in explaining rates of alcoholism for different groups or cultures. On the other hand, this does not mean that sociological findings are irrelevant in the explanations of individual cases. Some symbolic interactionists, social psychologists, and interdisciplinary theorists maintain that sociological knowledge helps explain the individual case, that is, factors studied by the sociologists (or anthropologist) provide partial answers to the question, "What causes alcoholism?"

THE SUPRA-CULTURAL ORIENTATION

There have been a number of theories and cross-cultural studies of drinking and alcoholism that attempt to cover most, if not all, cultures. Horton[4] maintains that the primary function of alcoholic beverages in all societies is the reduction of anxiety. His theorems and their corollaries follow:[5]

1. Drinking tends to be accompanied by release of sexual and aggressive impulses.

2. The strength of the drinking response in any society tends to vary directly with the level of anxiety in the society.

3. The strength of the drinking response tends to vary inversely with the strength of the counter-anxiety elicited by painful experiences during and after drinking. The sources of such painful experiences are (a) actualization of real dangers as a result of impairment of physiological functions, (b) social punishments for impairment of functions, (c) social punishments invoked by release of sexual impulses, and (d) social punishments invoked by the release of aggressive impulses.

He attempted to test these hypothetical statements through an examination of data from the files of the Cross-Cultural Survey in the Institute of Human Relations at Yale University. Adequate information on drinking was available for 77 societies. A scale of drinking behavior was constructed, based on data showing the degree of insobriety commonly reached by adult male drinkers. Horton reports that the literature furnished strong evidence of the release of aggressive impulses as a result of drinking; it also furnished less strong but significant evidence of sexual responses following drinking. He claimed that Theorem 1 was tentatively verified.

One of the measures of anxiety in a society was based on each society's dominant subsistence activity. The more primitive that a society's food-getting techniques are, the greater the danger of food shortages, and the more difficult are life conditions. These conditions, according to Horton, should create a relatively high amount of anxiety in such cultures. Primitive subsistence techniques were thus assumed to be conducive to high anxiety levels. Hunting and gathering economies were thought to be more conducive to this "subsistence anxiety" than were more advanced herding and agricultural economies. The degree of insobriety in the societies studied were found to be positively related (at a statistically significant level) to type of subsistence economy, and thus also to anxiety. As a further test of this second theorem, the societies were divided into two groups: those where there was evidence of acculturation in process, and those that showed no signs of acculturation in process. If acculturation had taken place in the past but reintegration had been accomplished, the society was placed in the second group. The process of acculturation was assumed to create high levels of anxiety. The results disclosed that all societies in the process of acculturation were characterized by extremely high levels of insobriety.[6] Theorem 2 was considered supported.

Theorem 3 holds that if drinking and insobriety (and the aggressive and sexual responses released while drinking) lead to punishment or unpleasant consequences, the act of drinking will become associated with negative consequences in the minds of the society's members. Drinking behavior (or thoughts thereof) will elicit anxiety about possible unpleasant consequences. This anxiety will counter anxiety from other sources that would be conducive to drinking. Thereom 3 and corollaries *a* and *b* were not tested statistically, but by a qualitative review of the material. Horton observed that the predicted counter-anxiety occurs, but does not effect a weakening of the drinking habit in most societies. Instead, it motivates a cultural solution to the problem presented by such actualization of objective dangers. The solution takes the form of special customary precautions against dangers, and the arrangement of drinking occasions to minimize interference with normal social and economic activities.[7]

Regarding corollary *b*, Horton claimed that social reaction to impairment of functions has operated to change the drinking situation in such a way that impairment of functions is controlled (and thus need not be punished). He concluded that corollaries *a* and *b* were incorrect, but that this did not necessarily invalidate the theorem.

The third corollary, c, stated that insobriety varies inversely with the counter-anxiety elicited by sexual responses released by drinking. It was predicted that insobriety would be inversely associated with the strength of punishments for premarital sexual behavior. The more strongly premarital sexual behavior is punished, the greater is the counter-anxiety, and thus the lower the level of insobriety. The expected relationship was observed but reached statistical significance only when societal anxiety motivating drinking was *not* especially strong. The counter-drive elicited by punishment of premarital sexual behavior was *not* strong enough to compete with *high* subsistence anxiety. Horton explained that the tendency for sexual counter-anxiety to be inversely associated with insobriety was clear enough to tentatively verify corollary c.

There was only slight evidence to support corollary d. The presence of sorcery was deemed indicative of a high level of aggression. There were only five societies with a high level of aggression (sorcery) and superordinate social control. It was assumed that in these societies, drunken aggression would be punished and that, therefore, drinking within them would be moderate.[8] The prediction was borne out, but data for a large-scale test was not available. Corollary d was considered unverified. Horton wisely attempted to test the alternative hypothesis that level of insobriety in a society was directly related to the type of beverage, and on the basis of his data reported that "strength" of beverage was not a determining factor of the customary degree of insobriety.

Field[9] reexamined Horton's theory and results by studying the ethnographic data on 56 of the same tribes with a new scale of insobriety which measured degree of drunkenness at periodic drinking bouts. He found no relationship between level of fear (fear of sorcerers, ghosts) and extent of drunkenness. His data confirmed Horton's[10] finding that tribes with very primitive hunting and gathering economies tend to have more drunkennesss than agricultural tribes. However, he reasoned that "subsistence anxiety" was not responsible for the relationship, but rather type of social organization. Field pointed out that the social organization of a hunting tribe is quite different (in some ways) from the social organization of tribes with advanced herding and agricultural economies. Similarly, Field claimed that other of Horton's results could be better explained through a social-organization perspective. He concluded, for example, that the concomitance of a lack of premarital sexual freedom and low levels of drunkenness found by Horton could result from a corporate social organization which maintained hierarchial control of marital choice. Field interpreted Horton's findings of a relationship between acculturation and insobriety not in terms of anxiety but in terms of the disorganization of social structure occurring during acculturation.

Some of the variables found to be associated with relative sobriety in primitive tribes were patrilocal residence at marriage, presence of a bride price, corporate kin groups with continuity over time, and collective ownership of property. Relatedly, it was found that drunkenness increases markedly if the authority of the male in the household is lessened or diffused, and if the nuclear family is (relatively) less integrated into larger kin structures through neo-local or bilocal residence. Field contended that the degree of drunkenness was substantially unrelated to the level of anxiety in the societies studied. He deemed social organization the key variable. Drunkenness was positively related to variables indicating a personal or informal, rather than a corporate or formal type of social organization.

Theory at the supra-cultural level most frequently mentioned in the literature is that of Robert F. Bales,[11] who based his formulations on a review of cultural and cross-cultural studies. According to Bales, there are three general ways in which culture and social organization influence rates of alcoholism:

1. The degree to which the culture operates to bring about acute needs for adjustment of inner tensions in its members (e.g. culturally induced anxiety, guilt, conflict, suppressed aggression, and sexual tensions of various sorts).

2. The sort of attitudes toward drinking which the culture produces in its members. The crucial factor here seems to be whether given attitudes suggest drinking to the individual as a means of reducing his inner tensions, or whether such a thought arouses a strong counter-anxiety.

3. The degree to which the culture provides substitute means of satisfaction. In other words, there is reason to believe that if the

inner tensions are sufficiently acute, individuals will become compulsively habituated to alcohol in spite of opposed social attitudes, unless substitute means of satisfaction are provided.

Bales' three factors and rates of alcoholism are discussed respectively:

1. One of the studies which probably helped inspire Bales and also supports his theory was that of Horton,[12] who concluded that the greater the level of anxiety and insecurity in a society, the greater the alcohol consumption. Bales cited Ireland as an example of a connection between high rates of alcoholism and culturally induced tension. Some of the factors contributing to high culturally induced tension in Ireland were the following: the average Irishman was a farmer exploited by the British and by an absentee landlord system which contributed to the general national poverty; Irish childrearing practices were ambivalent and contradictory, combining lavish displays of affection with intense parental anger and hostility; only one son inherited the family farm and the others were expected to leave home and make their own way in a country with little opportunity; and economic realities made marriage impossible until relatively late age, while sexual expression outside of marriage was strictly prohibited.

2. Bales outlined four types of cultural attitudes toward drinking that influence rates of alcoholism in conjunction with factors one and three: (a) complete abstinence; (b) the ritual attitude toward drinking, which requires that alcoholic beverages, sometimes a particular one, should be used in the performance of religious ceremonies or imbibed at religious festivals; (c) the convivial attitude toward drinking, which involves a social rather than a religious ritual (this type of drinking is a mixed type; it tends toward the ritual in that it symbolizes social unity and solidarity, and tends toward the utilitarian drinking attitude in that it loosens up emotions which make for ease and good will; this type of attitude may break down into the utilitarian attitude; examples of convivial drinking would include drinking at nonreligious social functions and celebrations); and (d) the utilitarian attitude is not strictly a cultural attitude, but is found in some subcultures or groups. The purpose of drinking is personal and self-interested rather than social (e.g. drinking to relieve a hangover or to forget

about personal problems). The utilitarian attitude toward drinking, if commonly held, is the one most likely to lead to "compulsive" drinking.

Bales cited the Moslems as a culture with an abstinent attitude but stated that there is no reliable data available on rates of alcoholism for these people. In his example of a ritual attitude, Bales turns to a subcultural group, the Jews, and suggests that their low rates of alcoholism are related to their ritual use of wine, which causes them to reject the idea of using alcoholic beverages for personal purposes. Their ritual attitude leads to a counter-anxiety, which lessens the chances of usage leading to addiction. The frequent ritual use of alcohol and low rates of alcoholism among Jews is confirmed by Snyder[13] in his study of Jewish drinking behavior.

In at least partial support of Bales' contention, Strauss and Bacon[14] studied drinking at 27 colleges and universities in the United States. The samples at each institution were selected so as to be representative of the school as a whole. They analyzed the responses of over 15,000 students and found that Jewish students had the lowest incidence of "being drunk more than 5 times" (when compared to Catholics, Protestants, and Mormons). Part of this difference they attributed to well-defined drinking customs closely integrated with the Jewish family and religious structures. These customs are introduced to the individual early in life.

The Irish, according to Bales, are a people with convivial attitudes toward drinking. The breakdown of convivial drinking into utilitarian drinking is found in marked form in the Irish culture. A drinking party is in order at all of the principal occasions in the life cycle: in the meeting of friends, in business dealings, political affairs, pilgrimages, and many other occasions when people come together. One writer of the last century says "Hallow-E'en, St. Patrick's Day, Easter and all extraordinary days are made apologies for a drinking bout; a week's excess is taken at Christmas."[15] The Irish use of alcohol as a medicine is also perceived as a manifestation of a utilitarian use of alcohol.

3. The third element of Bales' theory, concerning the availability of substitute means of satisfaction, was not easily tested empirically. In support of this contention, Bales cited (without supporting data)

the supposedly high rates of neuroses and drug addiction among the Jews in contrast to their low rates of alcoholism.

Another supracultural hypothesis, similar to that of Bales, was formulated by Glad.[16] His hypothesis was derived from the results of a study of Jewish and Irish-American drinking behavior. Glad's "affectivity-instrumentality hypothesis" is as follows:[17] "Uses of alcohol for affective consequences will contribute to a high incidence of inebriety, while uses of alcohol for secondary or associated purposes, to which the affective consequences of alcohol *per se* are incidental or inimical [instrumental consequences], will contribute to a low rate of inebriety."

Cultures or subcultures with attitudes and customs conducive to the use of alcohol for affective consequences will have high rates of alcoholism, while those with customs conducive to the use of alcohol for instrumental purposes will have low rates of alcoholism. By affectivity, Glad refers to the social and personal feeling consequences of drinking (drinking to promote sociability or to deal with personal problems). Instrumentality refers to drinking for ritual purposes or because it is socially practical, i.e. instances in which the effects of alcohol per se are not the primary intended consequences.

Ullman[18] has also presented a hypothesis relating cultural attitudes and rates of alcoholism. He maintains that in any group or society in which the drinking customs, values, and sanctions, together with the attitudes of all segments of the society are well established, known to, and agreed upon by all and are consistent with the rest of the culture, the rate of alcoholism will be low.[19]

In a society where drinking norms are well supported, the drinker is under social pressure to conform to the standards. Examples of this situation in America are found among Orthodox Jews and Italians. These two groups have relatively low rates of alcoholism in contrast to the Irish-Americans who possess unintegrated drinking customs. If the culture does not have a well-integrated system of controls, the individual is left in a situation of ambivalence which may be conducive to alcoholism. Ambivalence about drinking is the psychological product of unintegrated drinking customs.

In other discussions Ullman expands this theoretical framework.

He contends that the formation of an addiction is dependent upon a psychological state made possible, in part, by the sociological variable of attitudes and the physiological fact of the tension-reducing effects of alcohol.[20] This framework was derived, in part, from the results of experimental studies on rats. More specifically, he claims[21] that alcoholism occurs when (1) there is emotional arousal with regard to drinking (2) such drinking is accompanied by a stress situation, and (3) these circumstances occur on several occasions when a significant amount of alcohol is imbibed to produce a tension-reducing effect. Emotional arousal with regard to drinking is the element perhaps most amenable to group influence. It is this ambivalence about drinking which may be one source of emotional arousal. It is generally true that sanctioned behavior arouses less anxiety and guilt than unsanctioned behavior. This is another way of saying that conflict of values with respect to drinking produces ambivalence. We should then expect to find a correlation between unsanctioned introduction to drinking and the occurrence of addiction.[22]

Ullman reports that the addiction process often begins with the first drink if the appropriate conditions prevail. On this basis, he hypothesized that "the conditions associated with the addictive drinker's first drink ought to occur relatively frequently in any population having a high rate of alcoholism."[23] In studies of alcoholics and ethnic groups with varying rates of alcoholism,[24] he found a number of results supporting his hypothesis.

Jellinek[25] theorizes that in societies proscribing large daily intakes of alcohol, only those persons with high psychological vulnerability suffer the risk of addiction. In societies accepting large daily amounts of alcohol, a small psychological vulnerability will suffice for exposure to the risk of addiction. The rate of alcoholism in a society is thus determined by the interaction of two factors: the degree of psychological vulnerability of the members and the amount of alcohol intake socially acceptable in that society.

THE SPECIFIC-CULTURES ORIENTATION

Although there is material available on drinking and alcoholism in many countries and cultures, we confine our analysis to the United States and Canada and to a comparison of Italy and

France.[26]

Alcoholism in the United States and Canada

Formulations Emphasizing Drinking Attitudes,
Drinking Norms, or Drinking Groups

One of the most obvious paths taken in the United States in an attempt to explain alcoholism is one that emphasizes social factors that influence drinking.[27] Myerson[28] notes the conflicting social attitudes about alcohol in the United States. Alcohol has been extolled in song and incorporated into the customs of many groups as the basis of good fellowship and social unity. The use of alcoholic beverages accompanies both celebration and sorrow. Alcoholic beverages are used to drown mental ills; they are, at the same time, the chief "social solvent" of everyday life in America. Ranged against this hedonistic attitude is a completely opposite one. Generally, those persons fiercely denouncing alcohol are puritanical and they believe in the sober activities, especially work, duty, and religion. They easily find scientific support for their perspective, since alcohol dulls the reflexes and curtails physical and mental performance. Alcohol is seen as a destroyer of personal achievement and dignity. According to Myerson, it is difficult for stable attitudes to develop in this atmosphere, and therefore control over drinking becomes difficult. When drinking occurs, it tends to take place in a hedonistic atmosphere. Drinking in such an ambivalent cultural situation very easily leads to alcoholism.

Trice[29] mentions ambivalence in his formulations but takes into account other factors. His discussion is, in part, a general summary of much that has been written about alcoholism in the United States. He states that alcoholism in America is a mixture of the following chief factors:[30] (1) prone personalities, who drink regularly in (2) drinking groups that reflect the functional value of alcohol in a complex society, but which exercise (3) widely varying norms about what is improper (or deviant) drinking— a social ambivalence. As a result there are (4) weak social controls, since a deviant drinker in one group can easily move to a new set of drinking companions more tolerant of excessive drinking. Finally, cultural values stressing the importance of self-control justify (5) a pattern of segregation of those who frequently become intoxicated. An explanation of each factor follows.

1. Cultural values play an important role in producing an alcoholism-prone personality. American culture stresses the sanctity of the individual and his independence as a free, responsible agent. On the other hand, parents (especially in the middle class) tend to encourage strong dependency in their children. These two situations result in an independence-dependency conflict that is often dealt with by the use of alcohol. Personality predispositions, however, are insufficient to explain alcoholism. They must be linked with influences that press the latent predispositions toward actual addiction.[31]

2. There are a multitude of formal and informal groups in which alcohol is used frequently in a casual manner. Alcohol functions by helping the individual to find relaxation in a complex world. The predisposed person in such a group might come to see alcohol as a readily available tool to deal with his problems.

3. and 4. In a heterogeneous country, there is little consensus about the propriety or impropriety of many aspects of drinking behavior. With this lack of consensus, social control over drinking is weak. Heterogeneity of tolerance levels about drinking provides new drinking groups for the person who exceeds his current group's drinking norms. When the prealcoholic increases his drinking to deal with his original problem (and those brought on by drinking itself), his current drinking group applies sanctions. However, the drinker is not compelled to conform, because he can find another group which will both satisfy his social needs and tolerate his drinking excesses.

5. The drinker's excesses finally become intolerable to even the most tolerant "normal" or nondeviant groups. Then the broad cultural value of self-reliance and self-control justifies a segregation which frees him even further from effective controls over his drinking.[32] This exclusion gives the alcoholic a deviant role within stigmatized groups (e.g. skidrow) and inadvertently encourages him to fulfill the role.

Formulations Emphasizing Social Disorganization, Alienation, or Anomie

In contrast to investigators who concentrate on social factors that influence drinking directly, there are those who focus on the more general negative sociocultural conditions in America to which alcoholism is viewed as a response.

Clinebell[33] claims that one of the significant factors in the etiology of alcoholism is the attempt to satisfy religious needs by a nonreligious means, alcohol. The source of religious needs is existential anxiety. Such anxiety is normal (nonpathological) and arises from the nature of human existence. For example, man is the only animal who knows that he will die, and he must painfully contemplate this inevitable event. Alcoholism is a pseudoreligion, an attempt to deal with existential anxiety. Existential anxiety can affect everyone and, as an end in itself, does not cause alcoholism. It may lead to alcoholism in certain sociocultural conditions, such as those which exist in the United States. Many find it necessary to deal with this anxiety with alcohol, because we live in a period of history when it is not easy to find genuinely religious answers.[34] In many parts of the western world, contemporary religion has lost much of its ability to handle existential anxiety. For many persons, social conditions and institutions exacerbate, or fail to provide answers to, the problems of human existence.[35]

Of course, this anxiety and the social crises affect many who do not become alcoholics. The alcoholic is one who is particularly impaired by the impact of his existential anxiety.[36] He differs from others in that he has a neurotic fear of death and an exaggerated dependency conflict. Because of this condition, he is unable to avail himself of the experiences in adolescence and young adulthood which could enable him to handle his anxiety constructively.[37]

Clinebell's formulations or assumptions based on the need for religion, dependency, and existential anxiety appear vague and visionary to the authorship. The substitution of alcohol for religious needs appears to be a simplistic, if not naive, explanation. All kinds of people have many different kinds of religious needs. And perhaps many people have few, if any, religious needs. We have been living in a secular society for a very long time. Moreover, the testability of these speculations appears impossible. Clinebell's postulates illustrate the wide generalizing methods of some writers who, in attempting to explain too much, explain too little.

Robert Merton[38] has focused on societies in terms of their culturally prescribed aspirations (ends) and their socially structured avenues for realizing these aspirations (means). Of the types of societies that can result from the independent variation of means and ends, Merton is primarily concerned with those in which there is an exceptionally strong emphasis on goals, without a corresponding emphasis on institutionalized means. Contemporary America is seen as a polar example of this type, with its great emphasis on monetary success. Merton outlined five possible modes of adaptation to this cultural disjointedness of means and ends. The alcoholic falls into Merton's category of "retreatist" adaptations, which also includes outcasts, tramps, and drug addicts. Retreatism is "an expedient which arises from continued failure to reach the goal by legitimate measures and an inability to use the illegitimate route because of internalized prohibitions, this process occurring while the supreme value of the success goal has not yet been renounced. The conflict is resolved by abandoning both precipitating elements, the goal and the means."[39]

Cloward[40] has expanded on Merton's framework by taking into account the conditions of access to both legitimate and illegitimate means. He has further specified the circumstances under which various modes of deviant behavior may arise. Merton hypothesized that the retreatist was unable to utilize illegitimate means because of internalized prohibitions. Cloward stipulated that retreatism can arise in another manner. There may be retreatists who are unable to utilize illegitimate means, not because of internalized prohibitions, but because of limited access to such means (e.g. limited chances to learn criminal skills or to be accepted into professional criminal groups). Thus, there may be alcoholics whose condition is related to their failure to attain life goals by both (or either) legitimate and illegitimate means.

The problem with Merton's and with Cloward's retreatism mode of adaptation embracing some alcoholics is obvious. Why do some retreatists utilize alcoholism as a vehicle of adaptation while other retreatists utilize other vehicles? Moreover, another question indicates a broader and perhaps a more fundamental criticism. How can a sociologist directly relate a "means end disjunction" (structural fault) with retreatism (in this case alcoholism), without considering intervening variables, i.e. intervening variables between the links social structure and deviant behavior (e.g. personality variables)? Certainly many people who face structural stress-strain do not resort to retreatism; and when they do, they do not necessarily close on alcoholism.

Kinsey and Phillips[41] investigated the relationship between alcoholism and anomy and noted that anomy might be a predisposing factor or one that develops concomitantly with alcoholism. They studied 81 male and 12 female patients at an alcoholism clinic in Canada. On the basis of a "phases of alcoholism" scale, their subjects were classed as being in either the "early," "middle," or "late" stages of alcoholism. Anomy was measured by use of the McCloskey-Schaar Anomy scale, a scale that deals with the respondent's feeling about the political and social community. It taps psychological conditions caused by discrepancies between socially defined goals and institutionalized means, e.g. "anomie" as defined by Merton.[42]

The early alcoholics had the lowest mean anomy score; the middle alcoholics, the intermediate score; and the late alcoholics, the highest mean anomy score. These relationships were statistically significant.

The authors investigated the possibility that anomy might be more closely related to some other variable than to alcoholism. The other variables tested for were religion, sex, age, marital status, number of years drinking, and number of years the respondent felt his drinking had been a problem. None of these variables were significantly related to anomy scores when phase of alcoholism was held constant. This result indicated that anomy was related to the subject's alcoholism and not to some other factor in their backgrounds which also might be expected to cause anomie.

Although Kinsey and Phillips were unable to give a conclusive answer to the question of whether anomie is a predisposing or concomitantly developing factor in alcoholism, the strong association between stage of alcoholism and anomy lends more credence to a concomitantly developing hypothesis (or to one positing a mutual feedback between the two).[43]

The authors think that any theory of alcoholism based on the construct anomie is shaky, for several reasons. First, the term is imprecise, in that it has been defined in various ways throughout the literature. Even when operationally defined, it has been hard to test for. As generally used, the construct seems to imply that once upon a time (halcyon days), the degree of anomie was much less than it is now. This is unsupported (historically), for man has never lived anywhere in "certitude." There has been no society yet where harmony exists among the culture goals (the wants or aspirations that men are taught by their culture); the norms prescribing the means that men may legitimately employ in the pursuit of these goals; and the actual distribution of facilities and opportunities for achieving the culture goals in a manner compatible with the norms. Interaction among these variables, according to Merton, determines the distribution of socially structured strain. If this be the case, structural strain is perennial. How does one measure it?

The straight line argument of many sociologists from anomie to deviant behavior makes little sense. Even accepting the anomie thesis, there must be intervening variables between such a condition and deviant behavior of whatever type. The overwhelming number of people, in whatever cultural milieu in which they might grow up, are not secondary deviants, i.e. their lives are not organized around deviant practices and groups.

Problem Drinking in the United States

This section is exclusively concerned with Don Cahalan's survey which utilizes several sociological and social-psychological variables. He devised a "current problems score" from combining the results on the eleven specific types of problems (see definition of drinking problems in the Introduction), with the individual problems being scored differently according to their presumed severity and the number of experiences within a problem area.[44] Fifteen percent of the men and 4 percent of the women (9% of the total sample) had a current problems score of 7 points or more. This 7-point level of problem-drinking score was used as the primary dependent variable in most of the analyses of the correlates of problem drinking. The prevalence of the 11 specific types of problems was measured in terms of their occurrence within a three-year period (1964-1967). Fifty-seven percent of the men and 79 percent of the women reported that they had not experienced any of the 11 types of drinking problems during the three-year period.[45]

Findings on Independent Variables

Cahalan disclosed that the major drinking related problems for men were frequent intoxication, symptomatic drinking behavior (i.e. "symptomatic" of possible addiction), problems with spouse or relatives, and psychological dependencey upon alcohol. Female interviewees responded differently in that none of the specific problems showed a "high rate" for them in excess of the 4 percent for health problems. The major problem reported by women was "that a physician had advised them to reduce their drinking for health reasons."

Cahalan discovered that there were differences in the types of drinking problems in various subgroups according to sex, age, socioeconomic status, urbanization, and ethnoreligious background. There was a higher rate of problem drinking among men than among women. The peak of prevalence for almost all types of drinking problems was among men in their twenties, rather than in older age groups. On the other hand, relatively few women in their twenties had drinking problems; problem drinking among women was concentrated among those in their thirties and forties. The sex differences in drinking are explained by the likelihood that men generally get introduced to heavier drinking by other men when they are young; women get involved in heavier drinking later in life, through the influence of husbands or men friends. A larger proportion of persons under 50 have drinking problems than do older persons. Drinking problems among men taper off sharply after age 50, indicating a "maturing out" process. Very few women have drinking problems after age 50. There was a greater (percentage-wise) "maturing out" of drinking problems among upper-status men after they reached 50 compared to lower-status men; therefore, the lower-status man in his fifties or sixties is probably contributing more than his share of the more serious types of drinking problems. For all ages, the frequency of problem drinking was higher among lower-status men than among higher-status men, even when all other variables were held constant. Lower-status women had much higher percentages of nondrinkers than upper-status women; however, if the tabulations had eliminated the nondrinkers, the ratio of problem drinkers among drinkers would have been higher for lower-status women.[46]

Higher proportions of heavy drinkers were found more frequently in larger cities than in smaller cities, small towns, or rural areas. The highest rate of having both interpersonal problems and implicative drinking behavior was in the group of younger men (in their 20's) of lower socioeconomic status. The lowest rate was in the group of older men of higher status in the small and medium-sized towns. The Irish Catholics, Latin Americans or Caribbeans, and Negroes showed the highest rate of social-consequence drinking problems. Jews had minimal drinking-problem rates.[47]

Multivariate Analysis of Four Independent Variables

Two separate multivariate analysis processes were conducted, using four variables in combination to predict problem drinking: sex, age, index of social position, and size of city. Ethnocultural origin was not used, because the numbers in some subgroups were too small for an analysis. A stepwise multiple regression technique showed that sex was the single most effective predictor of current drinking problems score, followed by age, city size, and index of social position. The cumulative multiple regression "R" was 0.27 (when squared, explains 7% of the aggregate variance on the current problems score). This interaction analysis showed that the highest proportion of persons with a "high" problem drinking score (35%) was for men of lower socioeconomic satus, under 60 years of age, and living in cities of more than 50,000. Cahalan interpreted these differences as a consequence of the differences in acting-out tendencies found among men in contrast to women, among younger, lower-status men (especially in the more abrasive and alienated larger cities), and among ethnoreligious groups which vary in their styles of expressing tensions and aggressive tendencies. Cahalan concluded on the basis of this analysis that we can make a "better-than-chance" prediction of problem drinking on the basis of these four demographic variables: sex, age, city size, and index of social position.[48]

The Social-psychological Intervening Variables

Cahalan reasoned that a considerable amount of additional variance in problem drinking could be explained by social-psychological intervening variables, i.e. variables that intervene between the independent demographic variables (sex, age, social status, and urbanization) and the rate of problem drinking. Independent variables generally precede the criterion to be predicted (in this case problem drinking) and intervening variables (in this case social-psychological variables). Drawing heavily on Richard Jessor's[49] model in the Tri-Ethnic Project, and Merton's[50] and some of Cloward and Ohlin's sociological concepts, Cahalan developed a social-psychological model to predict problem drinking.[51]

Six social-psychological molar intervening variables were developed out of combinations of 150 items which were applied to the same respondents in both the 1964-1965 and 1967 interviews.[52] The rationale for each of these variables and a summary of their content follows.

1. *Attitude toward drinking.* Cahalan found that highly favorable attitudes toward drinking are strongly correlated with problem drinking. Individuals acquire habits through reinforcement of their behavior, which means, in this case, that favorable attitudes toward drinking are acquired because drinking is rewarding to the individual. Cahalan views attitudes as dynamic forces that cause behavior. He found that attitudes are more important in the development of habits of drinking than drinking is important in the development of attitudes toward drinking. The items comprising this variable included the following: a four-item "social drinking" Guttman scale (e.g. "I drink because the people I know drink"); single items on how much the respondent would miss drinking if he had to give it up; the opinion that "Drinking does more good than harm"; the opinion that "Good things can be said about drinking"; the interviewee's selection of an above-average number of drinks as appropriate for his drinking; the interviewee's agreeing that "I enjoy getting drunk once in a while."

2. *Environmental suport for heavy drinking.* One learns drinking behavior from others. Significant others teach us how and when and how much to drink. Significant others also reinforce drinking

behavior (positively or negatively) by their example and by their attitudes toward drinking. Heavy drinking is an acquired taste that is taught by others. Those exposed to heavy drinking and to the permissiveness on the part of associates toward heavy drinking will be more likely than others to become problem drinkers. Questions making up this molar variable included 21 items. Two sets of questions comprise the main elements of this variable: first, four items which ask the interviewee whether he knew, or could guess, whether four of his significant others (father, mother, spouse, and another important person in his life from without his household) ever had drunk as many as four drinks at any one time. The second series of items requested the respondent to guess what would be the largest number of drinks that these significant others would think apropriate for him to drink at any one time.

3. *Impulsivity and nonconformity.* Since heavy drinking is deprecated by society, the individual's persistent indulgence in heavy drinking indicates that he is either impulsive and short-term-oriented or that he is a deliberate nonconformist (unless he is successful in ordering his environment so that it consists of persons who are tolerant of heavy drinking). Those who are impulsive or rebellious, or who have flexible moral codes would be expected to drink more heavily than others, either as a shortcut toward goals (pleasure or to escape from unpleasant reality) or as an expression of defiance. In this study, several sets and items were combined to form this molar variable: a 4-item religious fundamentalism Guttman scale; a 4-item impulsivity Guttman scale; a 7-item impulsivity scale from an earlier California study; a 2-item anger score; an 11-item internal-external control scale; and a 12-item attitudes-toward-deviance scale.

4. *Alienation and maladjustment.* Cahalan reasoned that those scoring high on this scale would be more likely than others to adopt the use of alcohol to relieve tensions, anxieties, and fears of failure. Several subscales were utilized to make up this variable: two neuropsychiatric complaints scales; a nonhelpfulness score (how much one could count on people in time of trouble); an irritability index, measuring the extent to which the respondent feels irritated by his environment; and single items on worrying about getting ahead, desire for a different occupation, and ratings

of one's childhood and present level of happiness.

5. *Unfavorable expectations.* Cahalan expected that those who feel they have (or can achieve) access to their expectations are less likely than others to drink excessively. This score was made up from 13 items, 10 of which constituted an expectation score related to prospects regarding future relationships with family and friends. The remaining items deal with general expectations regarding the meaning of life goals.

6. *Looseness of social controls.* Cahalan hypothesized that the greater the number of close primary-group ties a person has, the more likely he will live up to the norm of moderation. Five items, including the interviewee's marital status, presence or absence of close friends from the neighborhood and primary-group ties, were utilized.

A Multiple Correlation of the Six Social-psychological Variables

A multiple correlation of the six preceding social-psychological variables, measured as Stage I against current problems score (for problems reported at Stage II as having occurred between the years 1964-1967), revealed a resultant multiple correlation of 0.28 between all six variables and problem drinking (0.31 for men and 0.22 for women).[53] A multivariate analysis of these six variables (social-psychological, "risk scores") against current problems score (when the six variables consisted of items which were applied at either Stage I or Stage II and combined) yielded a multiple correlation of 0.38 for the total sample. The first four variables accounted for virtually all of the variance in the multiple correlation. The latter two variables (unfavorable expectations and looseness of social controls) had negligible correlations with the current problems score, after taking into account the partial correlations of the first four variables. These two variables, however, had a significant correlation with problem drinking, when considered alone.

The greatest share of the multiple correlation between the six variables and problem drinking was accounted for by one variable, attitude toward drinking, e.g. would the respondent miss drinking if he had to give it up, did he agree that drinking does more good than harm, did he feel good things could be said about drinking; and did he feel that drinking was associated with sociability. Cahalan claims that this finding shows that *attitudes* cause behavior.[54]

A Multivariate Analysis of the Combined Variables

Next, Cahalan combined the six social-psychological variables and the demographic variables (sex, age, socioeconomic status, and urbanization) and correlated them with current problems scores.[55] This was accomplished by a multivariate analysis of background variables and social-psychological risk scores against current problems scores. The multiple regression for the four independent variables combined with the six intervening variables was 0.42. Attitude toward drinking, alienation and maladjustment, sex, and index of social position were the four leading variables. Very little additional variance was explained by the remaining variables. Cahalan thinks that the predictive utility of the combined independent and intervening variables was underestimated for various reasons, including problems with the multiple regression technique as utilized for his type of skewed distribution sample.

The AID Analysis

Finally, Cahalan analyzed the predictive power of the 10 combined independent and intervening variables with the AID (Automatic Interaction Detector) procedure. The AID procedure provided information which assisted in delineating significant subgroups of high and low rates of problem drinkers in ways not provided by multiple regression. By the AID method, a group of 60 persons was isolated, 63 percent of whom had a high (7 plus) current problems score. This group was comprised of men with highly favorable attitudes toward drinking who were also high on two other variables: impulsivity and nonconformity, and environmental support for heavy drinking.

The AID multivariate analysis[56] revealed that the variable of *attitude toward drinking* was the strongest predictor on problem drinking. The second most powerful predicting variable was *environmental support for heavy drinking*. The powerful predictability of these two variables is explained in part by the fact that both are specific to alcohol, while stresses related to the other four variables may be coped with in many ways other than by drinking. The four other psychological variables were found to interact with attitudes and environments in being associated with a high level of problem drinking among specific subgroups. AID analysis selected out those men with extremely low rates of problem drinking: men with an unfavorable attitude toward drinking, who were also low in impulsivity and nonconformity, and who were also not highly maladjusted, or who were over fifty. Interactions for women revealed that the highest scores were found among those who had a very favorable attitude toward drinking and also had either higher alienation and maladjustment scores, or lived in large cities. Cahalan concluded that his analysis demonstrated the principle that interactions between psychological and demographic factors can be important in predicting problem drinking. The chief single variable in predicting problem score is "the person's attitude toward the usefulness and importance of alcohol in his life." This means, according to Cahalan, that we should concentrate upon the origin of the "exact characteristics and causal sequence of the development of attitudes about drinking as such attitudes relate to the onset and changes in the severity of problem drinking over a period of time."

Changes Over Time

Stages I and II included enough questions to enable Cahalan to measure change between the two stages, in reference to two elements in drinking problems: psychological dependence and frequent intoxication—which were combined into an index of problem drinking. The index revealed that 22 percent of the men and 9 percent of the women had changed their problem-drinking status appreciably within the short period of three years. This finding shows that more people go into and out of the problem-drinking category than was once thought. Moreover, a high rate of change in drinking behavior as measured on a retrospective basis was borne out by separate measurements in the 1964-1965 and 1967 surveys. During this short period, 15 percent of the total persons interviewed had moved into, or out of, the group reporting drinking five or more drinks per occasion at least some of the time.[57]

An above-average proportion of the respondents with a higher level of problem drinking began drinking earlier in life than those with lower levels of problem drinking. The reasons given for drinking less or more emphasized environmental and role factors rather than psychological factors. Tensions associated with more drinking, feelings of guilt associated with less drinking, and ethical, moral, religious, or guilt-related reasons for cutting down on drinking were reported infrequently. This disclosure, along with Cahalan's failure to find a strong correlation between problem drinking and psychological maladjustment, does not support the theoretical relevance of a clinical model for the study of alcoholism.[58]

Cahalan's Conclusions

Cahalan certifies that sociological and psychological variables are important in the development of problem drinking. The sociological variables (external environmental) determine whether the individual is encouraged or permitted to drink heavily; the psychological variables operate to help cause or maintain a level of drinking which may be above that normally encouraged or permitted for the person's social environment. Excluding the attitude-toward-drinking variable, the sociological variables played a much more significant role among the correlates of problem drinking than did the psychological variables. The variable of alienation and maladjustment played a more important role for women than did the sociological variables. Cahalan hypothesizes that the general disapprobation of heavy drinking for women explains the finding that women with drinking problems have higher scores on psychological maladjustment than men with drinking problems. He speculates that it takes more psychological pressures for women than it does for men to persist in problem drinking, in the face of society's condemnation of heavy drinking for women. On the other hand, Cahalan emphasizes that his overall findings failed to demonstrate a strong correlation between problem drinking and psychological maladjustment.

Cahalan's Theoretical Paradigms

Cahalan, on the basis of his social-psychological orientation and his findings in *Problem Drinkers,* offers two interesting theoretical paradigms to explain (1) the process of becoming a problem drinker and (2) the process of becoming psychologically dependent on heavy amounts of alcohol.[59]

1. The process of becoming a problem drinker involves the following steps: first, the culture must permit drinking and heavy drinking, at least occasionally, before the individual can place himself into a position to become a problem drinker. Second, given a culture permissive of heavy drinking under at least some circumstances, the individual may become a heavy drinker under conditions accorded him, specific to his sex, age, ethnic, and social-class roles. Third, an individual may be suddenly defined a problem drinker because of a change in his cultural environment, e.g. he may move, marry, or "age out" of an environment permissive of heavy drinking into a nonpermissive environment. His drinking habits remain the same in the two cultural environments, but the definitions of problem drinking change. Fourth, given that the individual forms a habit of heavy drinking which he finds to be maladaptive in his environment, he may continue as a heavy drinker under`one or more of the following conditions: If his social adaptability is impaired by his impulsivity toward resorting to short-term gratifications, he may continue to drink heavily even in the face of social condemnation; if the gradient between his usual subjective conditions when not drinking and the way he feels when drinking is steep (stemming from either an alienated, neurotic or depressive personality or living under conditions of subjective deprivation), he may persist in heavy drinking because of the powerful reinforcements obtained from drinking and the dearth of rewards for not drinking. Fifth, assuming that the individual's heavy drinking has caused problems for him in his environment, he may continue heavy drinking if that environment is rendered more permissive, e.g. he may become separated from significant others, such as his family, work associates, and cultural peers. On the other hand, he may stop heavy drinkng if the environment continues to exert counterpressure through significant others. Consequently, individuals with severe drinking problems are more likely to shed such problems if they maintain social ties which support them and do not reinforce the problem behavior.

2. Operant conditioning appears to be of prime importance in the development of dependence on heavy amounts of alcohol. Cahalan thinks that it is likely that most problem drinkers become conditioned at a very early age to expect that alcohol can do great things for them. The regular drinker begins to get psychologically addicted (loses control over drinking) when the positive reinforcement of the alcoholic effects (euphoria) is consistently further enhanced by contrast with the negative effect of the physiological and psychological letdown, or hangover, which develops when the alcohol's positive effects wear off. The individual learns that the aversive effect of the hangover can be forestalled by continued drinking. This knowledge may explain the compulsive behavior of the addictive drinker. Alcohol is a drug which not only helps to temporarily erase anxiety, malaise, and self-doubt, but it also erases simultaneously the memory of past self-resolution to limit drinking and the memory of past hangovers. Thus, we see that alcohol as an addicting drug fits the operant conditioning mechanism.

Comments on Cahalan's Problem Drinkers

The national survey on which *Problem Drinkers* is based is far and away the most significant work of its type to date (in both research design and analysis of data). Though Cahalan is primarily interested in problem drinkers rather than alcoholics, we hope that the third stage (Stage III) will indicate a demarcation between problem drinkers who are alcoholics and those who are not. This distinction must be made eventually, and Cahalan and his associates are in a position to do just this. Perhaps this delineation calls for an interdisciplinary approach, including the help of scholars who adhere to the medical model of alcoholism. The findings in Stage III, yet to come, will undoubtedly augment and enhance the very significant findings disclosed in "problem drinkers." As Cahalan acknowledges, it is difficult to determine in survey research, "Which comes first, the drinking or the problem?" Certainly the results of Stage III will help solve this problem. Hopefully, many questions in Stage III will be directed toward two problems: (1) the origin of attitudes and values that influence drinking behavior, and (2) how attitudes and values influence drinking behavior, and how changes in attitudes and values influence changes in drinking behavior. Cahalan's operant conditioning approach to the etiology of alcoholism (or more specifically, problem drinking) appears plausible. Again, we hope the results of Stage III will shed more light on the efficacy of the operant conditioning model. Perhaps more questions should be directed to the parents, relatives, and significant others of problem drinkers about their drinking habits in Stage III. Lastly, and probably not importantly, we think the criterion of "four drinks" by significant others in the presence of the respondent is a little shy of comprising environmental support for heavy drinking.

ALCOHOLISM IN FRANCE AND ITALY

France and Italy are two nations with many things in common, including the widespread use of wine; however, they differ markedly in rates of alcoholism. Keller and Efron[60] estimated the rate of alcoholism (with and without complications) to be 2,850 per 100,000 in France and only 500 per 100,000 in Italy. This great difference in rate of alcoholism despite many similarities invites comparative investigations.

Sadoun, Lolli, and Silverman[61] compared and analyzed drinking patterns in the two countries and found the following:[62]

1. Although France is reputedly the nation in which wine is used most commonly by all segments of the population, it is actually imbibed by a larger proportion of the population in Italy.

2. The quantities of wine consumed with meals in France and in Italy are approximately the same, but the use of wine between meals is substantially greater in France than it is in Italy.

3. Alcoholic beverages other than wine (cider, beer, aperitifs, and especially distilled spirits) are used more frequently in France than they are in Italy. It is not suggested that these other beverages are more or less toxic than wine, but the evidence is that some of them, particularly distilled spirits and aperitifs, are more likely to be consumed on an empty stomach in France.

4. Early childhood exposure to alcohol is viewed differently in the two nations. Among the French, rigid parental attitudes, either strongly in favor of or against childhood use prevail. Italian parents, in contrast, regard this matter unemotionally, as a normal and relatively unimportant part of a child's development.

5. The inebriating or otherwise harmful potential of alcoholic beverages is made more clearly apparent to the Italians, who set much lower "safe limits" than do the French for the amount of wine which may be taken without harm by adults or by children.

6. Among the French, there is a wide acceptance of the notion that drinking, particularly copious drinking, is in some way associated with virility. Among Italians no such concept is noted.

7. Among the French, there is wide social acceptance of intoxication as fashionable, humorous, or at least tolerable. Among Italians, intoxication is consistently regarded as a personal and family disgrace.

One of the differences thought to be among the most important in terms of rates of alcoholism is the greater traditional concomitance of eating and drinking in Italy. In Italian customs, wine is viewed as a food and is consumed almost exclusively with meals. This is not the case in France. Laboratory research has shown that the effects on the nervous system are more marked when the subject has an empty, rather than full, stomach. The physiological protection provided by the dietary use of alcohol (the drinking of wine with meals) has evidently been known and understood in Italy for many centuries. It has been less appreciated in modern France, and this may be one factor largely responsible for the remarkable difference between the alcoholism rates of the two countries.[63]

Two other factors were considered important in understanding the difference in rates of alcoholism between France and Italy. First, the high degree of immunity to alcoholic excesses demonstrated by Italians may be related to the features of their introduction to alcohol, which consistently takes place in the home with meals, and within the framework of the family. In such circumstances, Italian children might adopt alcoholic beverages from the outset as a foodstuff in liquid form, to be consumed in association with solid food, and in an environment marked by mutual responsibility and affection of the family.[64] Secondly, it was postulated that alcoholics have often exhibited premonitory difficulties during adolescence. In France this tendency is marked by leisure time activities centered around alcohol; drinking away from the moderating influences of the family; drinking apart from meals;

attributing characteristics of virility or manhood to drinking, and especially to heavy drinking; and by repeated episodes of intoxication or immoderate drinking.[65]

Jellinek[66] also compared the results of studies of French and Italian drinking behavior. He reasoned that the lower rates of alcoholism in Italy might, in part, be traced to the lower social pressure for drinking and less tolerance of drunkenness. In Italy polite refusal of a drink is met with indifference, while in France such a refusal might elicit contempt and disapproval. In France, drinking is a must, while in Italy, it is a matter of choice. Jellinek considered more important the fact that in France there is a wider acceptance of relatively great daily consumption of alcoholic beverages than in Italy. This was also one of the points emphasized by Sadoun, Lolli, and Silverman above. They reported[67] that the "average" Frenchman consumed more alcohol during the course of a day, and set the "safe" limit of wine which could be drunk daily by a heavy laborer at 1800 cc. The safe limit set by the "average" Italian was only 1400 cc. Given this greater acceptance of heavy daily intake, a Frenchman with psychic difficulties is more likely to become an alcoholic than an Italian with comparable psychic difficulties.

THE SUBSTRUCTURAL ORIENTATION

The two social institutions most frequently discussed as playing an important part in the causation of alcoholism are religion and the family.[68] Other sociological variables frequently analyzed in their relationship to alcohol are social class, ethnicity, sex, age and urbanization.

Drinking and Alcoholism in the Major American Religious Groups

Jewish Drinking and Alcoholism

1. *Jewish drinking patterns.* The Jewish group is the American religious group whose drinking behavior has been the most thoroughly investigated. Three national drinking studies placed the percentage of drinkers in the adult Jewish-American group at 87 percent,[69] 90 percent,[70] and 92 percent.[71] In all there studies, this was the highest percentage of any major religious group. In

their study of American college students, Straus and Bacon[72] found that heavy drinking was not as frequent among Jewish students as among Catholic and Protestant students. Cahalan, Cisin, and Crossley[73] estimated that 10 percent of all Jewish persons in the United States were heavy drinkers. This was below the national rate of 12 percent. However, their breakdown by religion and sex revealed that 25 percent of Jewish males were heavy drinkers. This was higher than the national rate for males of 21 percent. The percentage of Jewish women who were heavy drinkers was zero. These authors concluded that the aggregate (combined sex) rate masked the fact of a relatively high rate of heavy drinking among Jewish men offset by an extremely low rate of heavy drinking among Jewish women.[74] However, they recommend caution in interpreting these findings because of their small sample (77 Jewish respondents). In Cahalan and Cisin's analysis,[75] 8 percent of Jewish drinkers were classified as "heavy escape drinkers" in comparison to the national rate of 9 percent. However, given a Jewish drinking rate of 92 percent, this figures out to be a relatively high rate of heavy escape drinking for all Jews.

Mulford's national survey results[76] showed that the rate of heavy drinking among all Jewish *drinkers,* 7 percent, was below the national rate of 11 percent. However, given a large percent of drinkers among all persons in the Jewish Group (90%), this constitutes a rate of heavy drinking among all Jews of over 6 percent. Skolnick[77] reanalyzed some of the data from Strauss and Bacon's college drinking study and found that 55 percent of Jewish student drinkers reported never being intoxicated, as compared to about 19 percent of drinkers of other religious groups. The Jewish students also reported the lowest percentage of drinkers having been intoxicated more than five times. Cahalan[78] found that the Jewish group in his national study of problem drinkers contained very few problem drinkers, even though it included a very high proportion of occasional drinkers.

2. *Alcoholism among Jews.* Bailey, Haberman, and Alksne[79] placed the rate of alcoholism among Jews in a New York City borough area at 2 per 1,000, the lowest rate of any group. Roberts and Myers,[80] in their study of all New Haven, Massachusetts, residents undergoing psychiatric treatment, found no cases

of alcoholism among 223 Jewish patients. The Jewish population accounted for 9.5 percent of the total population of the area, yet accounted for zero percent of the alcohol and drug addiction cases. Snyder reviewed the literature on Jewish drinking patterns and concluded:[81] "In terms of percentages, there are probably more users of alcoholic beverages in the Jewish group than in any other major religio-ethnic group in America. Yet, as has been shown repeatedly, both in this country and abroad, rates of alcoholism and other drinking pathologies for Jews are very low."

3. *Theoretical considerations.* The interesting question is, of course, how can it be that so many Jews drink (a fairly high percentage of Jewish males *may* be heavy drinkers) and yet their rate of alcoholism is quite low (in both absolute and relative terms)? There have been a number of theoretical attempts to explain Jewish drinking patterns. Noting the solidarity of the Jewish group, it has been suggested by Durkheim that this solidarity insulates the Jew from the forces of alienation of anomie that are conducive to alcoholism. Others have attempted to relate Jewish sobriety to Jewish values on education, self-control, and rational behavior.[82]

Bales reported[83] that rates of alcoholism are low among Jews because they have a "ritual" attitude toward drinking. The frequent ritual use of wine prompts the Jew to reject the idea of using alcoholic beverages for personal reasons. This ritual attitude leads to an anxiety about drinking for personal reasons, which militates against the use of alcohol for purposes conducive to alcoholism. Drunkenness is a profanity and a perversion of the sacred use of wine. Hence the idea of drinking to intoxication for some individualistic or selfish reason arouses a counter anxiety so strong that few Jews ever become alcoholics.

Glad[84] studied 49 Jewish senior high school students and compared them with two control groups (all matched on age, I.Q., and socioeconomic status). He tested a number of possible explanations for low rates of inebriety among Jews. One of these was the "group protection" hypothesis, which states that the low Jewish rate of inebriety results from the need for Jews to conform to the best standards of society in order to avoid censure and blame. This was not supported by his data.[85] He also evaluated a "parental permissiveness" hypothesis, i.e. a permissive attitude on the part of parents toward children's drinking contributes to a low rate of inebriety; and that a restrictive parental attitude contributes to a high rate of inebriety. He claims that his data partially supports this hypothesis. Glad found that Jewish subjects differed from the two control groups in being significantly younger (in average age) when they first felt that they had parental permission to drink, and in tending to drink in more casual, matter-of-fact, and parentally acceptable situations.[86]

Glad also reported that Jewish students looked upon drinking as socially practical (not only ritualistically as Bales contended) and concluded that the low rates of alcoholism among Jews could be attributed to their use of alcohol for "instrumental" reasons rather than for personal or "affective" reasons.[87] The Jewish students were found to use alcoholic beverages for reasons that were instrumental in religious or social situations and not for results thought to be related to alcoholism.

Snyder,[88] from his extensive analysis of the literature and from his study of 73 Jewish males, drew a number of conclusions. He reports that most Jews perceive moderate drinking and sobriety as "Jewish virtues" and intoxication and hedonistic drinking as "Gentile vices." It is not so much fear of the out-group which motivates the Jew to moderation as it is the Jewish group itself which pressures the individual into conformity to Jewish norms and customs. The effectiveness of the Jewish group's control over its memberships' drinking is directly related to the solidarity within the group. Solidarity is heightened when tensions between Jews and Gentiles rise. Influences on the individual from outside are generally conducive to greater heavy drinking. As in-group relationships are weakened and out-group contacts are increased, heavy drinking among Jews increases. Synder also maintains that the "ritual" attitude toward drinking (as suggested by Bales) is also an important factor in the regulation of Jewish drinking; through the ceremonial use of beverage alcohol, religious Jews learn how to drink in a controlled manner. Through constant reference to the hedonism of outsiders in association with a broader pattern of religious and ethnocentric ideas and sentiments, Jews also learn how not to drink.[89]

Cahalan's unpublished data[90] report group scores on social-psychological variables (hypothesized to be positively related to problem drinking) that demonstrate the effectiveness of Jewish drinking controls. When compared with the mean scores of the total sample, the Jewish group scored slightly higher on positive attitudes toward drinking and scored higher on exposure to a permissive drinking environment. Jews also had one of the highest overall mean scores for all six social-psychological variables thought to be conducive to alcoholism. Whatever it is that "insulates" the Jewish drinker from problem drinking seems to be extremely effective. Cahalan found that Jews have a very low problem-drinking rate.

The authors think that it is often overlooked that Jews do not constitute a homogeneous group. We need additional comparative drinking studies among Orthodox, Conservative, and Reform Jews (from various countries) and perhaps between Eastern and Western Jews. Further concentration is also required on "whatever it is" (defined in testable form) in Jewish culture that precludes heavy problem drinking and alcoholism. We must also take into account the fact that there has been a considerable amount of intermarriage between Jews and other religious groups. Perhaps Jewish mixed-marriage drinking rates should be compared with Jewish and non-Jewish drinking rates.

Keller[91] recently noted the relative infrequency of drunkenness and alcoholism among the Jews as reported from several countries. He recognizes that social scientists attribute these Jewish drinking patterns "to the religious-cultural integration of drinking by the Jews with their important ceremonies and rites of passage" (rather than to genetic factors). He notes, however, that there has been no attempt to account for the historical frequency of drunkenness among the ancestors of the Jews during the age of the Prophets, nor for the time and manner of its disappearance. Keller suggests from an examination of post-Biblical sources that the transition occurred in the 200-year period after the return from the first (Babylonian) exile. At this time, the competing Canaanite gods, with their orgiastic-drunken festivals, were successfully banished, the Bible was formally adopted by the Jews, their established local synagogues were adopted as places of popular education and worship, and the ritual use of drink was fixed and sanctified. Keller reports that by the Middle Ages in Europe neither drunkenness nor the fear of it survived within Jewish communities.

Protestant Drinking and Alcoholism

SOME PRELIMINARY STUDIES AND HYPOTHESIS. In contrast to the situation with American Jews and Catholics (these two groups are not completely homogeneous), the term *protestant* covers a much more heterogenous collection of subgroups, with widely varying official and unofficial stands on drinking. Materials and data on Protestant drinking practices in the literature are frequently not specific to any one denominational group. Moreover, the preciseness and objectivity of research design and findings about alcohol are quite uneven. We begin with the more general studies and hypotheses and move to the specific.

Skolnick hypothesized that there was a positive relationship between abstinence teachings and the (conjectured) intemperance among drinkers from abstinence groups. He utilized data from Straus and Bacon's college drinking study and randomly selected around 100 *drinkers* from each of the following religious groups: Jewish, Episcopalian, and Methodist. He also utilized 44 non-church-affiliated persons from abstinent backgrounds (NAAB). The Methodist group was selected because of that church's abstinent stand; the Episcopalian group, because of that church's permissive stand; the Jewish group, because of that group's strong stand against drunkenness, and its ritual incorporation of drinking. The NAAB group was chosen to represent an abstinent group like the Methodists but without religious ties.[92] Skolnick found that Episcopalians had the greatest percentage (31%) of total persons in the heaviest drinking category. The Jewish group had far and away the lowest percentage in the heaviest drinking category, and the two other groups had around 22 percent in this category. The percentage of drinkers "being intoxicated more than five times" was only 15 for the Jews and around 62 for the three other groups. The findings showed that the Methodist and NAAB drinker groups had fewer heavy drinkers than the Episcopalians, yet had just about as many drinkers admitting intoxication more than five times. Skolnick reasoned that a high ratio of intoxication to drinking indicated that drinking is viewed by the user as leading to intoxication; and that if one drinks, he drinks, whether consciously or not, to become intoxicated.[93]

Skolnick also found "troubles due to drinking" least frequently among Jews, intermediate among the Episcopalians, and most frequently among the Methodists and NAAB's. This tenuous finding represents the only positive finding supporting Skolnick's thesis.

Skolnick noted that Straus and Bacon[94] found a relatively high incidence of heavy drinking and intoxication among Mormon students (who also come from an abstinence background). Straus and Bacon viewed these high rates as a reaction against the prohibitive pressures of the Mormon church. They theorized, in short, that Mormon student drinking was a type of rebellion. Straus and Bacon concluded that drinking by members of abstinence groups is not controlled by any drinking norms; therefore, alcoholism is likely among such a membership. If drinking behavior is adopted, variation must be the rule, since there is no norm. Extremes in drinking are likely since the behavior itself represents the rejection of social rules. The models for behavior are either members of other groups or dissident members of their own group. Individual or situational factors cannot be restrained by sociocultural definitions of what is proper for drinking, because such definitions do not exist.[95]

Skolnick claimed that, in contrast to the lack of norms as stipulated by Straus and Bacon, there was a norm. In short, frequent and emotionally charged abstinence teachings foster a norm of "extreme drinking." Drinking is regarded as sinful and harmful. Even nominal use is prohibited. There is, thus, no such thing as moderation. The role model of the user is usually the extreme example, the person who uses alcoholic beverages and suffers consequent degradation. Skolnick conjectured that the more religious the student, the greater the anxiety and guilt he would feel when breaking rules of abstinence. Unfortunately for this line of reasoning, Skolnick found (on the basis of interviews) that most Methodists who drank, whether religious or not, felt little guilt about drinking and perceived the religious injunctions to be a "matter of preaching rather than a matter of practice." Skolnick's use of Mormon abstinence patterns as somewhat analgous to

Methodist and NAAB groups' abstinence patterns (at least for illustrating the abstinence syndrome) is questionable because of the great difference in attitudes toward drinking among Methodists, NAAB groups, and Mormons. The Mormons are much more adamantly opposed to drinking than the other two groups.

Preston shares Skolnick's point of view. In one study he found that high school students in two southern communities from "prohibitionist" religious backgrounds were less likely to be drinkers than others, but, if drinkers, they tended to drink more than students from more "tolerant" backgrounds.[96] Preston thought that this finding demonstrated a relationship between heavy drinking and an ambivalent attitude toward drinking. He claimed also that a prohibitionist religion fosters ambivalent attitudes toward alcohol. The U. S. culture encourages the teenager to drink; if his religion says no, the adolescent drinks and feels guilty about it; consequently, he drinks more to salve his conscience. Furthermore, such drinking must be secretive, which contributes to overconsumption. The teenager from a prohibitionist background must not have any alcohol left over; therefore, he must drink it all before he returns home.[97] These findings appear to be overdrawn and conflict with other findings which follow.

Knupfer et al.[98] offers a similar formulation to Preston, although it is expressed in more general terms. They analyzed "escape drinking" in California among persons who might be expected to be under social pressure to avoid such drinking (e.g. persons belonging to conservative Protestant denominations, such as Methodists and Baptists). In each instance, when heavy drinkers from groups that had cultural sanctions against heavy drinking were compared "on their reasons for drinking" with the reasons given by heavy drinkers from groups without such sanctions, it was found that relatively higher proportions of the groups with "cross-pressures" against heavy drinking were escape drinkers.[99] Knupfer's results were consistent with the "cross-pressures" hypothesis, which states that "those who drink heavily in defiance of group sanctions proscribing such drinking are more likely than other drinkers to drink to escape from personal problems."[100] According to this viewpoint, persons from groups which proscribe drinking tend to have different motives for heavy drinking than do persons from more permissive groups. Drinking by members of "proscriptive" groups is often (supposed to be) for personal or escape reasons, while drinking by members of other groups may be (supposed to be) for matters of convention and socializing. The etiological implications are that given equal amounts of personal (or alcoholism-conducive) problems in two groups, drinkers who are members of the group proscribing drinking (or heavy drinking) are more likely to utilize alcoholic beverages for purposes conducive to alcoholism than drinkers who are members of the group not proscribing alcohol. Drinkers in proscriptive groups should thus have higher rates of problem drinking and alcoholism. It is important to note, however, that the rates of problem drinking or alcoholism for *all* persons (drinkers and nondrinkers) should be *lower* in groups proscribing alcoholic beverages than in those groups not proscribing alcohol, because large numbers of persons in proscribing groups may not drink.

The "Protestant Ethic" is claimed by some writers (in a loose way) to influence the drinking behavior of some Protestant groups. The quality of asceticism in Protestantism is stressed by those adhering to this very etherial construct, "the Protestant Ethic." The essence of the ascetic pattern (according to Max Weber's analysis of asceticism as a typological construct characteristic of certain branches of Protestantism) is hostility toward spontaneous enjoyment of life and what it has to offer; active and purposive control over emotions, with a consideration for the ethical consequences of one's actions; and a lifelong, systematic rational ordering of the moral life, oriented toward, and subordinated to, a supernatural goal.[101]

Thorner[102] claimed that ascetic Protestantism was one of the major thrusts behind prohibition. He pointed out that Jellinek's data on rates of alcoholism in different states[103] showed that these rates were inversely proportional to the percentage of votes against repeal of the 18th Amendment. The five states with anti-repeal majorities (North Carolina, Kansas, Mississippi, Oklahoma, and South Carolina) had the lowest rates of alcoholism eleven years after the referendum.

Cahalan, Cisin, and Crossley[104] hypothesized that those scoring higher on their "Protestant Ethic scale" would be less likely than others to be heavy drinkers because of a greater concern for long-term goals rather than short-term gratifications. They found, however, that Protestant Ethic scores were not highly related to drinking when age, sex, and social position were held constant. They discovered a slight tendency for men with lower scores to be heavy drinkers, while women with higher scores were more likely to be abstainers or infrequent drinkers. On the other hand, a comparison of "heavy" and "heavy-escape" drinkers showed only a slight tendency for those scoring high on the Protestant Ethic scale to fall into the heavy-escape drinker category.[105] These slight data trends may suggest that those who are members of groups bearing the Protestant Ethic are less likely to drink, but more likely to become problem drinkers or alcoholics if they should drink. This is, of course, similar to the hypotheses of Skolnick and Knupfer et al. The evidence is slight and weak.

The utilization of the theoretical construct "The Protestant Ethic" by some researchers in alcoholism is unfortunate from the viewpoint of this authorship. Many scholars have demonstrated that Weber's linkage of Protestantism and capitalism, from the historical as well as the theoretical point of view, is spurious. There never was any meaningful correlation between Protestantism and capitalism. Moreover, many scholars question the validity of the so-called Protestant Ethic.[106] Therefore, the term had an illegitimate birth. Hypothetically admitting the presence of the Protestant Ethic, who is to say that it makes for more asceticism (among Protestants) than is found among some other religious groups in the United States or elsewhere? Many Protestant groups are obviously much less ascetic than, for example, Roman Catholics, for whatever it is worth (and probably very little). Furthermore, should the Protestant Ethic have the ascribed force purported by some, would it not strongly influence the behavior (including drinking behavior) of us all, of individuals in all religious groups?

It is significant to note that some researchers use the Protestant Ethic to explain why some religious groups drink less than other groups, while other researchers use it to explain why memberships in some groups drink to excess. Actually, what seems to be at stake here is the puritan ethic (at one time prevalent among members of various religious groups) currently passé among most Protestants, as well as among many other religious groups. Additionally, historians have well documented the fact that there has always existed a wide gap between religious preachments of whatever kind and behavior (including heavy drinking as well as other deviant behaviors).

A review of the more precise data on Protestant drinking which follows reveals (among other things) probable answers to three important questions: Are drinkers from abstinence-oriented religious groups heavy or heavy-escape drinkers? Are drinkers from abstinence-oriented religious groups heavy or heavy-escape drinkers more frequently than drinkers from nonabstinence religious groups? What religious groups have the highest rate of heavy or heavy-escape drinkers? The answers to these questions will not constitute theoretical formulations, but they might indicate the errors in past theoretical formulations about the relationship between drinking and religion; and they might indicate, if nothing else, directions we should not pursue further in "drinking-religious formulations."

The percentage of Protestants estimated to be users (nonabstainers) of alcoholic beverages was placed at 59% and 63% in 1946[107] and 1963,[108] respectively. In both of these national studies, these rates were lower than those of either Jews or Catholics. In their Iowa study, Mulford and Miller[109] found that only about 14 percent of the presumed alcoholics were classified as members of a specific Protestant denomination; 12 percent of the presumed alcoholics were Protestants without denomination specification. Both of these groups comprised a smaller proportion of the total alcoholics than they did of the total sample; therefore, these groups were under-represented in terms of presumed alcoholics. Roberts and Myers[110] found that Protestants in New Haven accounted for nearly the same percentage of alcohol and drug addiction cases as they did for the total population.

DRINKING PATTERNS OF SPECIFIC PROTESTANT GROUPS. There are many Protestant denominations with widely differing attitudes about drinking and rates of drinking. Cahalan and Cisin[111] found that 91 percent of Episcopalians were drinkers, while only 31 percent of their respondents classed as "other conservative Protestant" were drinkers. Thus, a breakdown into specific denominations is necessary.

The Methodist Church is the largest single religious organization representing the total abstinence position and has been (historically) the most strongly organized and influential of the "temperance" religious groups.[112] Mulford and Miller[113] found in Iowa that 40 percent of Methodists were drinkers; 16 percent of these Methodist drinkers were heavy drinkers. This percentage was higher than that for Lutherans (13%), but lower than that for Catholics (20%) Mulford [114] found that 61 percent of Methodists nationwide were drinkers and that only 5 percent of Methodist drinkers were heavy drinkers. Both percentages were below the national, Lutheran, and Catholic rates. Cahalan, Cisin, and Crossley[115] estimated that 66 percent of persons who were Methodists or of similar denomination were drinkers, and that only 10 percent of these were heavy drinkers. This former figure was below the national rate of 68 percent, and "the heavy drinking rate" was below the national rate of 12 percent. Cahalan and Cisin[116] found that 7 percent of all Methodists and similar denomination drinkers were "heavy-escape" drinkers in comparison to the national rate of 9 percent. The rate of heavy-escape drinking for *all* Methodists was below the national average.

The Baptists are another group that generally frowns upon the use of alcoholic beverages.[117] Mulford[118] found that 48 percent of Baptists were drinkers and that only 9 percent of these drinkers were heavy drinkers. Both figures were below the Catholic and national averages. Cahalan, Cisin, and Crossley[119] found that 47 percent of Baptists were drinkers, and that 7 percent of these were heavy drinkers. Both figures were below the national averages. Cahalan and Cisin[120] reported that 10 percent of Baptist drinkers were heavy-escape drinkers as compared to the national rate of 9 percent. This percentage was also higher than that of Jews (8%) and Episcopalians (6%), who have a percentage of drinkers twice as high. However, the rate of heavy escape drinking for *all* Baptists is very low because of their high percentage (53%) of nondrinkers. Bailey, Haberman, and Alksne[121] reported that *Negro* Baptists had far and away the highest rate of alcoholism (40/1,000) in their New York City area studies.

The Lutherans, a large Protestant denomination, have a more "liberal" or "permissive" view of alcoholic beverages than many other Protestant denominations. In both Mulford's[122] and Cahalan, Cisin, and Crossley's[123] national studies, Lutherans had percentages of "drinkers" and "heavy drinkers" substantially larger than the corresponding rates for Baptists and Methodists. Cahalan and Cisin[124] found that 7 percent of Lutheran drinkers were heavy-escape drinkers as compared to 7 percent of Methodist (and similar denominations) and 10 percent of Baptist drinkers. Given the high percentage of drinkers in the Lutheran group (81%), this points to a higher rate of heavy-escape drinking for *all* Lutherans than that for all Methodists and Baptists.

The Episcopals comprise another religious group that has a permissive attitude toward drinking. The Episcopal Church sanctions moderate drinking, but opposes drunkenness; however, its admonitions relating to alcohol use are not as severe as those of the Methodists and Jews.[125] Cahalan and Cisin[126] found that Episcopalians had a percentage of drinkers (91%) that was exceeded by only one other religious group, the Jews. Thirteen percent of Episcopalian drinkers were heavy drinkers, as compared to the Methodist rate of 15 percent. Only 6 percent of Episcopal drinkers were heavy-escape drinkers as compared to the Methodist and national rates of 9 and 7 percent, respectively. Since Episcopalians have a relatively high percentage of drinkers (compared to other religious groups), their "6% heavy-escape drinkers' rate" constitutes a relatively high rate of escape drinkers to total persons (greater than that of both Methodists and Bapists).

Cahalan, Cisin, and Crossley[127] divided their Protestant respondents into two groups, liberal and conservative, in reference to the group's general stand on abstinence. The conservative Protestant group had more than twice as many abstainers and only about half as many heavy drinkers as the liberal group. The percentage of all drinkers who were heavy drinkers was 16 percent for the conservative Protestants. Even the liberal Protestant percentage was below the national rate of 18 percent. When comparisons were made by subgroups defined by similar age, social position, and sex, the conservative Protestants had the highest proportion of persons who drank less than once a month (abstainers and infrequent drinkers). The liberal Protestants displayed a pattern of drinking remarkably close to that of Catholics in terms of percentage of drinkers, but the former had a lower percentage of heavy drinkers among drinkers. As might be expected, a high score on Cisin, Cahalan, and Crossley's "religious fundamentalism" scale was associated with a low percentage of drinkers, and low percentages of heavy drinkers among all persons.

THEORETICAL CONSIDERATIONS. The hypotheses of Skolnick and others, built upon a supposed relationship between abstinence teachings and intemperance among drinkers, are not supported by the data reviewed. Although a number of comparisons (e.g. Baptist vs Episcopalian and Methodist vs Episcopalian) in Table VI could be construed as partially supporting such a relationship, the differences are small, and an overwhelming number of comparisons from other studies negate the relationship. For example, the percentages of heavy drinkers and heavy-escape drinkers for the Methodist group (the group most explicitly proscribing drinking) are consistently lower than those percentages for the Catholic group (the group that takes a very permissive stand on drinking). This is not what would be expected, if an abstinent normative stand is solely and consistently associated with intemperance and/or alcoholism among those who drink. On the other hand, Cahalan, Cisin, and Crossley[128] found a *trend* in their data, suggesting that there were slightly greater proportions of "heavy-escape drinkers" among Baptist and Methodist "heavy drinkers" than among other Protestant heavy drinkers. Whether or not drinkers in such groups are more likely to become escape drinkers or alcoholics than other Protestants is still an open question. It may be that the hypotheses of Skolnick, Knupfer, and others with similar frames of reference are only applicable in comparative studies of specific and homogeneous Protestant groups in specific areas of the nation.

The following summary statements on Protestant drinking behavior should be kept in mind by those interested in the theoretical relationship between religion and drinking practices: (1) Protestants appear to have the lowest drinking rates among religious groups in the United States; (2) national rates of alcoholism appear to be lowest among Protestants and Jews; (3) Protestant drinkers have lower rates of "heavy" and "escape" drinkers than do many other religious groups; (4) the Protestant rate of "heavy" and "escape" drinking among drinkers is well below the national rate;

TABLE VI
RATES OF DRINKING AMONG ADULTS OF
MAJOR AMERICAN RELIGIOUS GROUPS

	Percent Who Drink (Nonab-stainers)	Among Drinkers	
		Percent Heavy Drinkers	Percent Heavy Escape Drinkers
Jewish			
Riley & Marden (USA, 1946)	87		
Mulford (USA 1963)	90	7	
Cahalan & Cisin (USA, 1964-65)	92	11	8
Catholic			
Mulford & Miller (Iowa, 1958)	79	20	
Riley & Marden (USA, 1946)	79		
Mulford (USA 1963)	89	12	
Cahalan & Cisin (USA, 1964-65)	83	23	11
Protestant			
Riley & Marden (USA, 1946)	59		
Mulford (USA 1963)	63		
Methodist			
Mulford & Miller (Iowa, 1958)	49	16	
Mulford (USA 1963)	61	5	
*Cahalan & Cisin (USA, 1964-65)	66	15	7
Baptist			
Mulford (USA 1963)	48	9	
Cahalan & Cisin (USA, 1964-65)	47	17	10
Lutheran			
Mulford & Miller (Iowa, 1958)	61	13	
Mulford (USA 1963)	85	13	
Cahalan & Cisin (USA, 1964-65)	81	19	7
Episcopalian			
Cahalan & Cisin (USA, 1964-65)	91	13	6

*Methodist and similar denominations

Sources: John W. Riley and Charles F. Marden: The social pattern of alcoholic drinking. *Quarterly Journal of Studies on Alcohol, 8*:270, September, 1947; Harold A. Mulford: Drinking and deviant drinking, U.S.A., 1963. *Quarterly Journal of Studies on Alcohol, 25*:637, 640, 1964; Harold A. Mulford and Donald E. Miller: Drinking in Iowa, I. Sociocultural distribution of drinkers. *Quarterly Journal of Studies on Alcohol, 20*:717, 1959; Harold A. Mulford and Donald E. Miller: Drinking in Iowa, II. Drinking in selected sociocultural categories. *Quarterly Journal of Studies on Alcohol, 21*:30, 1960; Don Cahalan and Ira H. Cisin: American drinking practices: Summary of findings from a national probability sample, I. Extent of drinking by population sub-groups. *Quarterly Journal of Studies on Alcohol, 29*:142, March, 1968.

and (5) the "liberal" Protestant rate of "heavy drinkers" is below the national rate, and below that of some other religious groups, including Catholics, even when age, social position, and sex are held constant. It should be kept in mind, however, that these statements are based on research data and survey reports at hand.

Catholic Drinking and Alcoholism

CATHOLIC DRINKING PATTERNS. Three national drinking surveys since 1946 placed the percentage of adult American Catholics who drink at 79 percent,[129] 89 percent,[130] and 83 percent.[131] In two of these studies this rate was exceeded only by that of the Jews, and in the other, only by that of Jews and Episcopalians. Mulford and Miller[132] placed the percentage of Catholics in Iowa who drink at 79 percent the highest of any religious group in the State. However, this survey did not include a report on any Jewish respondents. Mulford[133] estimated that 12 percent of Catholic drinkers in the United States are heavy drinkers, compared to the national rate of 11 percent. Cahalan, Cisin, and Crossley[134] estimated that 19 percent of *all* Catholics are heavy drinkers. This is well above the national average of 12 percent.

Special calculations by Cahalan, Cisin, and Crossley[135] on the drinking practices of various religious and ethnic groups showed that Catholics had comparatively higher percentages of heavy drinkers even when ethnic affiliation was held constant. The exception was in the case of Irish liberal Protestants, who were more likely to be heavy drinkers than were Irish Catholics. When Catholics were compared with liberal and conservative Protestants (within comparable age-sex-social position groups), the Catholics had higher rates of heavy drinking. Cahalan and Cisin[136] reported that 11 percent of Catholic drinkers were heavy-escape drinkers; this rate exceeded that for Jews and the total national sample rate of 9 percent. In their college drinking study, Straus and Bacon[137] found that a higher percentage of Catholics (when compared to Jewish, Protestant, and Mormon students) fell into the two heaviest drinking categories.

ALCOHOLISM AMONG CATHOLICS. Mulford and Miller[138] found that in Iowa the Catholic group had far and away the highest percentage (54%) of the total presumed alcoholics. This group constituted only 20 percent of the total sample. Bailey, Haberman, and Alksne[139] estimated that the rate of alcoholism for Catholics in a New York City area was around 24 per 1,000. This exceeded the rate for other Protestants (20 per 1,000) and Jews (2 per 1,000), and was exceeded only by the rate for Negro Baptists (40 per 1,000). In their study of New Haven residents undergoing psychiatric treatment, Roberts and Myers[140] found that Catholics accounted for 68.5 percent of the patients with alcoholism or drug addiction, yet constituted only 57.5 percent of the total general population.

THEORETICAL CONSIDERATIONS. In comparison to the amount of theoretical work on Jewish and Protestant drinking and alcoholism, there is relatively little theoretical treatment of Catholic drinking patterns. In contrast to the ramifications of the "Protestant Ethic," the strong injunctions of conservative Protestant groups, and the obvious Jewish norms and traditions, the Catholic ideology seems to be associated with a relatively more tolerant attitude toward drinking (similar to that of liberal Protestant groups). This relative lack of a clear-cut normative stand may have discouraged potential theorists. It might be conjectured from Catholic drinking patterns that their high rates of drinking, problem drinking, and alcoholism result from the lack of a strong normative position on the use of alcohol. Some might contend that Catholics have high rates of heavy drinkers and alcoholics because of a positive-normative position toward alcohol.

Drinking and Alcoholism in the Major American Religious Groups: Conclusions

The data in Table IV shows a number of logical trends. First, it is obvious that the controls over drinking associated with religious group membership are effective to a certain extent. The two groups taking the most unfavorable official view of alcoholic beverages, Methodists and Baptists, have the lowest percentages of drinkers. The Jewish, liberal Protestant, and Catholic groups, with more permissive attitudes, have consistently higher percentages of drinkers. In general, those groups with high percentages of persons who drink have higher percentages of heavy drinkers among drinkers. The outstanding exception is the Jewish group, which has the highest percentage of drinkers, and a relatively low percentage of heavy drinkers among drinkers. This may be because Jewish customs and group norms are not concerned so much with "drinking" or "not drinking", but with "drinking to excess." This is in contrast to the Methodist approach of drawing the line at the point of drinking or not drinking. Cahalan found that a very small percentage of Jews (in comparison with other religious groups) reported being exposed to significant others who ever drank as many as four drinks per occasion.

Unfortunately, there is no comprehensive, reliable, nationwide data available on rates of alcoholism for different religious groups. Any summary statements are thus tentative at best.

It appears from the Jewish case (probably the only case) that a high rate of drinking does not necessarily lead to high rates of heavy drinking and alcoholism. In the Catholic case, high percentages of drinkers are associated with high rates of heavy drinking and alcoholism. Both groups have relatively permissive attitudes about drinking, but the Jewish group is more cohesive, has a more intolerant attitude toward intoxication, and has more effective sanctions against excessive drinking. It may be this relatively "greater intolerance" and more "effective sanctions" keep rates of alcoholism low where rates of drinking are high. The group cohesion contributes to the strength of drinking controls and may insulate the individual from life factors conducive to alcoholism. The Catholic drinking patterns suggest that a permissive drinking position without strong or effective sanctions against heavy drinking is conducive to alcoholism. Cahalan,[141] in his national survey, found that on "attitude toward drinking" Irish-Catholics, as a group, had the most favorable attitudes toward drinking. He also reported this group as having an above-average rate of problem drinking. In environmental support for heavy drinking, Catholics were shown to be above average, and conservative Protestants, below average. A significantly higher proportion of Catholics, particularly Irish-Catholics, reported being exposed to significant others who drank at least four drinks on some occasions.

Finally, there is always the possibility that religious group differences in rates of drinking and alcoholism are contaminated to some degree because certain other variables are not held constant in many cases (e.g. race, ethnicity, age, sex, social class, area of domicile). Cahalan[142] discovered that when he held risk score (based on socialpsychological intervening variables) constant liberal Protestants, conservative Protestants and Catholics had similar drinking problem rates. Catholics had a higher aggregate proportion of persons with higher problems scores. They also had a higher proportion of persons with higher-risk scores than did the other two religious groups.

There is a growing secularism and materialism among the memberships of most all religious groups, coupled with a growing similarity among them. Therefore, it is likely that religious differences will increasingly become less important as determinants of drinking practices as well as other behaviors. Drinking patterns among Jews, the group that has been the most thoroughly analyzed in regard to drinking, may be related to ethnic variables unrelated to religion per se.

The Family of the Alcoholic

A common assumption among most behavioral scientists is that the individual's family of orientation is one of the most important factors in determining behavior. Given this assumption, it seems logical to examine the families of alcoholics in any attempt to understand the causes of alcoholism. At this level of analysis, the data of sociology and psychology merge. Many psychoanalytic and alcoholic personality studies have dealt with the alcoholic's family background. Since the family is a group and at the same time a social institution, it is legitimate to include family studies in a sociological discussion. This inclusion seems further justified by the fact that much of the literature analysis in this area is in terms of role models. On the other hand, some of the family data deals with the personalities of the parents of the alcoholic. In most cases, research on alcoholism and the family has been concerned with interpersonal relations that are within the province of sociology and psychology. Irrespective of how this interdisciplinary question is resolved, studies on family influences upon alcoholism may help explain personality factors in alcoholism (as well as social factors); they may also disclose the influence of family types on alcoholism rates.

Obviously, the alcoholic's family often includes members beyond the alcoholic and his parents; the alcoholic usually has siblings or other relatives living in his family.[143] Since there is a dearth of data in the literature on the alcoholic's siblings and other relatives, only the parents of alcoholics are considered.

Parent-Child Situation in the Families of Alcoholics

Several researchers have attempted to correlate alcoholism with parental deprivation. Kinsey[144] found in his study of 46 hospitalized female alcoholics that in 50 percent of the cases the parents were not living together regularly during the patients' childhood, and that in 35 percent of the cases either the mother or father, or both, had died during the patients' childhood. Pittman and Gordon[145] studied 187 males arrested for inebriety and reported that in 39 percent of the cases the family unit was broken by death, divorce, or separation before the inebriates' tenth birthday. Moore and Ramseur[146] noted in their study of 100 hospitalized alcoholic veterans that the loss of at least one parent in childhood occurred in 45 percent of the cases. On the other hand, when Oltman and Friedman[147] compared 500 hospitalized alcoholics with 600 schizophrenics, 4 other diagnostic (patient) groups, and 230 controls, they found that parental deprivation was no more frequent among alcoholics than among the six other groups.

Wittman[148] reviewed much of the literature (especially psychoanalytic) of the 1930's on the family of the alcoholic. The majority of these studies portrayed similar etiologic developmental factors in the chronic alcoholic's history, e.g. a doting, oversolicitous mother and a comparatively stern, forbidding father; the latter, a person who inspired respect and awe or fear, and who displayed inconsistent tendencies of severity and indulgence, thus producing in the child a feeling of insecurity and helpless dependence.[149]

Wittman, in her own study, compared the histories of 100 male alcoholics with those of 100 volunteers. The experimental and the control group were matched for age, education, and nationality. Her results virtually substantiated the descriptions in the literature: a domineering and idealized mother was paired with a stern autocratic father who was feared by the child. This child, who later became an alcoholic, had disproportionately greater love for the mother than for the father; he came from a family where strict unquestioned obedience was demanded.

Several subsequent studies have supported Wittman's results, while others have not. Kinsey[150] found that 24 percent of 46 female alcoholics recalled paternal rejection, while none recalled paternal overprotection. Thirty-six percent of the male alcoholics in Pittman and Gordon's study[151] felt rejected, while none felt overprotected or overindulged by their fathers. Moore and Ramseur[152] observed that 22 percent of the fathers of 100 male alcoholics in their study were recalled to be rejective and only 2 percent to be overindulgent. One-third of the mothers in Kinsey's study[153] were reported to be highly rejective, while none were overprotective. Moore and Ramseur[154] noted that 26 percent of the mothers were overindulgent, while 13 percent were rejective. Pittman and Gordon[155] characterized the typical mother-son relationship among inebriates in their study as follows: "The general thread that runs through the cases is an emotionally impoverished relationship between mother and son, with consequent deprivation of social and psychological gratifications which are usually found in the primary group of the family."

McCord, McCord, and Gudeman[156] found in their longitudinal study that boys strongly encouraged by their mothers to be dependent were not more likely to become alcoholics than were boys not so encouraged (boys relatively independent of their mothers). The mothers were also rated on the extent to which they controlled or restricted the child's activities (e.g. sheltered him from adversity, selected his friends). Restrictive and controlling mothers produced a smaller proportion of alcoholics than less restrictive mothers; the highest proportion of alcoholics came from families where the mother was "subnormally restrictive." The prealcoholics, during adolescence, were more likely to have been disapproving of their mothers than were the nondeviants.

McCord, McCord, and Gudeman[157] contended in their theoretical explanations that both maternal and paternal role playing contributed to alcoholism. Their alcoholics were often reared in antagonistic, conflictful homes by emotionally erratic and unstable mothers. Consequently, the prealcoholics' dependency desires were erratically met, lending to the development of strong dependency needs among them during adolescence. The prealcoholic boy was deprived of a clear perception of the male role because of paternal antagonism and escapism and the presence of an inadequate father. Deprived of a male role model, the boy accepted the role (or self-image) of an aggressive and independent male, as found in the mass media and social stereotypes. However, his strong dependency needs (brought on by the mother) conflicted with this self-image. Thus, McCord viewed alcoholism as a compromise, between two conflicting personality elements: independence, and dependence.

Specifically, McCord found significant statistical differences distinguishing prealcoholics' home backgrounds from the home backgrounds of his nondeviants (nonalcoholics and noncriminals). The following conditions were found more frequently in the homes of the prealcoholics; intense parental conflict; neural disorder, especially in combination with intense family conflict; families characterized by incest or illegitimacy; maternal alternation between active affection and rejection; maternal escapism (from crisis situations); deviant mother (criminal, promiscuous, or alcoholic behavior); denigration of the mother by the father; antagonistic relationship between parents; maternal resentment of her family role; overt paternal rejection; paternal escapist behavior in crisis situations; absence of high paternal demands for the boy; influence of outsiders who were in conflict with the parents; subnormal maternal restrictiveness; and dearth of supervision of the boy.[158]

McCord[159] devised a scoring system which selected the six most critical variables that most strikingly differentiated the alcoholics from nondeviants: maternal alternation of affection and rejection, maternal deviance, paternal antagonism, parental escapism, and an "outsider" in conflict with parental values.

Parental Drinking Attitudes and Behavior in the Families of Drinkers and Alcoholics

Cahalan, Cisin, and Crossley[160] observed a high correlation between the drinking and frequent drinking of parents and the drinking and heavy drinking of their children (respondents). For example, among males who reported that their fathers drank three or more times a week, 84 percent were drinkers and 35 percent were heavy drinkers, compared to 64 and 12 percent respectively for males who reported that their fathers never drank or drank less than once a year. Their data also showed that as mothers' or fathers' attitudes toward drinking became more favorable, the percentage of drinkers and heavy drinkers increased. For example, among men whose fathers were reported to have approved of drinking, 84 percent drank, and 28 percent were heavy drinkers; among men whose fathers disapproved, only 63 percent drank, and only 12 percent drank heavily. An analysis of the characteristics of heavy drinkers who were or were not "escape" drinkers demonstrated that (for males and females) the percentage of "escape" drinkers was higher among those respondents whose mothers and fathers disapproved of drinking than among those respondents whose parents approved.[161] For example, among male "heavy drinkers" whose fathers disapproved of drinking, 59 percent were "escape drinkers"; for those "heavy drinkers" whose fathers approved of drinking only 47 percent were "escape drinkers."

Jackson and Conner[162] claim that attitudinal structures are important in attempting to understand alcoholism, and that parental attitudes toward drinking are the chief source of children's attitudes towards drinking. They hypothesized that the parents of alcoholics would have different attitudes about drinking than the parents of nonalcoholics. The alcoholics in their study were drawn from three sources, and a comparison group was selected from among contributors to the Washington Temperance Association. Persons in the comparison group were divided into "nondrinker" and "moderate drinker" categories. They found that nondrinkers more frequently came from homes in which neither parent drank, and where both parents disapproved of drinking. Moderate drinkers also came frequently from nondrinking homes but almost as often from homes in which both parents drank. Jackson and Conner claim that those who came from nondrinking homes developed either negative attitudes toward drinking or negative attitudes toward loss-of-control drinking. The moderate drinkers from homes where parents drank moderately may have learned specific and detailed definitions of appropriate types of drinking behavior. Alcoholics, on the other hand, came most frequently from homes in which one parent drank (usually the father). These researchers held that in this "ambivalent environment" the individual who has since become an alcoholic failed to develop a consistent and well-organized attitudinal structure which could restrain him from excessive drinking.[163] Jackson and Conner stipulated that their alcoholics may have developed ambivalent and hence anxiety-provoking attitudes toward drinking because their parents disagreed markedly in their attitudes toward the use of alcohol. This ambivalence and anxiety led to subsequent excessive drinking.[164]

MacKay[165] studied 20 adolescent problem drinkers (17 male, 3 female) referred to an alcoholism clinic. Analysis of these cases led him to five hypotheses based on the parental and family situation:[166]

1. Alcoholism was a frequent parental trait; thus the role models for identification that these prealcoholic children had were perceived by them persistently in relation to the model's alcoholism.

2. The child brought into the first and early drinking situations a high degree of ambivalence, uncertainty, and concern based on his observations of the effects of alcohol in his own family. He learned early that alcohol relieved some of his many tensions.

3. The children felt both overt and covert hostility toward their parents because of the parents' inability to provide love and maternal needs, and because of the parents' inconsistencies and other weaknesses. One of the major ways in which the weaknesses of the parents were demonstrated was in their pathological use of alcohol. In an attempt to demonstrate independence from their parents, (especially during adolescence) the children had to prove their ability to drink successfully as compared to the way in which their parents drank. In this way, added value was placed on the use of alcoholic beverages.

4. The depriving family situation produced among the children a feeling of not belonging. The need to belong was strong in these adolescents, and their drinking associates filled at least a semblance of this need. It may be that the primary satisfaction was on a social level, while the secondary drinking behavior may have become addictive because of the related factors discussed.

5. Somewhat related to the second point was the effect that alcohol had in temporarily filling the emptiness physically felt by these children and ameliorating their passive feelings of depression.

Alcoholism among the parents of alcoholics has been considered (among other things) by several studies. For example, Kinsey[167] found that one-third of the 46 female alcoholics he studied had an alcoholic father, while only one had an alcoholic mother. Moore and Ramseur[168] found 35 alcoholic fathers and 6 alcoholic mothers in the histories of their sample of 100 alcoholics.

Robbins, Bates, and O'Neal[169] conducted a longitudinal study of children seen at a psychiatric clinic. The family histories of children who later became alcoholics were compared with those of children who later became heavy drinkers or showed no excessive drinking. When the father demonstrated a pattern of antisocial behavior, 40 percent of the offspring became alcoholic, 29 percent became excessive drinkers, and 31 percent showed no excessive drinking. When the fathers' antisocial behavior was in the specific form of drinking, 38 percent of the offspring became alcoholics, 34 percent became heavy drinkers, and 28 percent showed no excessive drinking. In contrast to authors who emphasize alcoholism on the part of the alcoholic's father, these authors concluded that[170] fathers who drink excessively were no more likely to produce alcoholic children than fathers who were arrested, who were erratic workers, who had deserted, who were guilty of sexual misbehavior, or who beat their wives or children. The presence of antisocial fathers in a family situation predisposes children to excessive drinking whether or not these fathers set an example of heavy drinking. The antisocial behavior of fathers was found to be the chief etiologic factor in the development of alcoholism.

McCord, McCord, and Gudeman[171] in another longitudinal study rated the mothers and fathers of their subjects as "approving" of drinking, "disapproving," or "neutral." This variable did not have statistically significant relationship to later alcoholism. They discovered that 15 percent of the 53 fathers who approved of drinking, and 10 percent of the 10 fathers who were neutral or disapproved of drinking had alcoholic sons. Thirteen percent of the 16 mothers who approved and 15 percent of the 40 who were neutral or disapproved had alcoholic sons. In those cases where direct evidence on parental drinking behavior was available, the parents were categorized as "abstainers," "moderate drinkers," or "excessive drinkers" (including alcoholics). None of the 5 families in which both parents abstained had alcoholic sons; but in 15 percent of the 13 families in which both parents were moderate drinkers, and in 20 percent of the 5 families in which both parents were alcoholics, there were sons who became addictive drinkers.[172] The data in this study indicated a trend for alcoholic parents to have alcoholic children.

Verbal parental conflict about alcohol and alcoholism was not found to be related to alcoholism at a statistically significant level, although there was a data trend in that direction. Only 12 percent of the 89 subjects whose parents agreed upon alcohol use became alcoholics compared to 21 percent of the 19 subjects whose parents evidenced some conflict about alcohol, and 25 percent of the 20 cases where conflict over alcohol was a basic problem. McCord also found a data trend suggesting that when the parents differed in actual drinking behavior, alcoholism in offspring was higher than when there was no difference in parental drinking patterns. He concluded that parental conflict concerning alcohol *may* have been conducive to alcoholism. The major weakness of this study, as well as many other similar studies, was the small number of cases available in the various categories (in categories compared with each other on various variables). Perhaps this dearth of cases in various categories precluded significant statistical differences.

Carman[173] administered questionnaires to 188 enlisted personnel (61 women) staff members at two U. S. Army hospitals. (San Francisco and Okinawa), all of whom reported some drinking behavior. He measured for factors, including family drinking models, family individual attitudes toward drinking, religious attitudes and involvement, drinking behavior in terms of self-reported motivations, quantity, frequency, and social complications related to drinking. He found that drinking patterns of the family were positively correlated with those of the respondents. This was more the case with men than with women, whose patterns were more closely related to the attitudes of the family toward drinking. Problem drinking in parents was correlated positively with problem drinking in respondents, except when the parents were religiously involved. On the other hand, attitudes of the churches to which respondents belonged did not correlate with their drinking behavior.

Theoretical Considerations

Studies on the families of alcoholics have dealt frequently with the lack of appropriate role models because of either parental deprivation, or the presence of inadequate or "pathological" role models; the antisocial behavior of the role models characterized by alcoholism or some other form of deviant behavior; the greater frequency of antisocial behavior among the fathers than among the mothers of both male and female prealcoholics; various constellations of parental attitudes toward alcohol that influence children to become alcoholics, such as ambivalence toward alcohol or strong approval of drinking. Almost all of the study findings indicate that either the parents of alcoholics were not "normal" parents or that they did not relate to their prealcoholic children in ways conducive to the children's successful adjustment.

It may be that the parents' role in the development of alcoholism is twofold: they help create in the child psychic or adjustment problems, and they directly or indirectly encourage the use of alcohol to deal with these problems. Most family studies have not reported consistent findings. Longitudinal family studies, probably the most objective, have not yielded enough statistically significant differentials upon which to base any etiological system of analysis. Family studies have not included enough respondents (alcoholics or parents of alcoholics). Terminology from study to study varies greatly and the selection and definitions of variables under study are frequently ambiguous. There is also a dearth of replication studies. Finally, many family studies have been marred by a clinical and/or psychoanalytical bias. We probably need more learning theory studies in this area. We certainly need to find out more about the alcoholism rates and problem drinking rates among the close relatives of alcoholics.

Social Class Factors in Drinking and Alcoholism

Preliminary Discussion

The drinking patterns of different American social classes[174] have been outlined by John Dollard,[175] who apparently based his descriptions on community and other studies and on personal observation. He contended that in the upper classes drinking is not a moral issue and that both sexes at the top of the social ladder drink a good deal. In the upper classes one is condemned not for drinking and not for drunkenness, but for antisocial behavior while drunk. The lower-upper class contains the "cocktail set," in which people drink more recklessly than in the old families of the upper-upper class. These families relatively new to wealth are in a rather insecure, frustrating position. According to Dollard, they constantly compare themselves with the people who socially "own" the territory in which they live, and suffer from helpless feelings of inadequacy. Dollard also claimed that parental controls are weak in the lower-upper class and that the scars from social competition are painful here. Therefore, lower-upper class young people may try to escape from their discomforts by drunkenness. Some case studies suggested to Dollard that there was some destructive drinking in this class.

The upper-middle class has a strong evaluation of wealth and talent. The men drink on social occasions and at casual gatherings. Women drink infrequently. The attitude toward drinking is influenced by an identification with the higher classes and is generally a neutral one. According to the impressions of Clinard,[176] drinking parties are increasing among the middle class as an escape mechanism from increasing tensions and insecurity brought about by high-speed living, industrial and commercial activity and high pressure salesmanship.

Dollard[177] depicted members of the lower-middle class as desperate strivers for recognition and status, and in fact for anything which would widen the gap between them and those whom they consider lower than themselves. Members of this class thus have strong taboos against drinking. This is particularly the case among women. Excessive drinking is associated in their minds with the behavior of the lower classes. Dollard claimed that the neutral or permissive attitudes of the higher classes tend to shift downward and that consequently the middle classes may become more tolerant of drinking and even imitative of higher-class drinking patterns.

In the upper-lower class, the chief labor group, there is more drinking and fewer restraints on drinking than in the lower-middle class. Drinking is frequent in both homes and taverns, the latter acting as social clubs. These class members have no "drink like a gentleman" prescriptions. Drunkenness is not a disgrace. In the lower-lower class drinking is socially unrestrained. Weekend drinking binges and chronic drunkenness is frequent.

On the basis of these descriptions, the middle and lower-upper classes might be expected to have high rates of alcoholism because of the tensions inherent in their positions. The lower classes would be expected to have high rates because of their supposed lack of controls on drinking. Following Dollard's outline, McCord, McCord, and Gudeman[178] reasoned that the upper- and lower-lower classes in America would most likely produce confirmed alcoholics. They conjectured that social control of drinking is weak in these two classes and therefore excessive drinking could be one major channel for the expression of anxiety and aggression.

One problem that confronts researchers (past and present) who study the association between drinking patterns (including alcoholism) and social class is the matter of social-class criteria. Sociologists utilize different methodologies and criteria in the stratification area. The four most frequently used indicators of social class are income, education, occupation, or some combination of these.

Income, Drinking, and Alcoholism

Riley and Marden[179] in their national study of 1946 classed their respondents as "poor," "average," and "prosperous." The percentage of "drinkers" and "regular drinkers" increased respectively with these income groupings. Straus and Bacon[180] found that percentage of "users" and "heavy users" increased with students' family (parental) income. The results of Mulford[181] and Cahalan, Cisin, and Crossley[182] also present a general pattern of increasing percentage of "drinkers" and "heavy drinkers" among drinkers with increasing income. Cahalan and Cisin[183] found no consistent relationship between family income and percentage of "heavy escape drinkers" among all drinkers. However, those with incomes of $10,000 or more a year had a markedly higher percentage of heavy- escape drinkers among all persons than did those with lower incomes. A special comparative analysis of "heavy-nonescape drinkers" and "heavy-escape drinkers" led Cahalan, Cisin, and Crossley[184] to conclude that the heavy-escape drinkers had relatively lower incomes, were more likely to have a family income of under $6,000 per year.

Bailey, Haberman, and Alksne[185] reported that the two lowest personal income groups (under $5,000 and under $3,000 per year) had a proportion of presumed alcoholics greater than the proportion of the total population they comprised. Groups with higher incomes were underrepresented in terms of proportion of presumed alcoholics. Families with an alcoholic were also more likely to be receiving public assistance (5.1% for families with an alcoholic versus 3.4% for all families). On the other hand, there were no significant differences in total family income between all households and those with a presumed alcoholic. Thus, other family members apparently compensated for the economic deficiencies of the alcoholic.[186]

Education, Drinking, and Alcoholism

The results of Riley and Marden,[187] Mulford and Miller,[188] Mulford,[189] Cahalan and Cisin[190] show that (usually) as amount of education increases, percentage of drinkers (nonabstainers) increases. However, in the latter three studies there is no strong consistent pattern between education and percentage of heavy drinkers among drinkers. Cahalan and Cisin[191] found that the grammar-school-or-less education group had the lowest percentage of drinkers (53%), yet the highest percentage of heavy drinkers among drinkers (20%). This group tied with the some-college group in reference to heavy-escape drinkers among all drinkers. Mulford's[192] earlier results do not show this pattern. Fewer people with a grammar-school-or-less education drink, but if they do, it *may* be that they are more likely to be heavy drinkers.

Overall, Cahalan and Cisin's[193] data on heavy-escape drinkers among all persons show no consistent pattern among educational groups. However, the highest percentages of heavy-escape drinkers to *total* persons is found in the completed-high-school and some-college groups. The highest and lowest percentages of heavy-escape drinkers among drinkers is found at the extremes of the distribution: in the lowest grammar-school-or-less (11%) and highest college-graduate (6%) education groups, respectively.

Locke, Kramer, and Pasamanick,[194] in their study of alcoholic psychosis first admissions to public mental hospitals in Ohio, found that rates of admission were higher among those with a grammar-school-or-less education than among those with more education. Bailey, Haberman, and Alksne[195] found that rates of alcoholism in a Manhattan area were highest (33/1,000) among those in the none-to-some-grade-school category and lowest (9/1,000) among high-school-graduates. The three groups with less education than a high school graduate had rates of alcoholism higher than the overall aggregate rate of 19/1,000. The high-school-graduate group and the two groups with more education had rates lower than 19/1,000. Similarly, in Iowa Mulford and Miller[196] found that the lowest education group (1 to 8 years of education) accounted for 44 percent of the presumed alcoholics but only for 25 percent of the total sample. The 9 to 12 years of education group was slightly underrepresented, and the 13-plus years group was heavily underrepresented in proportion of alcoholics to proportion of total sample.

Occupational Status, Drinking and Alcoholism

Both Mulford's[197] and Cahalan and Cisin's results[198] show that that there is a slight (but inconsistent) tendency for percentage of drinkers to increase with increasing occupational status. They found even less of a consistent pattern for heavy drinking. Mulford's[199] occupational breakdown is for both males and females, but "house-wives" were omitted. The lowest ranking occupational group in Mulford's study (laborers, janitors) had the lowest percentage of drinkers (69%) and the second lowest percentage of heavy drink-ers among drinkers (10%). The highest percentage of drinkers (87% and 100%) fell into the two highest occupational categories. The percentage of heavy drinkers in the highest occupational group (lawyers, judges, physicians) was *lowest* in the study (zero). The second highest ranking group (scientists, college professors, engineers) had the *highest* percentage of heavy drinkers among drinkers (24%). The next highest percentage of heavy drinkers among drinkers (19%) was found in the third lowest category, which included shipping clerks, cabinet makers, and mechanics. The two lowest groups averaged only 10.5 percent. The percentages of heavy drinkers among drinkers for other categories ranged between 11 and 15 percent.

Cahalan, Cisin, and Crossley[200] arranged their data by "occupa-tion of chief breadwinner" for both men and women. They found that for men the highest percentage of drinkers (86%) was found in the service-worker category (the second lowest status category).

The two highest categories (professional and manager-proprietor-official) had the next highest percentages of drinkers, 82% and 81% respectively. Farm owners were clearly the least drinking group, 40 percent were classed as abstainers. The highest percentages of heavy drinkers to all drinkers (38%) and total persons (29%) were found in the semi-professional-technical group where 76 percent were drinkers. Drinkers in this category, and to a certain extent in the operative category, were relatively more likely to be heavy drinkers than drinkers in other categories.

The data for women (by occupation of chief breadwinner) showed that women in the highest category (professional) had the highest percentage of users (81%), while the lowest percentage of drinkers (26%) was found in the farm-owner category. Women in the laborer category had the second lowest percentage of users (42%); however, they showed very high rates of heavy drinking in the service-worker category.[201] Cahalan, Cisin, and Crossley interpreted the drinking of women in the service-worker category as another illustration of heavy drinking among women drinkers at the lower status level.[202]

Multiple-variable Indicators of Social Class, Drinking, and Alcoholism

Cahalan, Cisin, and Crossley utilized a variant of the Hollingshead Index of Social Position (ISP).[203] This index takes into account the respondent's education, the occupation of the family breadwinner and the status position of that occupation. When respondents were divided into ten ISP groupings, percentage of drinkers increased with increasing status. In general, percentage of "heavy drinkers" among "drinkers" increased slightly with increasing status. The percentage of heavy drinkers among all persons ranged from 10 to 14 percent and was generally higher in the higher ISP groups. When the sample was broken down into four ISP groups, and when sex and age were controlled, the proportion of drinkers was consistently higher in higher ISP groups. There was also a steady *decrease* in the proportion of light or moderate drinkers going down the ISP scale in almost every ISP group. There was very little difference in distribution of heavy drinkers and heavy-escape drinkers by ISP for various age and sex groups. The two middle ISP groups showed very little difference from either the lowest or highest ISP groups in percentage of heavy drinkers among drinkers and all persons. This finding refutes the legend of the "abstemious middle classes" described by Dollard, who claimed that those in the upper and lower classes drink more than those in the middle class.[204]

A comparison of data on heavy-escape drinkers and heavy drinkers showed that the former were more likely to be from lower ISP groups. Cahalan, Cisin, and Crossley also discovered that more well-to-do and middle class people report drinking at least occasionally than lower ISP groups, but that fewer of those who do drink, drink heavily.[205]

Cahalan[206] also utilized ISP in his national survey. Special correlation analyses revealed that ISP was one of the four variables most predictive of problem drinking. Problem drinking rates did not differ markedly between upper and lower status women; however, lower status women had much higher percentages of non-drinkers than did upper status women. Both groups had the same rates for three types of drinking problems: psychological dependence, implicative drinking (e.g. drinking binges), and social consequence (interpersonal problems due to drinking). Said another way, there is a smaller proportion of moderate drinkers among the lower status women; and if the tabulation had set aside the nondrinkers, the rates of "problem drinkers" among "drinkers" would have been higher for lower status women.[207]

Cahalan[208] found the highest proportion of problem drinkers among men of lower socioeconomic status. Moreover, he also discovered that the frequency of lower-status problem drinking and heavy drinking is compounded when one adds age (21-44) and urban area (large cities). Furthermore, Cahalan's respondents of lower status had higher risk scores on the social-psychological variables than did those of higher status. Alienation and maladjustment scores were positively correlated with problem drinking scores. This two-factor variable was one of the four most predictive of problem drinking. Lower status persons showed more alienation and maladjustment than did higher status persons. The impulsivity and nonconformity (lack of ego controls) variable was also positively correlated with problem drinking scores, but there were no marked differences in this variable between status groups. The variable "environmental support for drinking" was also predictive of problem drinking. This variable dealt with the number of heavy drinkers among "significant others" and with the number of drinks significant others would tolerate the respondent's drinking on one occasion. Perhaps somewhat unexpectedly, it was found that upper status groups demonstrated higher environmental support for drinking. Some of the conditions thought to be conducive to problem drinking were more characteristic of lower status groups, while others were more characteristic of upper status groups.

Men of upper and lower status were found to be quite dissimilar in their problem patterns even when age was held constant. There was a greater "maturing out" among those of higher socioeconomic status as they got older than there was among men of lower status. This was particularly the case for frequent intoxication, symptomatic drinking, and interpersonal problems (with relatives, friends, neighbors, police).

The reasons for a higher prevalence of problem drinking among the lower status men were interpreted as arising from a combination of factors involving relative lack of tolerance from one's society and one's significant others; fewer options for recreation and tension release; a greater level of alienation and anxiety; a greater tendency to act out aggressiveness than those of higher status; and the possibility that some of the problem-drinking lower status men in the sample had skidded to a lower status because of their drinking.[209]

McCord, McCord, and Gudeman[210] in *Origins of Alcoholism* categorized their subjects into social classes on the basis of the occupation and education of the respondents' fathers. No individuals in the upper classes were included in the sample. They expected that the strong controls over drinking attributed to the middle classes would insulate boys from such families against alcoholism, and that the supposed lack of controls attributed to the lower class would be conducive to alcoholism. The authors found, however, that the middle and lower-middle classes produced a significantly higher proportion of alcoholics than did the lower class. Their results[211] are contrary to the expectations derived from Dollard's observations on drinking practices. Either social control over the use of alcohol is not as weak in the lower classes as has been described or Dollard's description of drinking in the various social classes is accurate, but social control, as such, is not the deciding factor. McCord's sample was skewed toward the lower class.

Robbins, Bates, and O'Neal[212] record a longitudinal study of 221 children examined at a psychiatric clinic. All subjects were assigned to one of five socioeconomic status categories, primarily on the basis of the occupation of the family's breadwinner. The percentage of alcoholics and excessive drinkers coming from each status group increased with decreasing status. The authors disclosed that not only do people of the lowest status group drink heavily, they are apparently much more likely to have social or medical problems resulting from their drinking than people in higher status groups.[213]

Theoretical Considerations

In general, survey results indicate that percentage of drinkers increases with increasing social status. On the other hand, rates of heavy drinking, heavy-escape drinking, and problem drinking among drinkers are highest in lower status groups. When persons in the lower classes (especially women) drink, they are more likely to drink heavily. The lower percentages of drinkers in the lower social classes and in the findings of Cahalan[214] indicate that controls over drinking by the lower classes are not as weak as once thought. Cahalan, Cisin, and Crossley[215] report that on every sex-age group comparison the higher percentage of drinkers reporting "that others had tried to get the respondent to drink less" was found in the lower status group. Lower status persons also had more negative attitudes toward drinking. The association of the lower classes with conservative Protestant and fundamentalist churches may help explain this group's large percentage of abstainers. The middle classes obviously drink more than the writings of Dollard and others suggest. It could be as Dollard conjectured, that the liberal drinking habits of the upper classes have been adopted by the middle classes. Dollard's claim that the lower-upper class drinks heavily because of relative deprivation and feelings of helplessness and inadequacy has not been borne out. In fact this postulate appears exceedingly spurious to the authors for several reasons. Given the presence of a lower-upper class, its prestige must be very high. Moreover, it must blend almost imperceptibly into the upper-upper class. The aristocracy of the so-called upper-upper class in the United States has been greatly exaggerated. Finally, in this vein, Dollard's use of Warner and Lunt's six-class system in a loose universal sense does not hold throughout the United States. Therefore, any hypotheses based on Dollard's observations are questionable.

Empirical studies of rates of alcoholism demonstrate that alcoholic rates increase with decreasing social status. In brief, problem drinking and alcoholism are found to be strongly associated with lower socioeconomic status. The most notable exception to this general finding is McCord, McCord, and Gudeman's[216] longitudinal study which reported that alcoholics were more likely to come from middle-class families than lower-class families. These results may indicate that lower-class status is not associated as strongly with the genesis of alcoholism as many have claimed. Some heavy drinkers drop in social status because of drinking problems. On the other hand, the longitudinal study of Robbins, Bates, and O'Neal[217] reports a very strong association between lower class status and alcoholism.

Unfortunately, for a number of reasons, there is no reliable national representative-sample data on rates of alcoholism available to provide concrete information on the degree of relationship existing between social class and alcoholism. Cahalan's work *Problem Drinkers*[218] comes closest; he shows that the association of problem drinking and lower social status is *not entirely* the result of downward mobility. He also establishes alienation (on some theoretical grounds thought to be conducive to alcoholism) as more characteristic of the lower classes, and as related to problem drinking. The fact that *lower status* persons who drink are more likely to be escape or problem drinkers than *high status* people who drink indicates differential drinking motivations for these two groups. We need an interdisciplinary endeavor (on the part of sociologists and psychologists) to explain differential drinking motivations among the social classes.

Drinking and Alcoholism in Two American Ethnic Groups[219]

Drinking, Alcoholism, and the American Negro

NEGRO-AMERICAN DRINKING PATTERNS. Cahalan, Cisin, and

Crossley[220] estimated that 62 percent of American Negroes were drinkers, as compared to 69 percent of whites. The percentage of heavy drinkers among all persons differed very little between Negroes and whites. Twenty-three percent of Negro drinkers were heavy drinkers as compared to 17 percent of white drinkers. Cahalan and Cisin[221] discovered that Negro rates of "heavy-escape drinking" among drinkers and among all persons were higher than that of whites for both sexes. Cahalan, Cisin, and Crossley[222] compared heavy drinkers and heavy-escape drinkers and found the heavy-escape drinking group included an above-average percentage of nonwhites.

NEGRO-AMERICAN ALCOHOLISM. Bailey, Haberman, and Alksne[223] computed rates of alcoholism per 1,000 persons aged 20 years and over in a Manhattan borough area. The rate for Negroes was 28 and that for whites 16 (a difference of 19). The racial differential decreased with increasing education. The difference between Negroes and whites with education of ten or more years was only 8 per 1,000 (20 for whites and 12 for Negroes). Locke, Kramer, and Pasamanick[224] found that rates of first admission to Ohio public mental hospitals for alcoholic psychoses were two or three times higher for Negroes than for whites. It seems logical to conclude, as did Sterne[225] (who reviewed over a dozen studies comparing white and Negro rates of alcoholism and problem drinking), that despite some evidence to the contrary, most studies demonstrate that alcoholism rates and problem drinking rates (whether crude or age standardized) are generally higher for Negroes than for whites.

THEORETICAL CONSIDERATIONS. A number of hypotheses have been advanced to explain the higher rates of heavy drinking and alcoholism among Negroes as compared to white rates. Most of these center on the frustration of the Negro in American society. Frazier[226] studied the *Black Bourgeoisie* and explained that excessive drinking seemed to provide one means of narcotizing the middle-class Negro against a frustrating existence. Strayer[227] found evidence of status striving among Negro alcoholics whose status position was below that attributed to the black bourgeoisie. Larkins claimed[228] that the position of the Negro in America has made him ready to engage in the excessive use of alcohol. According to

Larkins, there have been, and continue to be, all the conditions fostering frustration and the desire to escape, namely the oppression of the rural and landless black farm population and the super-exploitation of the urban proletariat. He points out that the economic and social discrimination of the Negro, in every phase of American life, has created fertile grounds for excessive drinking.

Hypothetical statements about the relationship of the Negroes' frustration and escape mechanisms to his heavy drinking rates (or alcoholism) leave much to be desired. Studies must demonstrate the claimed relationship. Additionally, the question arises, Why not select some other means (than alcohol) to assuage frustration and escape needs? Moreover, other ethnic minority groups in the United States have faced similar facets of discrimination without resorting to the heavy use of alcohol (Japanese-Americans for one). Fortunately, we have some specific "hypothetical" findings.

Cahalan,[229] in his study of problem drinking, found that his "alienation and maladjustment" variable was positively correlated with problem-drinking scores. This variable was one of the strongest predictors of problem drinking; the Negro group was one of the groups with a relatively high average score on this variable. The Negro group also had the highest mean score on the "unfavorable expectations" variable (e.g. unfavorable outlook regarding future relationships with family and friends and life goals).[230]

McCord[231] interviewed 1,454 Negroes randomly selected in the cities of Los Angeles (Watts), Houston, and Oakland in 1966-1967. He also drew upon 426 additional unstructured interviews in Watts. McCord claims to have uncovered a social type, "the defeated." The defeated have been crushed by life and escape from intolerable ghetto reality into a world of drugs, alcohol, and hallucination. McCord,[232] in the discussion of the ghetto Negro male as an alcoholic, maintains that ghetto life magnifies the same causative factors that lead to alcoholism in the general population. The Negro in American culture experiences an unusually high degree of stress. McCord also says that in many Negro families the father neither reinforces nor exemplifies the male role and its responsibilities. Negro boys often react to this confusion by creating an independent facade. In adulthood, white society continually undermines the Negro male's tenuous conception of manhood. Alcoholism is seen as a response to these factors.

Strayer[233] presented a similar formulation. Many of the Negro alcoholics he studied grew up in strongly matriarchal families. He claimed that this created strong dependency needs among Negro males which became a source of conflict when a masculine independent role was expected. He explained alcoholism in several instances as a revolt against dependency on a mother-figure. According to Strayer, the strong dependency trait in the male Negro alcoholic is not peculiar to him; it is also present among white male alcoholics. In the former, however, it is derived from the matriarchal family background, and in this sense it differs from the maternal dependency of white men. In the latter, the dependency is expressive of emotional pathology resulting from the cultural mores of a people, with deep-seated historical antecedents.[234]

Strayer's split explanation for the same phenomenon poses methodological as well as hypothetical problems. The ubiquitous matriarchal Negro family is (and has been) held responsible for many of the Negroes' problems. No empirical correlation between the Negroes' matriarchal family (his consequent dependence) and his alcoholism has been made to date. This is not to say that no such connection exists. The fact remains that many nonalcoholics come from matriarchal homes.

FEMALE NEGRO ALCOHOLISM AND THE ALCOHOLISM SEX RATIO.

Cahalan, Cisin, and Crossley[235] observed that the white and Negro men in their national sample differed very little in percentage of "drinkers" and "heavy drinkers" among drinkers and among all persons. However, Negro women differed from white women both in their much higher proportion of abstainers and their higher rate of "heavy drinkers" (among drinkers and all women).[236] Sixty-one percent of white females drank as compared to only 49 percent of female Negroes; however, 11 percent of all Negro women were heavy drinkers. The percentage for white females was only about a third as high. Cahalan, Cisin, and Crossley[237] found that 16 percent of Negro female drinkers were heavy-escape drinkers as compared to 4 percent of white female drinkers. This female Negro percentage (heavy-escape drinkers among drinkers) was higher than that for white males (13%), but not as high as the percentage for Negro males (20%). The heavy and heavy-escape drinking patterns of Negro females are much closer to the patterns of Negro males than these same drinking patterns of white females are to white males. The drinking pattern of female Negroes is characterized by relatively low rates of drinking, but relatively high rates of heavy drinking and escape drinking among drinkers. Thus, although fewer Negro women drink, when they do drink they are more likely (than white women) to be heavy drinkers.

Bailey, Haberman, and Alksne[238] reported that the rates of alcoholism per 1,000 adults in a New York City area for white males and females were 31 and 5 respectively (a difference of 26), while the rates for Negro males and females were 37 and 20 respectively (a difference of 17). The sex ratio of alcoholics for whites was 6.2 men to one woman, while that for Negroes was 1.9 to 1. Locke, Kramer, and Pasamanick[239] reported a ratio of rates of first admissions for alcoholic psychosis to Ohio public mental hospitals for nonwhite and white males of 30.8 to 13.1. The ratio for nonwhite and white females was 8.9 to 2.9. Negro males thus had a rate of admission slightly less than two and one-half times that of white males, while Negro females had a rate roughly three times that of white females.

Strayer[240] noted that 41 percent of Negro patients admitted to an alcoholism clinic in Connecticut were female, while only 16 percent of white patients were females. Sterne[241] reviewed much of the literature in this area and concluded that rates of alcoholism for Negro females are uniformly higher than those of white females. She reported that although Negro and white females always reflect a lower alcoholism rate than the males of their respective races, the sex ratio of alcoholic males to females differs considerably by race. The ratio for Negroes is much lower than that for whites; therefore Negro females run a much higher risk of incurring alcoholism, relative to Negro males, than do white females compared to white males.

THEORETICAL CONSIDERATIONS (NEGRO FEMALE). We have a few conflicting attempts to explain the relatively high rates of alcoholism in Negro women and the low alcoholism sex ratio among Negroes. Strayer[242] maintains that historical and economic factors have made the Negro family strongly matriarchal, thus placing heavy additional burdens on Negro females. These responsibilities have given Negro women more motivation for sobriety[243] and therefore explain the high rates of abstinence among them. On the other hand, Bailey, Haberman, and Alksne[244] claim that the Negro women they studied in a New York area lived in a permissive drinking culture for women, and that they fulfilled two roles in this culture, that of major breadwinner and that of housekeeper and mother. This situational burden led to alcoholism among these women.

Knupfer et al[245] poses a highly plausible reason to explain the differential sex-ratio drinking rates among Negroes and whites. They maintain that in groups where women are relatively less economically dependent on men, their behavior more closely resembles that of men; and where men are economically superior to women, they can better control the behavior of women. Thus, given the relative economic independence of Negro women, it might be predicted that their drinking behavior would resemble that of Negro men.[246] Certainly there is greater similarity between Negro female and Negro male rates for other forms of deviant behavior (e.g. crime rates) than there is between such rates for white females and white males. Negro females throughout their history in the United States have had more freedom in terms of all kinds of behavior vis-à-vis Negro males than have white women vis-à-vis white males.[247]

The fact that fewer than 50 percent of Negro females drink may indicate that their decision to drink or not drink is subject to a certain amount of social control. Yet among Negro women the rates of heavy drinking and heavy-escape drinking among drinkers are relatively high. It may be that drinking for "social" reasons is relatively uncommon among Negro women, and that when they drink, they drink heavily for personal or "escape" purposes. Certainly Negro women do not enjoy as high a social status among Negro men as white women do among white men. Sex and social-status anxiety among Negro women vis-à-vis Negro men may motivate for heavy drinking among Negro women who drink. This area needs further investigation. At first blush, this explanation may appear to conflict with our summary statement on Knupfer's foregoing thesis. This is not the case, for despite the Negro females' (historical) relative lack of economic dependence upon Negro men (and relative sexual freedom), her status vis-à-vis Negro men is lower than is the status of white women vis-à-vis white men.

The differential sex-ratio drinking patterns between Negroes and whites offers a fruitful area for future research. In short, we are dealing here with real significant differences. Moreover, as indicated, plausible explanatory hypotheses are available both at the cultural and psychological levels.

Drinking, Alcoholism, and the Irish-American

IRISH-AMERICAN DRINKING PATTERNS. Cahalan, Cisin, and Crossley[248] reported the drinking behavior for various groups by country of origin of the respondent's father. When age was held constant, those whose fathers were born in Ireland had the highest percentage of drinkers (93%), highest percentage of heavy drinkers (31%), and highest percentage of heavy drinkers among drinkers (33%). However, categorical tabulations based on the question, "Which one nationality did most of your family come from?" revealed that only 64 percent of those who responded "Irish" were drinkers. This was below the national (U. S.) rate of 68%. However, the percentages of heavy drinkers (13%) and heavy drinkers among drinkers were slightly above the national averages. Tabulations by both national identity and religion showed that the highest percentages of heavy drinkers (30%) and heavy drinkers among all drinkers (37%) were for liberal Protestants of Irish national identity.[249] The percentages for conservative Protestants of Irish national identity were well below the national averages, while Catholics of Irish national identity had percentages of drinkers and heavy drinkers well above the national averages. The drinkers and heavy drinkers in the Irish group are thus concentrated among those of liberal Protestant and Catholic religious groups. Further, the data also show that, as generational distance from birth in Ireland increases, percentages of heavy drinkers decreases, although Irish rates remain relatively high. This last point suggests that the Irish-American immigrant to the United States brought with him a heavy drinking pattern.

Straus and Bacon[250] in their college drinking study determined that 84 percent of males and 64 percent of females of Irish nationality were drinkers. Both figures were above the averages for the total college samples but were exceeded by some other ethnic groups.

However, 62 percent of Irish males who drank fell into the heaviest drinking category. This was the highest percentage of any ethnic group. On the other hand, percentages of Irish male student drinkers falling into various "incidence of intoxication" categories were roughly intermediate with respect to the percentages for other ethnic groups.[251] Cahalan, Cisin, and Crossley[252] found that 11 percent of those heavy drinkers of Irish national identity were heavy escape drinkers, as compared to the total sample rate of 9 percent. Cahalan[253] also found that the group of Irish origin was among those groups with the greatest prevalence of "problem" drinking.

IRISH-AMERICAN ALCOHOLISM. Roberts and Myers[254] in their study of psychiatric illness in New Haven discovered that the Irish-born constituted 2 percent of the total population of the area, yet accounted for 4.9 percent of the alcohol and drug addiction cases. This proportional overrepresentation (4.9:2) was the highest of any ethnic group. The Irish-born constituted 2.9 percent of the total *psychiatric* population. They were thus only slightly overrepresented in terms of all types of mental illness, yet heavily overrepresented in terms of alcoholism and drug addiction. The Irish were slightly overrepresented for most other specific types of mental illness. These findings either show that the Irish are more prone to alcoholism and drug addiction than to other types of illness or that mental illness in the Irish-born is manifested by alcoholism and drug addiction.

Skolnick[255] analyzed rates of arrest for inebriety in New Haven and discovered that the observed rate of arrest among Irish was greater than the expected rate (1.3:1). However, four other ethnic groups were overrepresented among arrests for inebriation to a greater extent than were the Irish. Robbins, Bates, and O'Neal[256] disclosed in their longitudinal study of children treated at a psychiatric clinic that the Irish had the highest rate of alcoholism and the greatest absolute number of alcoholics among ethnic groups represented, though they were not the largest ethnic group in the area under study. McCord, McCord, and Gudeman[257] in their longitudinal study determined that the Irish had the highest rate of alcoholism.

Glad[258] reviewed the literature on Armed Forces rejection rates for alcoholism, relative proportion of inebriates in hospital admissions, and rates of arrest or conviction for inebriety and concluded that rates of alcoholism among Irish-Americans were relatively high (especially when compared with rates for Jews).

THEORETICAL CONSIDERATIONS. The Irish and Irish-Americans like the Jews are frequently used as examples in general theories of the supracultural, specific cultures, and subcultural variety. Some writers claim that the high Irish rates of heavy drinking and alcoholism are a carry-over from Ireland. Bales[259] claims that high alcoholism rates in Ireland are the result of a high level of culturally induced tension, and a "convivial" attitude toward drinking later translated into a utilitarian attitude conducive to alcoholism. Bales also claims[260] that family factors in the Irish-American situation have also contributed to the high Irish rates of alcoholism in America. Irish fathers, as recent immigrants, found themselves for many years at the bottom of the occupational ladder. This and other factors, such as the more equalitarian relationship of men and women in the United States, decreased the influence and importance of the Irish father. The mother consequently became dominant in the family and bound the sons closer to her (as was usual and natural in Ireland). In America, however, a strong attachment between mother and son made it difficult for the sons to make a successful transition to adult status. These difficulties contributed to the sons' later alcoholism. The problem here is that many of these conditions have operated in the case of other ethnic groups in America with lower rates of alcoholism than the Irish.

Glad[261] compared Irish-American (Catholic) youth with Jewish and Protestant youths. The results disclosed that Irish-American attitudes toward alcohol were characterized by at least two semantically homogeneous attitude clusters. On two of these clusters, "excitement" and "conviviality," Irish youth differed markedly from the two other groups. The "excitement" cluster included drinking for fun and pleasure, while the "conviviality" cluster involved drinking for social facilitation and increased friendliness. Glad concluded that these two clusters embraced purposes for drinking in which the affective consequences of drinking are the most important. Drinking for affective consequences was seen to be conducive to alcoholism.

Knupfer and Room[262] compared Irish-American and Jewish-

American drinking patterns in California. They found that Irish men are more likely to choose alcoholism as a symptom than other ethnics are, because Irish men drink more heavily than others, and thus are more vulnerable to alcoholism. The custom of heavy drinking is viewed within a social context conducive to the development of alcoholism. Heavy drinking as a custom, in turn, is promoted by the existence of attitudes favorable toward drunkenness. The Irish highly value drunkenness under certain circumstances. They never regard drunkenness with as much contempt as do the Jews. Attitudes favorable to drunkenness, in turn, are promoted by a larger complex of modal character and values differentiating the Irish from Jews. Traits commonly attributed to the Irish, e.g. impulsiveness, sentimentality, and fantasy, are more compatible with seeking drunkenness than are traits such as intellectualization, realism, and pessimism (commonly attributed to Jews).

Knupfer and Room's results and hypotheses appear significant and plausible. Their terminology needs to be refined and operationalized in order that replication studies may follow. The core of their thesis rests on the acceptance of "drinking to drunkenness." Logically, one would expect groups which accept drinking to drunkenness to have higher alcoholism rates than those groups which proscribe this behavior. Perhaps further investigation based on Knupfer and Room's social-psycological paradigm will help explain what it is in Irish culture that makes for the condonation of drinking to drunkenness. Paradoxically enough, however, it must be kept in mind that many individuals, as well as cultural groups under certain circumstances, drink to drunkenness without alcoholism. The certain circumstances probably is the key here. Perhaps the Irish (and there is evidence for this point of view) and other groups with high rates of alcoholism condone (or even applaud) drinking to drunkenness more frequently (within a wide range of social situations) than do groups with lower rates of alcoholism.

Cahalan[263] affirms the importance of religion in Irish-American attitudes and drinking. He utilized six social-psychological variables assumed to be conducive to problem drinking and found that Irish-Americans from conservative Protestant backgrounds had a mean score (28) on all six variables, slightly lower than the mean of the total sample (30). Irish-Americans of Catholic background had a mean score (32), slightly higher than the total sample average. On the variable found to be most strongly related to problem drinking scores, "positive or favorable attitude toward drinking," the Irish-conservative Protestant score was below the national mean, and the Irish-Catholic score was above the mean. The same general pattern appeared for two other variables positively related to problem drinking, "exposure and permissiveness of environment toward heavy drinking" and "impulsivity and nonconformity."

The findings of various investigators (e.g. Cahalan's and Glad's) and the hypothetical postulates of many researchers indicate that the relatively high rates of heavy drinking and alcoholism among Irish-Americans may be partially attributed to Irish-American attitudes toward drinking. These findings and formulations may apply only to Catholic Irish-Americans and need to be checked with additional studies, including Irish drinking patterns in Ireland and perhaps elsewhere (e.g. England). The possibility of genetic factors should not be overlooked.

Problem Drinking Related to Age, Sex, and Urbanization

Age and Sex

These variables and their relationship to problem drinking have occurred throughout this chapter in several contexts. We will confine this critical discussion of them to Cahalan's recent national survey.

Men in all age groups have a higher frequency of drinking problems than do women. Cahalan holds that role differences between men and women explain men's heavier drinking. The frequency of drinking problems in the aggregate among men was found to be highest among those in their twenties, significantly lower among those in their thirties and forties, and tapering off among those in their fifties. When risk score (based on social-psychological variables) is held constant, however, there is a remarkably similar presence of drinking-related problems from age group to age group.[264]

Problem drinking differs between younger and older men in the area of health. Men over 50 have a higher rate of symptomatic drinking compared to those in their forties. Very few men over 70 have drinking problems. Though not mentioned by Cahalan, this may be explained by the fact that people with serious drinking problems (alcoholics) probably die much earlier than other men, more frequently before their seventies. It also could be that men over 50 who do not report drinking problems still continue to drink heavily, but have learned to cope with their drinking problems, e.g. they may have learned defensive techniques which permit them to continue drinking heavily, in terms of drinking places, drinking times, and drinking companions. Men over 50 who appear to "mature out" of drinking problems may be physiologically and/or biochemically different from those who do not "mature out." Certain body types may be more capable of withstanding heavy dosages of alcohol than others; that is, some bodies may become more readily physiologically adjusted to alcohol. Some men who drink heavily develop all sorts of mental and physical health problems. On the other hand, some very heavy drinkers do not appear to have physical, mental, or interpersonal problems related to drinking.

Cahalan compares the "maturing out" of drinking after age 50 with that of other deviants who "mature out" of drug use and sex activities. This so-called "maturing out" process may reflect higher death rates among drinkers and other deviant types. The heavy use of alcohol and drugs may result in both direct and indirect attrition rates. One does not expect to find many sex deviants upwards of 50 to 70 years old, for obvious physiological reasons.

Women who incur drinking problems have drinking-related problems more frequently in their thirties and forties. Very few women report drinking-related problems in their twenties. Relatively few women have drinking problems after their fifties. A relatively small proportion of women over 50 and men over 70 appear to have serious drinking problems. Women in their forties have a higher frequency of drinking because of psychological dependence than do younger or older women. Women problem-drinkers have higher risk scores in relation to alienation and maladjustment than do men. Therefore, Cahalan thinks that psychological motivations for heavy drinking are more frequently found among women than among men. The authors suggest that the short-term and long-term alcoholic effects on men and women drinkers may vary physiologically and psychologically because of innate physiological and other constitutional differences between men and women.

Urbanization

Cahalan[265] finds that size of city is important in the prevalence of problem drinking, especially among men between 40 and 49 years of age. He reports that this age group in small towns and rural areas avoids interpersonal complications in association with drinking more than do men in their forties (and fifties) living in cities over 50,000. Drinking-related problems involving psychological dependence are higher in larger cities than in smaller cities or rural areas. The degree of urbanization is related in certain ways to drinking behavior, depending upon the two variables—age and social status.

Cahalan, Cisin, and Crossley report that the highest proportion of abstainers and infrequent drinkers are found in the 45-and-over lower status/lower urbanization group. They thought that these variations reflect different social pressures regarding drinking on the part of those of lower status with greater social control in the smallest cities and rural areas. Interaction between socioeconomic status and urbanization in the rate of problem drinking exemplified a similar pattern.

Cahalan calculated a higher risk score for men in the larger cities than for those in smaller towns. He thinks that men in the larger cities, in his study, showed a high prevalence of drinking problems, because this group includes a higher proportion of higher risk people; larger cities per se do not cause problem drinking. Cahalan also finds the level of environmental support (social-psychological variable) to be significantly higher for both men and women in the larger cities and very low for respondents in towns and rural areas.

Several factors, then, appear to account for a higher frequency of problem drinking in cities than in small towns and rural areas: (1) variations in social pressures and social control; (2) differentials in social-psychological risk scores; (3) variation in drinking climate; and (4) variation in environmental support for drinking. As mentioned before, Cahalan's multivariate analysis revealed that problem drinking occurs more frequently among the following groups than among other groups: lower-socioeconomic status men under 60 in cities of 50,000 or more; Irish-Catholics; those of Latin-American or Caribbean origin; and Negroes.

COMMENTS ON THE SOCIOLOGICAL APPROACH

The Structure of Sociological Works on Drinking and Alcoholism

The three types of sociological theory and research analyzed in this monograph may be visualized in terms of three pyramid levels. *Substructural* theories and works should provide the base of knowedge necessary for theory building on drinking behavior and alcoholism in specific cultures. More general theories applying to an increasingly greater number of cultures could be built upon these *specific-culture* theories and studies. Hopefully, this process would eventually lead to a theory explaining alcoholism and drinking behavior in all cultures (*supracultural theory*). Ideally, each level would interact with every other level and thus contribute to theory building at all levels. Unfortunately, testable sociological theories of alcoholism beyond the substructural level are not as yet available. Perhaps for a long time to come, the realistic sociologist will have to settle for substructural and specific-culture theory building (middle-range theory) based on modest, empirical substructural studies. Even at this level an interdisciplinary approach appears necessary. Several sociological studies either indicate or demonstrate that specific, necessary sociological variables can predict drinking rates among and between certain population groups. These necessary variables, however, do not constitute sufficient variables. Intervening variables from other disciplines are required, in combination with sociological variables, to explain and predict problem drinking and/or alcoholism. Don Cahalan has demonstrated this fact with his sophisticated multivariate analysis of both sociological and social-psychological variables.

Some Comments on the Three Approaches

Most of the supracultural orientation theories or hypotheses may be applauded for their utilization of both sociological and psychological variables in attempting to explain rates of alcoholism. Moreover, many of these formulations also apply to single cultures and subcultures. While there is partial support for some of these postulates, many are imprecise and defy empirical confirmation. Specification is difficult to maintain in supracultural theory building; nonetheless, attempts must be made to operationalize all theoretical concepts involved. On the positive side, supracultural theories may focus attention on important phenomena overlooked or not discernible in approaches involving single cultures. Cross-cultural studies have proven fruitful in other behavioral studies, and therefore it is likely that they might contribute to an understanding of drinking and alcoholism. *Eventual* supracultural theories of alcoholism and drinking behavior may even contribute to an *eventual* theory of human behavior. In the meantime, most of us will continue to live on this earth and content ourselves with middle-range theory.

Many of the specific-culture theories, like most supracultural theories, are without supporting data, and are based on uncontrolled observations and speculation. Again, there is a need for hypotheses in more testable forms. The findings or techniques relevant to one culture may be used to guide further investigations of other cultures, e.g. if a significant drinking pattern is found in one culture, it can be sought out in others. If we are unable to find which variables explain drinking behavior in at least one or two cultures, we may not expect to find variables that explain supracultural drinking behavior.

The substructural studies, unlike the supracultural and specific-culture works, deal with a considerable amount of empirical data; unfortunately most of this data is neither presented in, nor guided by, suitable (clearly spelled out) theoretical frames of reference. Don Cahalan's theoretical frame comes closest in this direction, though his paradigms (in the main) follow, rather than precede, his national survey. The authors do not view this dearth of theory as an insuperable problem. One needs many bricks to build a brick house. Of course architects are also needed, but sociology has a plethora of them (also cathedrals and cathedrals full of theoretical high priests). We need more patient and competent brick layers.

Specific Comments on Substructural Works

In studies of religion, and drinking and alcoholism, the grouping of all Jews (or Catholics or Protestants or Methodists) in one category may be misleading because of the large number of variables (age, sex, degree of urbanization, social class, race) that crosscut religious groups in an uneven manner. Further, in many studies there seems to be little effort to discriminate between the "nominal member" and the "dedicated, conscientious believer."

Family background studies of alcoholics have received much attention by researchers, but most of them have glaring methodological weaknesses. First, we do not know if the families of alcoholics studied are representative of the families of alcoholics. Much of the data (e.g. that in Kinsey's[266] and Pittman and Gordon's[267] studies) was drawn from the alcoholics' memories of their families. There is no way to estimate the extent to which these recollections are blurred or biased. Many family studies to date utilize no control groups. In these circumstances, how do we know that the families of nonalcoholics may not be just as "bad" as the families of alcoholics? Rejective or overprotective parents and parental deprivation have not only been found in the families of alcoholics, but also in the histories of other types of patients, especially schizophrenics.[268] Obviously, more research is needed to differentiate the pathological family patterns found in the histories of alcoholics vis-à-vis those found in the history of other deviants— and those found in the histories of nondeviants. Constitutional factors, including genetic behavior, must be included in the future studies of alcoholics' families.

The generalizations about drinking controls and behavior, as well as the tensions peculiar to certain social classes, may be contaminated by the influences of ethnicity, religion, and other factors which influence drinking behavior. The relatively high rates of social mobility and vagueness of class lines in the United States render class generalizations difficult. Moreover, there has been little or no discussion of whether it is the social class in which the alcoholic was reared or the social class of the alcoholic himself, or both, that is of etiological significance. Social class studies must also deal with the probability that the association of problem drinking and alcoholism with lower social status might result (in part) from the downward mobility of the drinker (caused by drinking excesses). Finally, the relatively high association of lower social status and drinking problems may be due to sampling or visibility biases inherent in many studies based on mental hospital, alcoholic ward, or other institutional samples.

Data used in the comparison of white and Negro rates of alcoholism must be interpreted with caution. Many investigators comparing Negro and white drinking and alcoholism patterns have not adequately controlled for differential variables between the two groups, such as socioeconomic status, religion and urbanization. The higher rates might be an artifact of the greater visibility of the Negro alcoholic in certain circumstances. Whites are better able to afford private, as opposed to public, care and are less likely to appear in the statistics based on alcoholic populations of public institutions. Some researchers maintain that, in comparison to whites, Negroes suffer the onset of alcoholism earlier, are institutionalized earlier, and are thus likely to have higher rates of institutionalization for alcoholism.[269] Locke, Kramer, and Pasamanick[270] note that hospitalization for Negroes may be sought earlier because of the unavailability of caretakers in the home. They also suggest that alcoholic-beverage purchases by the Negro alcoholic are likely to cause curtailment of his other expenditures which may preclude the purchase of food and health care and therefore lead to the early onset of alcoholic complications. They also think that the Negroes' earlier termination of schooling and entry into the job market (as compared with whites) may cause greater personal strain and earlier drinking freedom. Thus, it may be that the differences reported in Negro and white drinking behavior may be truly reflective of reality, regardless of sampling and statistical considerations (for the reasons mentioned here or other reasons).

Don Cahalan's multivariate analysis (including R, the Coefficient of multiple regression and Automatic Interaction Detector procedures) of several substructural, sociological variables (age, sex, socioeconomic status, degree of urbanization, ethnicity, religion) meets many of the foregoing problems, and permits the measurement of the predictive power of single variables as well as that of combined variables. In our opinion, Cahalan's greatest contribution inheres in his success of combining, measuring, and predicting variables at two levels of analysis—the sociological and social-psychological levels. This methodology makes possible the construction and measure of an interdisciplinary model in the study of problem drinking and alcoholism. Multivariate analysis of variables at different levels of analysis enables the researcher to control and predict. This problem of control and prediction has been the sociologists' (as well as other behavioral scientists') greatest barrier in research on drinking behavior and alcoholism.

A Sociological Preliminary Framework

As the reader is well aware, the sociological material reviewed was not presented in terms of any overall analytic or explanatory framework. The material is presented in terms of level of theory rather than in terms of factors thought to be relevant to an understanding of the many types of drinking behavior. It might have been possible to adopt one of the theories available and present the material in terms of that theory or paradigm. Unfortunately, not all theories deal with all the material available and others deal with areas that have received little research attention. That is, no theory does justice to all the material and there are some theories to which the material does not do justice. The authors could, of course, have created their own theoretical framework in which to present the material and/or to expand or modify the theory in light of the material. (This same point also applies to the constitutional and psychological chapters.) This, of course, is not the primary purpose of this work. Nonetheless, the reader is entitled to the presentation of some attempt at providing a framework to reorganize and summarize these and future materials.

The authors were hard-pressed to find a beginning framework superior to that of Robert F. Bales. Bales' theoretical statements can incorporate, directly or indirectly, most of the *sociological* elements which appear repeatedly in the literature.

Bales contended that attitudes toward drinking are important in understanding all types of drinking behavior. This is, of course, almost a truism. The important element is isolating the specific types of attitudes conducive to specific types of drinking. For the type of attitude thought to be conducive to alcoholism, Bales used the term "utilitarian." Glad used the term "affectivity" and more recent authors have described it as "escape" drinking. All of these terms involve a conception of the reason or motivation for drinking. The common element they contain is the idea of drinking to deal with personal problems—drinking to escape. Horton, in a similar vein, maintained that the function of alcohol in all societies is the reduction of anxiety. The alcoholic is assumed to be dealing with his problems (perhaps by escaping them) by the use of alcohol. He chooses alcohol as the means of his escape partially because of his attitude about alcohol. These attitudes, in turn, are molded by the groups which impinge upon the drinker's existence. For example, the cross-pressures hypothesis of Knupfer, et al., the formulations of Skolnick and others suggest that persons from abstinence backgrounds who drink tend to use alcohol for its escape producing potential.

The second element in Bales' theory is "culturally induced tension." Horton pointed out that two sources of such anxiety or tension are acculturation and the problems of subsistence. Field, in contrast to Horton, emphasized social organization rather than anxiety. However, anxiety and social organization would seem to be closely interrelated. For example, in a society undergoing acculturation there might be more culturally induced tensions and/or fewer means of dealing with such tensions than there were before acculturation began. Clinebell mentions "existential anxiety." This type of tension is culturally induced and would seem to be most conducive to alcoholism with the breakdown of conventional social means of dealing with such anxiety.

The discrepancy in a culture between emphasis on means and ends, as propounded by Merton, results in a type of culturally induced tension. One of the responses to this anomie is retreatism in the form of alcoholism.

Bales' third element, the availability of substitute means of satisfaction, has not received as much attention from behavioral scientists as has the first two elements. This element deals with the extent to which there are alternate means of dealing with the culturally induced tension. These substitutes need not be pathological or undesirable (e.g. opiate addiction). Clinebell's formulation and the success of Alcoholics Anonymous suggest that religion may be a substitute means of satisfaction. Cahalan, for example, contended that one of the factors contributing to the higher rates of problem drinking in lower socioeconomic groups might be their fewer opportunities for recreation and tension release.

In summary, the culturally induced tensions provide the psychic state which alcohol can relieve. The amount of tension is determined by social structure and conditions. The choice of alcohol to relieve these tensions is determined by (1) attitudes toward alcohol and (2) the availability of substitute means of satisfaction or tension release. Once drinking is adopted as a means of dealing with the tension the pattern of drinking behavior is influenced by changes in tension levels, the availability of substitute means of satisfaction and by the drinker's attitudes.

Other factors which must be taken into account are the availability of alcohol and the extent to which drinking behavior is controlled formally or informally by others. Obviously, an inmate in solitary confinement in a maximum security prison will probably be restrained from drinking no matter how high the tension, how favorable his attitudes or how unavailable substitute means of satisfaction might be.

This framework is, of course, sketchy and far from complete. Its completion requires, at least, the consideration of the following factors. First is the extent to which (and manner in which) physiological and psychological factors influence the following: (a) the individual's reaction to the conditions which created the tension, e.g., no two people will have exactly the same reaction to the same social conditions, nor will they experience or interpret the resulting tension in the same way; (b) the individual's reaction to alcohol itself; (c) his attitude toward drinking; and (d) his attitude toward and reaction to substitute means of satisfaction. Secondly, the possibility that the "tension" afflicting the alcoholic is primarily physiological in origin and course (i.e., having little direct relationship with social or psychological factors) must be considered. Finally, there is the question posed by Smith, Williams and others about the extent to which heredity plays a part in the etiology of alcoholism.

SUMMARY STATEMENT

The theories and works herein reviewed (constitutional, psychological, and sociological) are not presented in any overall analytic or explanatory framework, but rather in a classification frame developed from the existing level of theory and research results found in the literature from 1940 to 1971. We did not think that any one behavioral theory analyzed was comprehensive enough to encompass the varied nature of all the studies examined throughout the literature. We have attempted to classify and analyze existing theory and research data that will pave the way for hoped-for interdisciplinary articulation of several levels of analysis in the etiological study of alcoholism and/or problem drinking.

Our analysis has demonstrated (at least to us) that the etiological factors in alcoholism comprise a combination of constitutional, psychological, and sociological variables. Therefore, we need matched group, longitudinal studies utilizing constitutional, psychological, and sociological variables. Several multivariate techniques will enable us to measure the potency of each variable, the degree of interaction between the variables, and the predictive power of combined variables. Obviously, we need competent interdisciplinary constitutionalists, psychologists, and sociologists to carry out these studies.

NOTES AND REFERENCES

1. Cahalan, Don, Cisin, Ira, H., and Crossley, Helen M.: *American Drinking Practices*. New Brunswick, N.J., Rutgers Center of Alcohol Studies, 1969, pp. 200-201.
2. Cahalan, Don, Cisin, Ira H., and Crossley, Helen M.: *Ibid.*, pp. 20, 196-199.
3. Kinsey, Barry A.: *The Female Alcoholic*. Thomas, Springfield, 1966, p. 40. Discussions of the sociocultural factors in alcoholism are found in: Pittman, David J., and Trice, Harrison M.: Social organization and alcoholism: A review of significant research since 1940. *Social Problems, 5*:294-308, Spring, 1958; Lemert, Edwin H.: Alcoholism: Theory, problem and challenge, III. Alcoholism and the sociocultural situation. *Quarterly Journal of Studies on Alcohol, 17*:306-317, June, 1956; Shalloo, Jeremiah P.: Some cultural factors in the etiology of alcoholism. *Quarterly Journal of Studies on Alcohol, 2*:464-478, December, 1941; Pittman, David J.: Drinking

patterns and alcoholism: A cross-cultural perspective, in Pittman, David J. (Ed.): *Alcoholism.* New York, Harper & Row, 1967, pp. 3-22; Snyder, Charles R.: A sociological view of the etiology of alcoholism, in Pittman, David J. (Ed.): *Alcoholism: An Interdisciplinary Approach.* Springfield, Thomas, 1959, pp. 32-39.

4. Horton, Donald: The function of alcohol in primitive societies: A cross-cultural study. *Quarterly Journal of Studies on Alcohol,* 4:199-320, September, 1943. Another cross-cultural study that may be of interest is Washburne, Chandler: *Primitive Drinking: A study of the Functions of Alcohol in Primitive Socities.* New York, College & University Press, 1961.

5. Horton, Donald: *Ibid.,* p. 293.

6. Horton, Donald: *Ibid.,* p. 269.

7. Horton, Donald: *Ibid.,* p. 295.

8. Horton, Donald: *Ibid.,* p. 296.

9. Field, Peter B.: A new cross-cultural study of drunkenness. In Pittman, David J., and Snyder, Charles R. (Eds.): *Society, Culture and Drinking Patterns.* New York, Wiley & Sons, 1962, pp. 48-74.

10. Horton, Donald: *op. cit.*

11. Bales, Robert F.: Cultural differences in rates of alcoholism. *Quarterly Journal of Studies on Alcohol,* 6:480-499, March, 1946.

12. Horton, Donald: *op. cit.*

13. Snyder, Charles R.: *Alcohol and the Jews.* Glencoe, The Free Press, 1958. Jewish drinking patterns will be discussed in more detail below.

14. Straus, Robert, and Bacon, Selden D.: *Drinking in College.* New Haven, Yale University Press, 1953.

15. Bales, Robert F.: *op. cit.,* p. 494. Drinking patterns of Irish-Americans are discussed in detail below.

16. Glad, Donald D.: Attitudes and experiences of American-Jewish and American-Irish male youths as related to adult rates of inebriety. *Quarterly Journal of Studies on Alcohol,* 8:406-471, December, 1947.

17. Glad, Donald D.: *Ibid.,* p. 452.

18. Ullman, Albert D.: Sociocultural background of alcoholism. *The Annals of the American Academy of Political and Social Science, 351*:22-30, January, 1958.

19. Ullman, Albert D.: *Ibid.,* p. 50.

20. Ullman, Albert D.: The psychological mechanism of alcohol addiction. *Quarterly Journal of Studies on Alcohol, 13*:602-608, December, 1952. See also Ullman, Albert D.: Sex differences in the first drinking experience. *Quaretrly Journal of Studies on Alcohol, 18*:229-239, June, 1957; The first drinking experiences of addictive and "normal" drinkers. *Quarterly Journal of Studies on Alcohol, 14*:181-191, June, 1953.

The Etiology of Alcoholism

21.Ullman, Albert D.: The first drinking experiences of addictive and of "normal" drinkers, *op. cit.,* p. 181.
22. Ullman, Albert D.: Ethnic differences in the first drinking experience. *Social Problems, 8*:45-56, Summer, 1960.
23. Ullman, Albert D.: The first drinking experiences of addictive and of "normal" drinkers, *op. cit.,* p. 181.
24. Ullman, Albert D.: Ethnic differences in the first drinking experience, *op. cit.,* pp. 45-56.
25. Jellinek, E. Morton: *The Disease Concept of Alcoholism.* New Haven, College & University Press, 1959, pp. 28-29.
26. These discussions of drinking and alcoholism in the United States and Canada also apply, to a certain extent, to the situation in Western European countries. For discussions of drinking and alcoholism in other countries or cultures see: Bunzel, Ruth: The role of alcoholism in two central American cultures. *Psychiatry, 3*:361-387, August, 1940; Chafetz, Morris E., and Demone, Harold W.: *Alcoholism and Society.* New York, Oxford University Press, 1962; Mac-Andrew, Craig, and Edgerton, Robert: *Drunken Comportment.* Chicago, Aline Publishing, 1969; Pittman, David J., and Snyder, Charles R. (Eds.): *op. cit.;* McCarthy, Raymond G. (Ed.): *Drinking and Intoxication.* New Haven, College & University Press, 1959. There is much research on alcoholism and drinking in the Scandinavian countries, especially in Finland where much of it is sponsored by the Finnish Foundation for Alcohol Studies. For example: Bruun, Kettil: Drinking behavior in small groups. *Alcohol Research in the Northern Countries.* Helsinki, The Finnish Foundation for Alcohol Studies, 1959. Much of the research on alcoholism in Europe is reported in the following two journals: *Acta Psychiatrica et Neurologica Scandinavica,* and the *British Journal of Addiction.*
27. Some of the studies in this general area are: Larsen, Donald E., and Abu-Laban, Baha: Norm qualities and deviant drinking behavior. *Social Problems, 15*:441-450, Spring, 1968; Maddox, George L.: Role making: Negotiations in emergent drinking careers. *Social Science Quarterly, 49*:331-349, September, 1968; Clinard, Marshall B.: The public drinking house and society, in Pittman, David J., and Snyder, Charles R. (Eds.): *op. cit.* A comprehensive discussion of the tavern or public drinking house from the standpoint of the value conflicts involved, types of taverns, functions of taverns, and the relation of the tavern to alcholism and delinquency; and Lemert, Edwin M.: Alcohol, values and social control, in *Society, Culture and Drinking Patterns,* pp. 553-571.
28. Myerson, Abraham: Alcohol: A study of social ambivalence. *Quarterly Journal of Studies on Alcohol, 1*:13-20, June, 1940.

29. Trice, Harrison M.: *Alcoholism in America.* New York, McGraw-Hill, 1962.
30. Trice, Harrison M.: *Ibid.,* p. 2.
31. Trice, Harrison M.: *Ibid.,* p. 3.
32. Trice, Harrison M.: *Ibid.,* p. 5. Articles of relevance to this aspect of Trice's formulation are Bahr, Howard M.: Drinking and disaffiliation. *Social Problems, 16:*365-375, Winter, 1969; and Bahr, Howard M., and Langfur, Stephen J.: Social attachment and drinking and attachment in skidrow life histories. *Social Problems, 14:*464-472, Spring, 1967.
33. Clinebell, Howard J.: Philosophical-religious factors in the etiology and treatment of alcoholism. *Quartery Journal of Studies on Alcohol, 24:*473-487, September, 1963.
34. Clinebell, Howard J.: *Ibid.,* p. 479.
35. Clinebell, Howard J.: *Ibid.,* p. 480.
36. Clinebell, Howard J.: *Ibid.,* p. 480.
37. Clinebell, Howard J.: *Ibid.,* p. 480.
38. Merton, Robert K.: *Social Theory and Social Structure.* New York, The Free Press, 1957, esp. pp. 121-159.
39. Merton, Robert K.: *Ibid.,* p. 153.
40. Cloward, Richard A.: Illegitimate means, anomie and deviant behavior. *American Sociological Review, 24:*164-176, April, 1959.
41. Kinsey, Barry A., and Phillips, Lorne: Evaulation of anomy as a predisposing or developmental factor in alcohol addiction. *Quarterly Journal of Studies on Alcohol, 29:*892-898, December, 1968.
42. Kinsey, Barry A., and Phillips, Lorne: *Ibid.,* p. 892.
43. Kinsey, Barry A., and Phillips, Lorne: *Ibid.,* p. 894.
44. Cahalan, Don: *Problem Drinkers.* San Francisco, Jossey-Bass, 1970, p. 137.
45. Cahalan, Don: *Ibid.,* p. 137.
46. Cahalan, Don: *Ibid.,* pp. 35-62.
47. Cahalan, Don: *Ibid.,* p. 139.
48. Cahalan, Don: *Ibid.,* pp. 56-62. The number of items per variable is the total for the two stages of the study to date. See also a preliminary study: Cahalan, Don: A multivariate analysis of the correlates of drinking related problems in a community study. *Social Problems, 17:*234-248, Fall, 1969. Some of the variables in Cahalan's studies were similar to those used by Jessor, Richard, et al.: *Society, Personality and Deviant Behavior.* New York, Holt, Rinehart & Winston, 1968.
49. Jessor, Richard, Graves, T. D., Hanson, K. C., and Jessor, S. L.: *Society, Personality and Deviant Behavior: A Study of a Triethnic Community.* New York, Holt, Rinehart & Winston, 1968. In a general and less specific sense, there are many studies of alcoholism and deviant behavior in the literature focusing on the

increased frequency of both in cultures conquered or dominated by other cultures for example native peoples' problems of subordination or acculturation resulting from contacts with European colonials; native Americans' (Indians) problems including social disorganization resulting from contact with Anglo-Americans. See Graves, T. D.: Acculturation, access, and alcohol in a tri-ethnic community. *American Anthropologist,* 69:306-321, June-Augcst, 1967.

50. Merton, Robert K.: *Social Theory and Social Structure.* Glencoe, Ill., The Free Press, 1967; Cloward, R., and Ohlin, L. E.: *Delinquency and Opportunity.* New York, The Free press, 1960.
51. Cahalan, Don: *op. cit.,* pp. 63-64.
52. Cahalan, Don: *Ibid.,* pp. 81-84.
53. Cahalan, Don: *Ibid.,* pp. 90-95.
54. Cahalan, Don: *Ibid.,* p. 97.
55. Cahalan, Don: *Ibid.,* pp. 105-106.
56. Cahalan, Don: *Ibid.,* pp. 107-113.
57. Cahalan, Don: *Ibid.,* pp. 144-145.
58. Cahalan, Don: *Ibid.,* pp. 149-153.
59. Cahalan, Don: *Ibid.,* pp. 151-154.
60. Keller, Mark, and Efron, Vera: The prevalence of alcoholism. *Quarterly Journal of Studies on Alcohol,* 16:634, December, 1955.
61. Sadoun, Roland, Lolli, Giorgio, and Silverman, Milton: *Drinking in French Culture.* New Brunswick, N.J., Rutgers Center of Alcohol Studies, 1965.
62. Sadoun, Roland, Lolli, Giorgio, and Silverman, Milton: *Ibid.,* pp. 119-120.
63. Sadoun, Roland, Lolli, Giorgio, and Silverman, Milton: *Ibid.,* p. 119.
64. Sadoun, Roland, Lolli, Giorgio, and Silverman, Milton: *Ibid.,* p. 121.
65. Sadoun, Roland, Lolli, Giorgio, and Silverman, Milton: *Ibid.,* p. 122.
66. Jellinek, E. Morton: *op. cit.,* pp. 28-30. This formulation about French and Italian drinking is a specific case of Jellinek's more general hypothesis which was based on a comparison of these two nations (see above p. 14).
67. Sadoun, Roland, Lolli, Giorgio, and Silverman, Milton: *op. cit.,* p. 122.
68. Discussions of other institutional factors in drinking and alcoholism are found in: Jellinek, E. Morton: *op. cit.;* Pittman, David J., and Snyder, Charles R. (Eds.): *op. cit.; Patterns;* and Clinard, Marshall B.: *The Sociology of Deviant Behavior.* New York, Rinehart & Winston, 1963.
69. Riley, John W., and Marden, Charles F.: The social pattern of alcoholic drinking. *Quarterly Journal of Studies on Alcohol,* 8:265-273, September, 1947.
70. Mulford, Harold A.: Drinking and deviant drinking, U.S.A. 1963. *Quarterly Journal of Studies on Alcohol,* 25:634-648, December,

1964.
71. Cahalan, Don, and Cisin, Ira H.: American drinking practices: Summary of findings from a national probability sample, I. Extent of drinking by population subgroups. *Quarterly Journal of Studies on Alcohol, 29:*142, March, 1968.
72. Straus, Robert, and Bacon, Selden D.: *Drinking in College.* New Haven, Yale University Press, 1953.
73. Cahalan, Don, Cisin, Ira H., and Crossley, Helen M.: *American Drinking Practices.* New Brunswick, N.J., Rutgers Center of Alcohol Studies, 1969, p. 56.
74. Cahalan, Don, Cisin, Ira H., and Crossley, Helen M.: *Ibid.*
75. Cahalan, Don, and Cisin, Ira H.: *Ibid.,* p. 142.
76. Mulford, Harold A.: *op. cit.,* p. 640.
77. Skolnick, Jerome H.: Religious affiliation and drinking behavior. *Quarterly Journal of Studies on Alcohol, 19:*452-470, September, 1958.
78. Cahalan, Don: *op. cit.,* p. 149.
79. Bailey, Margaret P., Haberman, Paul W., and Alksne, Harold: The eqidemiology of alcoholism in an urban residential area. *Quarterly Journal of Studies on Alcohol, 26:*19-40, March, 1965.
80. Roberts, Bertram H., and Myers, Jerome K.: Religion, national origin, immigration and mental illness. In Weinberg, S. K. (Ed.): *Sociology of Mental Disorders.* Chicago, Aldine Publishing, 1967.
81. Snyder, Charles R.: Culture and Jewish sobriety: The ingroup-outgroup factor. In *Society, Culture and Drinking Patterns, op. cit.,* p. 188.
82. A review of a number of explanations of Jewish drinking patterns is found in Snyder, Charles R.: *Alcohol and the Jews.* Glencoe, Ill., The Free Press, 1958.
83. Bales, Robert F.: *op. cit.,* pp. 263-267.
84. Glad, Donald D.: Attitudes and experiences of American-Jewish and American-Irish male youths as related to adult rates of inebriety. *Quarterly Journal of Studies on Alcohol, 8:*406-471, December 7, 1948.
85. Glad, Donald D.: *Ibid.,* p. 460.
86. Glad, Donald D.: *Ibid.,* pp. 460-461.
87. This is a specific example of Glad's more general "Affectivity-Instrumental" hypothesis discussed above (see p. 147.)
88. Snyder, Charles R.: *op. cit.*
89. Snyder, Charles R.: *Ibid.,* p. 182.
90. Cahalan, Don: Supplementary tables and scoring procedures, Addendum to *Problem Drinkers* (unpublished), p. 13.
91. Keller, Mark: The great Jewish drink mystery. *Quarterly Journal of Studies on Alcohol, Part B, 31:*779, September, 1970.
92. Skolnick, Jerome H.: *op. cit.,* pp. 452-470.

93. Skolnick, Jerome H.: *Ibid.,* p. 463.
94. Straus, Robert, and Bacon, Selden D.: *op. cit.*
95. Straus, Robert, and Bacon, Selden D.: *Ibid.,* p. 465.
96. Preston, James D.: Religiosity and adolescent drinking behavior. *Sociological Quarterly, 10*:372-383, Summer, 1969.
97. Preston, James D.: *Ibid.,* p. 380.
98. Knupfer, Genevieve, et al.: Factors related to amount of drinking in an urban community. *California Drinking Practices Study Report No. 6.* Berkeley, Division of Alcohol Rehabilitation, California State Department of Public Health, 1963, pp. 52-57. See also Cahalan, Cisin, and Crossley: *op. cit.,* p. 174.
99. Cahalan, Don, Cisin, Ira H., and Crossley, Helen M.: *Ibid.*
100. Cahalan, Don, Cisin Ira H., and Crossley, Helen M.: *Ibid.*
101. Thorner, Isidor: Ascetic Protestantism and alcoholism. *Psychiatry, 16*:167, May, 1953.
102. Thorner, Isidor: *Ibid.,* p. 167.
103. Jellinek, E. Morton: Recent trends in alcoholism and alcohol consumption. *Quarterly Journal of Studies on Alcohol, 8*:1-42, June, 1947.
104. Cahalan, Don, Cisin, Ira H., and Crossley, Helen M.: *op. cit.,* p. 155.
105. Cahalan, Don, Cisin, Ira H., and Crossley, Helen M.: *op. cit.,* p. 182.
106. Wax, Murray M.: Myth and interrelationship in social science: Illustrated through anthropology and socialogy. In Sherif, Muzafer, and Sherif, Carolyn W. (Eds.): *Interdisciplinary Relationships in the Social Sciences,* Crapter 5. Chicago, Aldine Publishing, 1969, pp. 93-97.
107. Riley, John W., and Marden, Charles F.: *op. cit.,* p. 270.
108. Mulford, Harold A.: *op. cit.,* p. 637.
109. Mulford, Harold A., and Miller, Donad E.: Drinking in Iowa, V. Drinking and alcoholic drinking. *Quarterly Journal of Studies on Alcohol, 21*:488, September, 1960.
110. Roberts, Bertram H., and Myers, Jerome K.: Religion, national origin, immigration and mental illness. In *Sociology of Mental Disorders,* p. 69.
111. Cahalan, Don, and Cisin, Ira H.: *op. cit.,* p. 142.
112. Skolnick, Jerome H.: *op. cit.,* p. 453.
113. Mulford, Harold A., and Miller, Donald E.: Drinking in Iowa, I. Sociocultural distribution of drinkers, *Quarterly Journal of Studies on Alcohol, 30*:717, December, 1959.
114. Mulford, Harold A.: *op. cit.,* p. 640.
115. Cahalan, Don, Cisin, Ira H., and Crossley, Helen M.: *op. cit.,* esp. pp. 56, 142.
116. Cahalan, Don, and Cisin, Ira H.: *op. cit.,* p. 142.
117. Skolnick, Jerome H.: *op. cit.,* p. 453.
118. Mulford, Harold A.: *op. cit.,* p. 640.

119. Cahalan, Don, Cisin, Ira H., and Crossley, Helen M.: *op. cit.*, p. 56.
120. Cahalan, Don, and Cisin, Ira H.: *op. cit.*, p. 142.
121. Bailey, Margaret B., Haberman, Paul W., and Alksne, Harold: *op. cit.*, p. 27.
122. Mulford, Harold A.: *op. cit.*, p. 640.
123. Cahalan, Don, Cisin, Ira H., and Crossley, Helen M.: *op. cit.*, p. 640.
124. Cahalan, Don, and Cisin, Ira H.: *op. cit.*, p. 142.
125. Skolnick, Jerome H.: *op. cit.*, p. 453.
126. Cahalan, Don, and Cisin, Ira H.: *op. cit.*, p. 142.
127. Cahalan, Don, Cisin, Ira H., and Crossley, Helen M.: *op. cit.*, esp. pp. 56, 57-61.
128. Cahalan, Don, Cisin, Ira H., and Crossley, Helen M.: *Ibid.*, p. 174. J. Midgley, in a recent study of Muslims living in their long- established quarter at Cape Town, found that Muslims remained faithful to the orthodox prohibition of alcoholic beverages. Using various measures of association, no significant relationship between attitude scores and age, sex, and place of residence could be found. The only factor that correlated significantly and negatively, with attitude toward drink was length of madressa attendance. Those persons who had experienced less secondary socialization through the madressa system (those who had had less opportunity to learn the norms and have them reinforced), were less likely to express rigidly negative attitudes toward drinking. This further indicates that strong prohibition against drinking results in less drinking. See Midgley, J.: Drinking and attitudes toward drinking in a Muslim community. *Quarterly Journal of Studies on Alcohol, 32*:148-158, March, 1971.
129. Riley, John W., and Marden, Charles F.: *op. cit.*, p. 270.
130. Mulford, Harold A.: *op. cit.*, p. 640.
131. Cahalan, Don, Cisin, Ira H., and Crossley, Helen M.: *op. cit.*, p. 142.
132. Mulford, Harold A., and Miller, Donald E.: *op. cit.*, p. 717.
133. Mulford, Harold A.: *op. cit.*, p. 640.
134. Cahalan, Don, Cisin, Ira H., and Crossley, Helen M.: *op. cit.*, p. 56.
135. Cahalan, Don, Cisin, Ira H., and Crossley, Helen M.: *Ibid.*, p. 188.
136. Cahalan, Don, and Cisin, Ira H.: *op. cit.*, p. 142.
137. Straus, Robert, and Bacon, Selden D.: *op. cit.*
138. Mulford, Harold A., and Miller, Donald E.: *op. cit.*, p. 488.
139. Bailey, Margaret B., Haberman, Paul W., and Alksne, Harold: *op. cit.*, p. 21.
140. Roberts, Bertram H., and Myers, Jerome K.: *op. cit.*, p. 69.
141. Cahalan, Don: *op. cit.*, p. 86.
142. Cahalan, Don: *Ibid.*, p. 103.
143. Other discussions of the families of alcoholics (including some material on the siblings and other relatives of alcoholics) are found in: McCord, William, and McCord, Joan: *op. cit.*, pp. 472-492;

McCord, William, McCord, Joan, and Gudeman, John: *op. cit.*, Bleuler, Manfred: Familial and personal background of chronic alcoholics. In Diethelm, Oskar (Ed.): *op. cit.*, pp. 110-166; Winokur, George, and Clayton, Paula J.: Family history studies, IV. Comparison of male and female alcoholics. *Quarterly Journal of Studies on Alcohol, 29*:885-891, December, 1968. This discussion is about the family in which the alcoholic was raised. Some articles relevant to the family to which the alcoholic, himself, creates are: McCord, William, and McCord, Joan: *op. cit.*, pp. 413-430; Jackson, Joan K.: *op. cit.* pp. 472-492; Burton, Genevieve, and Kaplan, Howard: Sexual behavior and the adjustment of married alcoholics. *Quarterly Journal of Studies on Alcohol, 29*:603-609, September, 1968; Haberman, Paul W.: Some characteristics of alcoholic marriages differentiated by level of deviance. *Journal of Marriage and the Family, 27*:34-36, February, 1965; Wolf, Irving: Alcoholism and mariage. *Quarterly Journal of Studies on Alcohol, 19*:511-513, September, 1958.

144. Kinsey, Barry A.: *op. cit.*

145. Pittman, David J., and Gordon, Calvin Wayne: *Revolving Door.* Glencoe, Ill., The Free Press, 1958.

146. Moore, Robert A., and Ramseur, Freida A.: A study of the background of 100 hospitalized veterans with alcoholism. *Quarterly Journal of Studies on Alcohol, 21*:51-67, March, 1960.

147. Oltman, Jane E., and Friedman, Samuel: A consideration of parental deprivation and other factors in alcohol addicition. *Quarterly Journal of Studies on Alcohol, 14*:49-57, March, 1953.

148. Wittman, Mary Phyllis: Developmental characteristics and personalities of chronic alcoholics. *Journal of Abnormal and Social Psychology, 34*:361-377, July, 1939. See also Fenichel, Otto: *The Psychoanalytic Theory of Neuroses.* New York, W. W. Norton, 1945.

149. Wittman, Mary Phyllis: *op. cit.*, p. 361.

150. Kinsey, Barry A.: *op. cit.*

151. Pittman, David J., and Gordon, Calvin Wayne: *op. cit.*

152. Moore, Robert A., and Ramseur, Freida A.: *op. cit.*

153. Kinsey, Barry A.: *op. cit.*

154. Moore, Robert A., and Ramseur, Freida A.: *op. cit.*, pp. 51-67.

155. Pittman, Donald, and Gordon, Calvin Wayne: *op. cit.*, p. 87.

156. McCord, William, McCord, Joan, and Gudeman, John: *Origins of Alcoholism.* Stanford, Stanford University Press, 1960.

157. McCord, William, McCord, Joan, and Gudeman, John: *Ibid.*, pp. 138-142.

158. McCord, William, McCord, Joan, and Gudeman, John: *Ibid.*, pp. 71, 82, 94.

159. McCord, William, McCord, Joan, and Gudeman, John: *Ibid.*, p. 94.

160. Cahalan, Don, Cisin, Ira H., and Crossley, Helen M.: *op. cit.*
161. Cahalan, Don, Cisin, Ira H., and Crossley, Helen M.: *Ibid.*, p. 174.
162. Jackson, Joan K., and Connor, Ralph: Attitudes of parents of alcoholics, moderate drinkers, and nondrinkers toward drinking. *Quarterly Journal of Studies on Alcohol, 14*:596-613, December, 1953.
163. Jackson, Joan K., and Connor, Ralph: *Ibid.*, p. 612.
164. Jackson, Joan K., and Connor, Ralph: *Ibid.*, p. 613.
165. MacKay, James R.: Clinical observations on adolescent problem drinkers. *Quarterly Journal of Studies on Alcohol, 22*:124-136, March, 1961.
166. MacKay James R.: *Ibid.*, pp. 132-133.
167. Kinsey, Barry A.: *op. cit.*
168. Moore, Robert A., and Ramseur, Freida A.: *op. cit.*
169. Robins, Lee N., Bates, William M., and O'Neal, Patricia: *op. cit.*, pp. 395-412.
170. Robins, Lee N., Bates, William M., and O'Neal, Patricia: *Ibid.*, p. 407; and Robins, Lee N.: *Deviant Children Grown Up: A Sociological and Psychiatric Study of Sociopathic Personality.* Baltimore, Williams & Wilkins, 1966. (A longitudinal study examining the childhood antecedents of adult sociopathic behavior) Robins found that the child who exhibited a variety of antisocial symptoms and who had a father whose behavior was antisocial (including alcoholism as well as other deviances) was highly likely to exhibit a pattern of adult deviance (including alcoholism as well as other deviant patterns).
171. McCord, William, McCord, Joan, and Gudeman, John: Some current theories on alcoholism: A longitudinal evaluation. *Quarterly Journal of Studies on Alcohol, 20*:727-744, December, 1959.
172. McCord, William, McCord, Joan, and Gudeman, John: *Ibid.*, p. 746.
173. Carman, R. S.: Drinking behavior as related to personality and sociocultural factors. Ph.D. dissertation, University of Colorado, 1968. University Microfilm No. 69-4316.
174. Other discussions of social class factors in drinking, alcoholism, and mental illness are: Cramer, Mary Jane, and Blacker, Edward: Social class and drinking experiences of female drunkenness offenders. *Journal of Health and Human Behavior, 7*:276-283, Winter, 1966; Clark, Robert E.: Psychoses, income and occupational prestige. In Bendix, R., and Lipset, S.M. (Eds.): *Class, Status and Power.* Glencoe, Ill., The Free Press, 1953, pp. 333-339; Hollingshead, August B., and Redlich, Fredrick C.: *Social Class and Mental Illness.* New York, John Wiley & Sons, 1958; Kleiner, Robert J., and Parker, Seymour: *op. cit.*, pp. 55-66; Lawrence, Joseph J., and Maxwell, Milton A.: *op. cit.*, pp. 141-145.
175. Dollard, John: Drinking mores of the social classes. In *Alcohol, Science*

and Society. New Haven, Quarterly Journal of Studies on Alcohol, 1945, pp. 95-104.

176. Clinard, Marshall B.:*op. cit.*, pp. 431-432.
177. Dollard, John: *op. cit.*, pp. 95-104.
178. McCord, William, McCord, Joan, and Gudeman, John: *Origins of Alcoholism, op. cit.*, p. 40.
179. Riley, John W., and Marden, Charles F.: *op. cit.*, p. 269.
180. Straus, Robert, and Bacon, Selden, D.: *op. cit.*, pp. 51, 109.
181. Mulford, Harold A.: *op. cit.*, p. 641.
182. Cahalan, Don, Cisin, Ira H., and Crossley, Helen M.: *op. cit.*, p. 29.
183. Cahalan, Don, and Cisin, Ira H.: *op. cit.*, p. 140.
184. Cahalan, Don, Cisin, Ira H., and Crossley, Helen M.: *op. cit.*, pp. 179-180.
185. Bailey, Margaret B., Haberman, Paul W., and Alksne, Harold: *op. cit.*, pp. 32-33.
186. Bailey, Margaret B., Haberman, Paul W., and Alksne, Harold: *Ibid.*, p. 32.
187. Riley, John W., and Marden, Charles F.: *op. cit.*, p. 270.
188. Mulford, Harold A., and Miller, Donald E.: *op. cit.*, p. 717.
189. Mulford, Harold A.: *op. cit.*, p. 640.
190. Cahalan, Don, and Cisin, Ira H.: *op. cit.*, p. 140.
191. Cahalan, Don, and Cisin, Ira. H.: *Ibid.*
192. Mulford, Harold A.: *op. cit.*, p. 640.
193. Cahalan, Don, and Cisin, Ira H.: *op. cit.*, p. 140.
194. Locke, Ben Z., Kramer, Morton, and Pasamanick, Benjamin: Alcoholic psychoses among first admissions to public mental hospitals in Ohio. *Quarterly Journal of Studies on Alcohol, 21*:473, September, 1960.
195. Bailey, Margaret B., Haberman, Paul W., and Alksne, Harold: *op. cit.*, p. 27.
196. Mulford, Harold A., and Miller, Donald E.: *op. cit.*, p. 488.
197. Mulford, Harold A.: *op. cit.*, p. 641.
198. Cahalan, Don, and Cisin, Ira H.: *op. cit.*, p. 140.
199. Mulford, Harold A.: *op. cit.*, p. 641.
200. Cahalan, Don, Cisin, Ira H., and Crossley, Helen M.: *op. cit.*, p. 30.
201. Cahalan, Don, Cisin, Ira H., and Crossley, Helen M.: *Ibid.*, p. 31.
202. Cahalan, Don, Cisin, Ira H., and Crossley, Helen M.: *Ibid.*
203. Cahalan, Don, Cisin, Ira H., and Crossley, Helen M.: *Ibid.*
204. Cahalan, Don, Cisin, Ira H., and Crossley, Helen M.: *Ibid.*, p. 26.
205. Cahalan, Don, Cisin, Ira H., and Crossley, Helen M.: *Ibid.*, p. 186.
206. Cahalan, Don: *op. cit.*, p. 85.
207. Cahalan, Don: *Ibid.*, p. 51.
208. Cahalan, Don: *Ibid.*, pp. 56-85.
209. Cahalan, Don: *Ibid.*, p. 87.
210. McCord, William, McCord, Joan, and Gudeman, John: *Origins of Alcoholism, op. cit.*

211. McCord, William, McCord, Joan, and Gudeman, John: *Ibid.*, p. 74.
212. Robins, Lee N., Bates, William M., and O'Neal, Patricia: *op. cit.*, pp. 395-412.
213. Robins, Lee N., Bates, William M,. and O'Neal, Patricia: *Ibid.* p. 404.
214. Cahalan, Don: *op. cit.*, pp. 85-89.
215. Cahalan, Don, Cisin, Ira H., and Crossley, Helen M.: *op. cit.*, p. 194.
216. McCord, William, McCord, Joan, and Gudeman, John: *Origins of Alcoholism, op. cit.*
217. Robins, Lee N., Bates, William M., and O'Neal, Patricia: *op. cit.*
218. Cahalan, Don: *op. cit.*, p. 187.
219. For discussions of drinking and alcoholism in other ethnic groups see: Barnett, Milton L.: Alcoholism in the Cantonese of New York City: An anthropological study, in *Etiology of Chronic Alcoholism, op. cit.*, pp. 179-227; Dozier, Edward P.: Problem drinking among American Indians. *Quarterly Journal of Studies on Alcohol, 27:72-85,* March, 1966; Whittaker, James O.: Alcohol and the Standing Rock Sioux Tribe, I. Pattern of drinking. *Quarterly Journal of Studies on Alcohol, 23:468-478,* September, 1962; Lolli, Giorgio et al.: The use of wine and other alcoholic beverages by a group of Italians and Americans of Italian extraction. *Quarterly Journal of Studies on Alcohol, 13:27-48,* March, 1952; Skolnick, Jerome H.: A study of the relation of ethnic background to arrests for inebriety. *Quarterly Journal of Studies on Alcohol, 15:622-630,* December, 1954; Ullman, Albert D.: Ethnic differences in the first drinking experience, *op. cit.*
220. Cahalan, Don, Cisin, Ira H., and Crossley, Helen M.: *op. cit.*, p. 48. Other studies relevant to Negro drinking, alcoholism, and mental illness are: King, Lucy Jane et al.: Alcohol abuse: A crucial factor in the social problems of Negro men. *American Journal of Psychiatry, 125:96-104,* June, 1969; Lewis, Hylan: *Blackways of Kent.* Chapel Hill, University of North Carolina Press, 1955; Maddox, George L., and Allen, Bernice: A comparative study of social definitions of alcohol and its uses among selected male Negro and white undergraduates. *Quarterly Journal of Studies on Alcohol, 22:418-427,* September, 1961; Parker, Seymour, and Kleiner, Robert J.: *Mental Illness in the Urban Negro Community.* New York, Free Press, 1966; Robins, Lee N., Murphy, George E., and Breckenridge, Mary B.: Drinking behavior of young urban, Negro men. *Quarterly Journal of Studies on Alcohol, 29:657-684,* September, 1968.
221. Cahalan, Don, and Cisin, Ira H.: *op. cit.*, p. 142.
222. Cahalan, Don, Cisin, Ira H., and Crossley, Helen M.: *op. cit.*, p. 179.
223. Bailey, Margaret B., Haberman, Paul W., and Alksne, Harold: *op. cit.*, p. 27.
224. Locke, Ben Z., Kramer, Morton, and Pasamanick, Benjamin: *op. cit.*, p. 472.

225. Sterne, Muriel W.: *op. cit.*, p. 89.
226. Frazier, E. Franklin: *Black Bourgeoisie*. New York, Collier Books, 1947, p. 190.
227. Strayer, Robert: A study of the Negro alcoholic. *Quarterly Journal of Studies on Alcohol, 22*:111-123, March, 1961.
228. Larkins, John R.: *Alcohol and the Negro*. Zebulon, Record Publishing, 1965, p. 239.
229. Cahalan, Don: *op. cit.*, esp. p. 86.
230. Cahalan, Don: *Ibid.*, p. 13.
231. McCord, William, et al.: *Life Styles in the Black Ghetto*. New York, W. W. Norton, 1969.
232. McCord, William, et al.: *Ibid.*, p. 77.
233. Strayer, Robert: *op. cit.*
234. Strayer, Robert: *Ibid.*, p. 120.
235. Cahalan, Don, Cisin, Ira H., and Crossley, Helen M.: *op. cit.*, p. 48.
236. Cahalan, Don, Cisin, Ira H., and Crossley, Helen M.: *Ibid.*
237. Cahalan, Don, and Cisin, Ira H.: *op. cit.*, p. 142.
238. Bailey, Margaret B., Haberman, Paul W., and Alksne, Harold: *op. cit.*, p. 27.
239. Locke, Ben Z., Kramer, Morton, and Pasamanick, Benjamin: *op. cit.*, p. 473.
240. Strayer, Robert: *op. cit.*
241. Sterne, Muriel W.: *op. cit.*, p. 112.
242. Strayer, Robert: *op. cit.*
243. Strayer, Robert: *Ibid.*, p. 119.
244. Bailey, Margaret B., Haberman, Paul W., and Alksne, Harold: *op. cit.*, p. 28.
245. Knupfer, Genevieve, et al.: *op. cit.*, p. 14.
246. Sterne, Muriel W.: *op. cit.*, p. 73.
247. Roebuck, Julian B.: Domestic service in the South; with particular attention to the Negro female. M.A. thesis, Duke University (Durham, N.C.), 1944.
248. Cahalan, Don, Cisin, Ira H., and Crossley, Helen M.: *op. cit.*
249. Cahalan, Don, Cisin, Ira H., and Crossley, Helen M.: *Ibid.*, p. 54.
250. Straus, Robert, and Bacon, Selden D.: *op. cit.*, p. 53.
251. Straus, Robert, and Bacon, Selden D.: *Ibid.*, p. 136.
252. Cahalan, Don, and Cisin, Ira H.: *op. cit.*, p. 142.
253. Cahalan, Don: *op. cit.*, p. 149.
254. Roberts, Bertram, and Myers, Jerome K.: *op. cit.*
255. Skolnick, Jerome H.: *op. cit.*
256. Robins, Lee N., Bates, William M., and O'Neal, Patricia: *op. cit.*, p. 403.
257. McCord, William, McCord, Joan, and Gudeman, John: *Origins of Alcoholism, op. cit.*, p. 38.
258. Glad, Donald D.: *op. cit.*

259. Bales, Robert F.: *op. cit.*
260. Bales, Robert F.: *Ibid.*, p. 486.
261. Glad, Donald D.: *op. cit.*
262. Knupfer, Genevieve, and Room, Robin: Drinking patterns and attitudes of Irish, Jewish and white Protestant American men. *Quarterly Journal of Studies on Alcohol, 29*:679, December, 1967.
263. Cahalan, Don: *op. cit.*, p. 13.
264. Cahalan, Don: *Ibid.*, pp. 41-57.
265. Cahalan, Don: *Ibid.;* the discussion on these variables is found in Chapter 5, Predicting problem drinking, pp. 96-105.
266. Kinsey, Barry A.: *op. cit.*
267. Pittman, David J., and Gordon, Calvin Wayne: *op. cit.*
268. Coleman, James C.: *Abnormal Psychology and Modern Life.* Chicago, Scott-Foresman, 1964, pp. 293-298.
269. Sterne, Muriel W.: *op. cit.*, p. 73.
270. Locke, Ben Z., Kramer, Morton, and Pasamanick, Benjamin: *op. cit.*, Quoted in Sterne, Muriel W.: p. 73.

NAME INDEX

Adamson, Robert, 76, 131
Adler, Alfred, 83
Alksne, Harold, 168, 178, 182, 195, 196, 203, 206, 207, 227, 229, 232, 233, 234
Amark, Curt, 26, 27, 28, 56

Bacon, Selden D., 14, 19, 146, 168, 172, 173, 182, 195, 208, 223, 227, 228, 229, 232, 234
Bailey, Margaret B., 168, 178, 182, 195, 196, 203, 206, 207, 227, 229, 232, 233, 234
Bales, Robert F., 144-146, 147, 169, 170, 210, 219-220, 223, 227, 234, 235
Bandura, Albert, 73-74, 78-80, 119, 120, 127, 131
Bandura, Alfred, 99
Barker, Michael J., 89-90, 133
Barr, Rosalie M., 66, 129
Bates, William M., 191, 201, 202, 209, 231, 233, 234
Bennett, Richard M., 65, 129
Berman, Sidney, 39, 44, 50, 59
Berne, Eric, 83, 132
Bertrand, Sharon, 88-89, 133
Black, Roger, 76, 131
Bleuler, Manfred, 22, 47, 55, 56
Blum, Eva Marie, 121, 137
Brady, Roscoe A., 36, 37, 58
Brown, Russell V., 37, 58, 75-76, 131
Buhler, Charlotte, 102-103, 136

Cobalis, Lori, viii
Cahalan, Don, 7-11 passim, 14, 17, 18, 19, 80, 131, 139, 154-165, 168, 171, 177-184 passim, 188, 195-205 passim, 208, 209, 211, 212-216, 218, 219, 221, 222, 225-235 passim
Carman, R. S., 192, 231
Carpenter, John A., 64, 98, 122, 129, 135, 137
Casey, A., 75, 131
Catanzaro, Ronald J., 100, 135
Cavan, Sherri, 15, 19

Chafetz, Morris E., 4, 18
Chordorkoff, Bernard, 92, 134
Cisin, Ira H., 8, 14, 17-20 passim, 139, 168, 175-182 passim, 188, 195-205 passim, 208, 209, 214, 222, 227-234 passim
Clayton, Paula J., 27, 56
Clinard, Marshall B., 4, 15, 18, 19, 194, 232
Coleman James C., 4, 17, 18, 20, 63, 129
Conger, John J., 71, 72-73, 80, 130, 132
Conner, Ralph, 189, 231
Crossley, Helen M., 8, 14, 18, 19, 139, 168, 175, 178, 179, 180, 182, 188, 195, 197-205 passim, 208, 209, 214, 222, 227-234 passim

Davis, Pauline A., 40, 41, 59
Demone, Harold W., 4, 18
De Vito, R. A., 112-113, 136
Diethelm, Oskar, 4, 18, 66, 129
Dollard, John, 71, 130, 193, 194, 199, 200-202, 231, 232

Edgerton, Robert, 117-118, 137
Efron, Vera, 17, 20, 165, 226
Eriksson, K., 35, 58
Eysenck, Hans Jurgen, 26, 28, 51, 55, 56, 60

Fenichel, Otto, 86-87, 90, 132-133
Ferster, C. B., 80, 131
Field, Peter B., 121-122, 143-144, 220, 223
Fleetwood, M. Friele, 39, 59
Frazier, E. Franklin, 203, 234
Freed, Earl X., 74, 75, 131
Friedman, Samuel, 186, 230

Garfield, Z. H., 67, 129
Gawienowski, A. H., 41-42, 59
Glad, Donald D., 147, 169-170, 209, 210, 212, 220, 223, 227, 234, 235

237

SUBJECT INDEX

Subject Index

Symptoms
  alcohol consumption, 32
  progression, 6

T

Taiwan, hereditary alcoholism studies, 29-30
Takashima, drinking customs, 117
TAT, field-dependence studies, 95
Taverns
  ethnographic study, 15
  liquor sales, 15
Teen-agers, alcohol use, 14
  see also Youths
Temperance religious groups, see Abstinent religious groups
Temple University, Institute for Survey Research, viii
Tennessee Self-Concept Scale, alcoholism study, 66
Tension
  alcohol consumption relationship, animal studies, 76-77
  alcoholics' inability to stand, 102-103
  blood studies, 39
  causes, 4
  cultural factors, 145
  cultural studies, 144
  culturally induced, 221
    Ireland, 210
  drinking spur, 194
  emotional, see Emotional tension
  physiological, studies needed, 221
  relief, 190
  sources, 220
Tension reduction
  alcohol's role, animal studies, 148
  role in drinking, 148
Tension release, recreation needed, 221
Terminology
  problems, 11-13
  variance, 220
Thematic Apperception tests, alcoholics, others compared, 100
Theoretical paradigms, problem drinking, 162-164
Theory dearth, comments, 216
Thiamine deficiency, animal studies, 77-78
Thought disorder, alcoholics studied, 108
Thought disturbance, high in alcoholics, 107
Tics, significance, 48
Toxic effect, sought by alcoholics, 45
Transactional orientation, theories and

studies, 81-86, 119-120
Treatment, alcoholics disinterested, 107
Treatment of alcoholism
  dietary approach, 36
  varied approach urged, 108
Tremors, significance, 48
Twins
  hereditary alcoholism studies, 22-26, 29
  similarities, 54, 55
  see also Siblings
Typing of alcoholics
  MMPI use, 113
  suggestions, 108
Typological approach, personality studies, 105-116

U

United States
  alcoholism, 149-154
    extent, 16-17
  class system inadequacy, 202
  drinking patterns, 13-16
  males, 168
  heavy drinking, 168
  heavy-escape drinking, 178
  hereditary alcoholism studies, 29-30
    with table
  problem drinking, 154-165
  upper-upper class, aristocracy exaggerated, 202
U.S. Army, enlisted personnel, hospital studies, 192
University of California, 7
  Cancer Research Genetics Laboratory, heredity studies, 33-34
University of Illinois, studies, 51
University of Lund, twin data, 22
University of Texas, studies, 51
Unpleasant stimuli, defenses against, 83
Upper classes, drinking customs, 193, 195, 201
Upper-lower group, drinking habits, 194
Upper-middle class, drinking attitudes, 194
Upper-upper class, United States, real status, 202
Urban areas
  drinking patterns, 199
  size, relationship to drinking, 156
Urbanization
  factor in drinking incidence, 139
  problem drinking factor, 214-215
Utilitarian attitude, relation to "compulsive" drinking, 146